Reading the Absurd

Reading the Absurd

JOANNA GAVINS

EDINBURGH
University Press

© Joanna Gavins, 2013

Edinburgh University Press Ltd
22 George Square, Edinburgh EH8 9LF

www.euppublishing.com

Typeset in 10/12 Times New Roman by
Servis Filmsetting Ltd, Stockport, Cheshire
printed and bound in the United States of America

A CIP record for this book is available from the British Library

ISBN 978 0 7486 6926 4 (hardback)
ISBN 978 0 7486 7001 7 (paperback)
ISBN 978 0 7486 6927 1 (webready PDF)
ISBN 978 0 7486 6929 5 (epub)

The right of Joanna Gavins
to be identified as author of this work
has been asserted in accordance with
the Copyright, Designs and Patents Act 1988.

Contents

List of Figures

Acknowledgements

The writing of this book has closely resembled a Sisyphean task at various stages, not least in the length of time I have taken rolling this particular scholarly rock uphill. Over the decade and a half that I have spent researching and writing what follows, numerous friends and colleagues have helped to shoulder the burden at different moments through their intellectual and personal encouragement. My colleagues in the School of English at the University of Sheffield continue to provide the collegial atmosphere which allows new ideas to thrive. I am also grateful for the support offered to this project and for the friendship offered to me by members of the Cognitive Poetics Research Group at Sheffield: Alice Bell, Joe Bray, Sam Browse, Richard Finn, Alison Gibbons, Andi Macrae, Helen Mort, Dave Peplow, Shelley Sikora and Isabelle van der Bom. Special thanks are also due to the undergraduate and postgraduate students who have taken my Cognitive Poetics and Absurd Prose Fiction courses at Sheffield and who have willingly subjected themselves to my academic experimentation over many years.

I have presented my research on the literary absurd at various venues far beyond the seven hills of Sheffield, most frequently at the annual international conferences of the Poetics and Linguistics Association (PALA), but also at the kind invitation of other colleagues in the many corners of the global village of literary-linguistic research. I owe thanks to Ron Carter, Cathy Emmott, Richard Gerrig, Geoff Hall, Laura Hidalgo Downing, Lesley Jeffries, Manuel Jobert, Vanina Jobert-Martini, Marina Lambrou, Sharon Lattig, Clara Mallier, Brian McHale, Dan McIntyre, Sara Mills, Rocio Montoro, Elena Semino, Mick Short, Michael Toolan and Katie Wales, all of whom have offered constructive feedback on my ideas at one stage or another. Special thanks are also due to Joke Bijleveld, Michael Burke, Helle Hochscheid, Lois Kemp, Ernestine Lahey, Gerard Steen and Peter Verdonk, who have in their assorted ways made Amsterdam, in particular, a home from home for me through many years of the warmest hospitality and intellectual support. David Herman and Paul Simpson both provided careful and insightful commentary on early plans and drafts of this book and their invaluable advice has directly shaped its final manifestation. I also owe an immense debt of gratitude to Sara Whiteley, who lent her perspicacity to later drafts and her unfaltering friendship throughout the writing of the manuscript. Thanks, too, to Simon Armitage for helping me to develop a perspective on the poetic absurd, for his friendship and for introducing me to the work of James Tate.

All the staff I have worked with at Edinburgh University Press have been, as usual, encouraging, professional and patient far beyond the call of duty. I am also grateful to Sheffield artist James Green for his permission to use 'Sleepwalker Encounters his Father as a Horse in the Tomato Plant Forest' on the cover of the book. Thanks too to Charles Simic for generously allowing me to reproduce two of his poems, 'Empire State' and 'Dream Avenue', in Chapter 5, and to James Tate for giving similarly kind permission for the reproduction of 'Red Dirt' in the same chapter. Also in Chapter 5, 'Bedtime Anecdote' by Ted Hughes is taken from *Collected Poems*, © Estate of Ted Hughes and reprinted by permission of Faber and Faber Ltd. Figure 4.2 is taken from *Breakfast of Champions* by Kurt Vonnegut, published by Jonathan Cape, and is reprinted by permission of The Random House Group Limited.

To my husband, Peter Stockwell, and our daughters, Ada and Edith, I owe more than I will ever be able to repay and far more than they would ever demand of me. My appreciation of all things absurd is learned entirely from my family; every word of this book is the result of their patience and support. Peter, Ada, Edith: I did it. It's finished. We can go to the park now.

1 The Literary Absurd

This book provides a rigorous and systematic account of the experience of reading the literary absurd. The term 'absurd' itself has its etymological roots in the Latin *absurdus*, meaning 'contrary to reason or inharmonious', an intensive of *surdus*, meaning 'irrational or deaf' (hence deaf to reason). The contemporary common use of 'absurd' still corresponds closely to this original sense and the term is ordinarily employed to identify and describe illogicality or incongruity in everyday life. The adoption of 'absurd' as a means of describing literary works is now also widespread and on the whole reflective of the primary meaning of the word as well. However, the boundaries around the term within literary criticism remain ill-defined: the literary absurd is a concept which has sustained critical interest for over half a century, but which is nevertheless highly nebulous. Most importantly, the substantial body of scholarly work dedicated to the examination of the phenomenon produced since the middle of the twentieth century has failed to agree on the temporal, generic or stylistic parameters which define the concept; the absurd has been identified in texts as diverse as Greek tragedy and multimodal science fiction, and in the works of authors from Amis to Voltaire. This book aims to address this critical imprecision by taking the theories and methodologies of stylistics as an analytical framework. The volume is grounded, more specifically, in a cognitive-stylistic approach to literary investigation, a method of analysis which aims to ensure that an account of literature is properly reflective of current knowledge about the workings of the human mind, based on linguistic evidence, and focused on the readerly experience of textual phenomena.

The absurd in philosophy

Having begun this book by pointing to the theoretical and technical imprecision which characterises most preceding literary criticism on the absurd, it is important now to emphasise that which all critics do agree upon: that the absurd as a literary phenomenon is an artistic expression of human beings' inability to find inherent meaning in their existence. The origins of

this viewpoint are multiple and can be seen to be drawn from a wide range
of nineteenth- and twentieth-century philosophy and theology (for a useful
survey see Cornwell, 2006: 2–14), as well as from ideas expressed within literary prose and drama. The origins of the vagueness surrounding the concept
of the literary absurd can be traced to the disagreement and discord which
permeate many of the movements, disciplines, and sub-disciplines which
have influenced its development. Having said this, Søren Kierkegaard's position as one of the key architects of the philosophical absurd is undisputed.
In *Fear and Trembling* (originally published in 1843), Kierkegaard (2006)
reflects upon the biblical story of God's command to Abraham to sacrifice
his son as a demonstration of his faith, presenting the anguished moment at
which Abraham cannot act, and yet must act, as the epitome of the absurdity
of human existence. His interest in such paradoxes also earned Kierkegaard
the title of 'Father of Existentialism', yet it is important to understand that
the majority of existentialists depart radically from the leap into Christian
faith that Kierkegaard makes as a result of his deliberations. Existentialist
philosophy and the absurd are closely related, not least in their shared recognition of the intrinsic meaninglessness of human life. However, existentialism
draws as much influence from the writings of Nietzsche and Heidegger as it
does from Kierkegaard. In very general terms, it holds that the responsibility
for the creation of an authentic existence lies with the individual (for a full
explication see Cooper, 1990), but this basic overarching proposition admits
a nuanced range of opinion and expression. As Macquarrie (1972: 14) points
out, existentialists do not subscribe to a single doctrine and existentialism
is better considered as a 'style of philosophizing' rather than as a unified
philosophy in itself.

Chapter 2 of this book explores the points of commonality and difference
between the absurd and existentialism in more detail and, in particular, looks
at the relationship between the two authors whose works are most frequently
cited as the point at which the absurd and the existential meet: Albert Camus
and Jean Paul Sartre. As we will see in Chapter 2, while being widely cred-
ited as one of the founding fathers of the absurd, Camus is also frequently
categorised as an existentialist writer. Most often, this categorisation is one
made in a critical context by those who view the absurd as just a single component within a wider existentialist perspective. These critics also tend to recognise that, for Camus, the absurd is a condition of existence to be explored
through writing, rather than a form of writing in itself. Camus's seminal text
Le Mythe de Sisyphe (originally published in 1942), for instance, is made up
of a series of essays in which Camus queries whether life has meaning, in
order to explore the further question of the legitimacy of suicide. He invokes
the Greek myth of Sisyphus as an allegory for the absurd human condition.
Sisyphus, having angered the gods, was condemned to roll ceaselessly a huge
stone to the top of a mountain, only to watch it roll back down again under
the force of its own weight. Camus explains:

Sisyphus is the absurd hero. He *is* as much through his passions as through his torture. His scorn of the gods, his hatred of death, and his passion for life won him that unspeakable penalty in which the whole being is exerted towards accomplishing nothing. This is the price that must be paid for the passions of this earth.

(Camus, 1975: 108)

Camus was also careful to point out, however, that the analogy for the human condition presented in *The Myth of Sisyphus* was intended simply to capture an 'absurd sensitivity that can be found widespread in the age' (Camus, 1975: 10). He goes on to emphasise that 'There will be found here merely the description, in the pure state, of an intellectual malady. No metaphysic, no belief is involved in it for a moment' (Camus, 1975: 10). The absurd is sketched out somewhat impressionistically by Camus in his philosophical essays, which, as we will see later in this book, leads to a longer-term problematic status for the concept within philosophy more broadly.

The absurd in literary criticism

Within *The Myth of Sisyphus* Camus directly addresses at some length the question of whether it is possible to have an absurd work of art. He offers the following polemic on the aesthetic form such works should take:

Thus I ask of absurd creation what I required from thought – revolt, freedom and diversity. Later on it will manifest its utter futility. In that daily effort in which intelligence and passion mingle and delight each other, the absurd man discovers a discipline that will make up the greatest of his strengths. The required diligence, the doggedness and lucidity thus resemble the conqueror's attitude. To create is likewise to give a shape to one's fate.

(Camus, 1975: 105–6)

For Camus, then, the creation of absurdity in art is a deliberate and revolutionary act and one which he goes on to identify in the literary works of a range of authors, including Shakespeare, Dostoevsky, Goethe and Malraux. Indeed, the first extended literary-critical application of Camus's notion that an absurd sensitivity pervades the modern era was made by Camus himself in his essay on Franz Kafka (also originally published in 1942: Camus, 1975: 112–24). Summarising Kafka's work, he offers the following initial definition of the literary absurd:

There is in the human condition (and this is a commonplace of all literatures) a basic absurdity as well as an implacable nobility. The two coincide, as is natural. Both of them are represented, let me repeat, in the ridiculous divorce separating our spiritual excesses and the ephemeral joys of the body. The absurd thing is that it should be the soul of this body which it transcends so inordinately. Whoever would like to represent this absurdity must give it life in a series of parallel contrasts. Thus it is that Kafka expresses tragedy by the everyday and the absurd by the logical.

(Camus, 1975: 115)

The idea Camus expresses here, that literary representations of the absurd human condition are based on 'parallel contrasts', was picked up most influentially by Martin Esslin in his 1961 study of contemporary drama, *The Theatre of the Absurd* (Esslin, 1980). Esslin coined this phrase to describe the dramatic works, primarily, of Samuel Beckett, Arthur Adamov, Eugène Ionesco, Jean Genet and Harold Pinter, and his evaluations of these writers led directly to a proliferation of 'absurd' criticism on experimental twentieth-century theatre which extended throughout the latter half of the twentieth century and into the twenty-first (for just a small sample see Barta, 1999; Bennett, 2011; Corfariu and Rovența-Frumușani, 1984; Ebewo, 2008; Esslin, 1965; Flegar, 2010; Freeman, 1996; Gerzymisch-Arbogast, 1988; Grol-Prokopczyk, 1979; Gunn, 2008; Haney, 2001; Hinden, 1981; Jakovljevic, 2010; Malinowska, 1992; Sherzer, 1978; Sikorska, 1994; Simpson, 1998, 2000; Srivastava, 1974; Vassilopolou, 2008). Many of these critical works (e.g. Sherzer, 1978; Simpson, 1998, 2000; Vassilopolou, 2008) have examined the language of absurd drama rigorously and in detail, which is one of the main reasons why the dramatic absurd does not form the focus of this book, although these studies are drawn upon at various points in the forthcoming discussion as I attempt to extend current understanding of the language of the absurd to encompass the read (rather than performed and witnessed) experiences of prose fiction and poetry.

An even greater explosion of literary criticism, one identifying the absurd in prose fiction, followed the trend for critical work on absurd drama soon after the publication of Esslin's study, resulting in a quite staggering range of literature being categorised and discussed in terms of its absurdist content (again, for only a sample, see Baker, 1993; Balogun, 1984; Bowen, 1971; Braun, 1974; Brodwin, 1972; Brombert, 1948; Brothers, 1977; Carroll, 2007; Cornwell, 1991a, 2006; Cuthbertson, 1974; Fink, 1998; Galloway, 1964, 1966; Hanțiu, 2010; Harris, 1972; Hauck, 1971; Hausdorff, 1966; Hinchliffe, 1972; Hoffmann, 1986; Hyles, 1985; Janoff, 1974; Karst, 1975; Kavanagh, 1972; Ketterer, 1978; Kiberd, 1986; Knopp, 1974; Komaromi, 2002; Kosinski, 1979; Lebowitz, 1971; MacNamara, 1968; Michel, 1961; Miller, 1967; Mistri, 1988; Morreale, 1967; Penner, 1978; Read, 1981; Safer, 1983a, 1983b, 1989, 1994; Seltzer, 1967; Spector, 1961; Waldmeir, 1964; Young, 1975). What all these accounts share is an almost complete neglect of the stylistic features which might characterise the literary absurd and which might help to define the tangible connections which exist between the disparate texts which have hitherto been included under this critical umbrella term. The present volume starts, then, from a point in literary-critical history, at which the state of the art in the examination of the absurd in literature might appear to be one in which almost anything goes. Delineating the absurd from the existential, the philosophical from the literary or the stylistic from the thematic does not currently appear to be a central or valued preoccupation in this area. The notion of the literary absurd within an academic context is now so all-encompassing, so vaguely defined, that its value as a descriptive and analytical term must surely be under question.

A new approach

My own approach to the literary absurd is one which focuses primarily and necessarily on language. It proceeds from an assumption that the only sensible way to advance our understanding of the absurd in literature is by beginning the systematic investigation of the linguistic features commonly exhibited by absurdist texts. I am choosing my words carefully here and I must emphasise at this point that the present study is only the *beginning* of this endeavour. In what follows, I am not aiming to provide a comprehensive survey of the stylistics of the literary absurd, since such a project is far beyond the practical constraints of this book. Instead, my discussion centres on a relatively small selection of key works which I examine in depth with the aim of formulating a workable template of significant aspects of absurd style. It is intended that this template eventually be applied and tested against a far broader spectrum of literary works than I have been able to devote my attention to here. For this reason, my focus is on ensuring that my account of the experience of reading the absurd is appropriately replicable rather than all-embracing. Important authors and major works of absurd literature have been overlooked in this process, but such is the compromise which must be made for the sake of precision of analysis and clarity of argument. Among those texts which necessarily fall outside the parameters of my enquiry are all those written in languages other than English. My own limited proficiency in any language other than my native tongue means that I am unable to offer an accurate or convincing analysis of the multitude of absurd works written in French, German, Polish or Russian, to name just a few of the languages through which the absurd has been expressed in literature. Where I do deal with absurd texts written by speakers of other languages, I do so in their translated form and always with the proviso that the claims I make are claims about that translation and not about the original text. Similarly, the arguments I put forward about reading, readers and the contexts which surround both of these are arguments made from the perspective of Western, English-speaking culture. A cross-cultural evaluation of the experience of reading the absurd again lies beyond the practical parameters of the present study.

As I have already mentioned, the analytical approach that I take throughout this book is one which combines stylistic enquiry with a cognitive perspective on language, literature and reading. It is based in the evolving discipline of cognitive poetics, which makes use of recent research in cognitive psychology, cognitive linguistics and neuroscience in order to better understand the human experience of literary reading (for useful introductions to this field see Brône and Vandaele, 2009; Gavins and Steen, 2003; Semino and Culpeper, 2002; Stockwell, 2002a). Stockwell (2009) provides a useful summary of the basic principles of the cognitive-scientific theories and disciplines which underpin cognitive poetics:

> to qualify as cognitivist approaches they all fundamentally share a commitment to *experiential realism*. This is the view that there is a world outside the body that exists objectively (realism), but our only access to it is through our perceptual and cognitive experience of it. Cognitivists thus do not deny that there are objects and relationships in the world that are available to be discovered and understood, but those phenomena can only be accessed, conceptualised and discussed within the constraints that our human condition has bequeathed to us.
>
> (Stockwell, 2009: 2)

The account of the literary absurd presented in this book, therefore, is essentially concerned with readers' perceptions and conceptualisations of textual phenomena. More specifically, much of the discussion which unfolds over the coming chapters uses Text World Theory as its central framework of analysis (for detailed introductions to the theory see Gavins, 2007; Werth, 1999). Since an exhaustive description of this theory is also beyond the practical parameters of the present volume, I will be explaining relevant aspects of the framework as they are needed. In brief, Text World Theory regards all discourse, including literary discourse, as the product of a purposeful interaction between participants in a real-world situation, known as the discourse-world (see Gavins, 2007: 18–34). The language the participants produce in the discourse-world and the way they understand that language is based both on their immediate perceptions and on the existing expectations and knowledge frames they bring with them to their interaction. Participants create mental representations, known as text-worlds (see Gavins, 2007: 35–72), of the language they encounter, and these mental representations have the potential to become as richly detailed and immersive as the real-world situations from which they spring. As a discourse develops, additional worlds may be created through language, often leading to a multiplex network of mental representations through which readers and listeners are able to conceptualise an array of different situations, beliefs and attitudes.

Text World Theory provides an ideal framework for the examination of the literary absurd since it aims to show how real-world contexts influence the production of discourse and how that discourse is perceived and conceptualised in everyday situations. It unifies text and context under one analytical apparatus, allowing the analyst to gain both an overall understanding of the interactional nature of a discourse and to achieve a precise explanation of its textual and conceptual components. Text World Theory is also a highly expansive and catholic model, which draws greatly from a wide range of other cognitive approaches to discourse and the mind, and which therefore allows for the combination of more than one perspective at once on a particular phenomenon. Adopting a text-world viewpoint on the literary absurd thus enables the concurrent examination of the imaginary worlds created by absurd texts, their relationships to their originating context, and the micro-textual elements through which they direct reader attention, facilitate immersion, manipulate emotion and so on.

Readers of the absurd

Like all the other works of literary criticism on the absurd which have preceded it, the present account is greatly based on my own subjective responses to the texts under scrutiny. However, like all the other works of *stylistic* analysis which have preceded it, it is also based on transparent and replicable methods of investigation. Furthermore, in order to push my investigation further beyond the limits of partial impressionism, at various points throughout the forthcoming discussion I consider responses to the absurd made by other readers. Over the coming chapters I examine both readings of the absurd offered in an academic context, in the form of literary-critical books, articles and reviews, as well as those reported by readers discussing literature in non-academic contexts. Within and around the discipline of stylistics, numerous analysts over the last thirty years or more have broadened the focus of literary studies beyond introspection to examine a far wider range of reader responses to literature (see, for example, Andringa, 1996; Bortolussi and Dixon, 2003; Bray, 2007; Emmott et al., 2006; Hanauer, 1998; Miall, 2008; Miall and Kuiken, 2002a, 2002b; Sanford et al., 2006; Sotirova, 2006; van Peer, 1983, 2008; van Peer and Andringa, 1990; Zyngier et al., 2008). As Swann and Allington (2009) point out, however, many of these studies examine readings produced in artificial reading or discursive environments by readers engaged in atypical reading behaviour and often interacting with atypical texts or textual fragments. More recently, though, a greater leaning can be identified towards what Swann and Allington (2009: 248) term 'naturalistic studies', with a focus on contextualised reading practices and on examining readers' behaviours in their usual environment, engaged in habitual reading behaviour and interacting with unmanipulated texts (see, for example, Allington, 2011, 2012; Allington and Swann, 2009; Peplow, 2011; Sedo, 2003; Stockwell, 2009; Swann and Allington, 2009; Whiteley, 2010, 2011a, 2011b). The specific non-academic reading environments examined in the present volume are online literary discussion websites, through which millions of readers all over the world currently share their experiences with texts. The reports readers offer about their experiences with absurd literature on these sites constitute voluntarily produced and often highly detailed accounts of habitual literary interaction, unaffected and unaltered by the analyst.

I am again being careful with my choice of words here and I refer throughout this book to 'reading contexts' rather than simply to 'readers' when differentiating between types of literary interaction. I do not claim at any point in this book that the readers participating in online discussions of literature are not necessarily academics. All of the literary websites examined over the course of the coming chapters offer their members anonymity and it is impossible to be certain of the age, gender, occupation, ethnicity or social background of the readers involved. However, for the purposes of the present study, this anonymity is immaterial, since what distinguishes the *context* of a website from that of a peer-reviewed academic publication is its informal and dynamic nature rather than (necessarily) the profiles of its participants. Even if the responses of academics happen to be included within the online responses I examine here, they are responses produced outside the usual highly formalised expectations of literary criticism and pedagogical practice. For this reason, then, online literary discussions report a useful and revealingly contrasting context of reading with which to compare those readings of the absurd produced in academic settings.

Of particular interest to the present project are the categorisations readers in non-academic online environments make of the literary texts they encounter, since the very definition of the concept of the literary absurd is the key focus of this study. The informal systems of classification which arise from such online categorisations are known within the discipline of information studies as 'folksonomies' and the processes by which readers arrive at their decisions over how to describe certain texts are currently a matter of significant scholarly interest within this field (see, for example, Bartley, 2009; Bates and Rowley, 2011; Maxymuk, 2007; Sinclair and Cardew-Hall, 2008; Thomas et al., 2010). Folksonomy is also a matter of great interest in my own investigation of the absurd in literature, not least because we shall see in the coming chapters how the concept of the literary absurd has multiple points of crossover with other literary concepts. Among these close cousins, two literary categories require special mention in this introductory chapter: postmodernism and surrealism. It is important for me to note from the outset that the present volume does not attempt a stylistic definition of either of these textual and cultural phenomena, since the refinement of current understanding of the literary absurd is a sufficient task in itself. However, postmodernism and the surreal do make their presence felt at various points over the course of the book, since readers in various contexts nominate these concepts as elements which, in one way or another, play an important role in their experiences of the absurd. As such, they cannot be ignored and I attempt at least to add some stylistic clarity to terms which, very much like the absurd, remain imprecise and nebulous in the majority of literary criticism. In the case of postmodernism, McHale (1987, 1992, 2012) remains an exception to this rule, presenting the most concerted attempts to add stylistic definition to what McHale (1987: 3–6) himself acknowledges is a term which by its very nature resists definition. The stylistics of surrealism has been similarly neglected until very recently, with Stockwell (1999, 2000, 2002b, 2012) providing a notable exception. The present volume, then, will rely on these accounts, where necessary, to provide the technical clarity needed to examine the relationships between the postmodern, the surreal and the literary absurd, rather than attempting discrete definitions of these other concepts.

The coming chapters explore the literary absurd as a linguistic and an experiential phenomenon, while at the same time reflecting upon its essential historical and cultural situation. In what follows, I present a series of case studies of the stylistic characteristics of absurd texts and examine a variety of readers' responses to them. I consider the diverse narrative and poetic means through which numerous authors have made manifest Camus's call for an absurd aesthetic of 'revolt, freedom and diversity' (Camus, 1975: 106) and attempt to provide an insight into the textual features which connect these works. In order to address the imprecision and lack of clarity which have typified criticism on the absurd in literature until now, I not only ground my discussion in replicable linguistic analysis but also consider the responses of readers for whom, as we shall see, encounters with the literary absurd habitually lead to long-lasting and profound emotional experiences. My core focus throughout is on the conceptual structures through which these experiences take place and on the cognitive complexities of reading the absurd.

2 Identifying the Absurd

In Chapter 1, I briefly outlined the reluctance in existing literary criticism to define the precise linguistic characteristics of absurd style, despite frequent references being made to such a concept in key critical works (for example Cornwell, 2006; Esslin, 1980; Harris, 1972; Hinchliffe, 1972). I also stated that the central aim of this book is to address this shortcoming through the systematic and transparent stylistic analysis of the phenomenon of the absurd in prose fiction and in poetry. One of the most likely reasons why no one, as far as I am aware, has sought to do this before now is the quite staggering range of texts, drawn from diverse historical moments and assorted literary genres, which have been categorised as 'absurd' in literary criticism. As I have already noted, the absurd has been identified in texts as distinct as Greek tragedy and multimodal science fiction, and in the works of authors from Amis to Voltaire. Until now, critics have seemed either unable or unwilling to establish the temporal, geographical, generic or stylistic boundaries of the absurd. While the notorious nebulousness of the concept is undoubtedly part of the irresistible appeal of the literary absurd for many academics, it is perhaps unsurprising that this vagueness has also led to a degree of analytical imprecision in preceding accounts of the phenomenon. This chapter begins the present attempt to clarify and refine our understanding of the absurd in literature through the systematic examination of some of the stylistic commonalities shared by absurd texts. In particular, what follows focuses on some of the techniques used to construct imaginary worlds through language in absurd prose fiction and on readers' experiences of these conceptual spaces. This chapter also examines the cognitive processes at the heart of readers' identifications of the absurd in literature in both academic and non-academic contexts and the ways in which complex concepts of genre are constructed in the mind.

Categories and categorisation

A search for academic publications on the phenomenon of the absurd in literature in the MLA International Bibliography (www.mla.org/biblio

graphy) suggests that the authors of prose fiction most frequently categorised as 'absurd' by literary critics include:

- John Barth (see Harris, 1972; Hauck, 1971; Hoffmann, 1986; Hyles, 1985; Janoff, 1974; Mistri, 1988)
- Samuel Beckett (see Barge, 1977; Kiberd, 1986; O'Neill, 1967; Swanson, 1971)
- Albert Camus (see Baker, 1993; Bersani, 1970; Braun, 1974; Brombert, 1948; Carroll, 2007; Christensen, 1962; McGregor, 1994, 1995; Morreale, 1967; Sagi, 2002; Sefler, 1974; Simon, 1960; Srigley, 2011)
- Joseph Conrad (see Cuthbertson, 1974; Michel, 1961; Young, 1975)
- Joseph Heller (see Harris, 1972; Janoff, 1974; Swardson, 1976; Waldmeir, 1964)
- Franz Kafka (see Cornwell, 2006; Karst, 1975; Kavanagh, 1972; Sollars, 2010)
- Daniil Kharms (see Cornwell, 1991a, 2006; Fink, 1998; Ostashevsky and Yankelevich, 2002)
- Herman Melville (see Bowen, 1971; Hauck, 1971; Seltzer, 1967; Spector, 1961)
- Thomas Pynchon (see Harris, 1972; Hausdorff, 1966; MacNamara, 1968; Safer, 1994)
- Mark Twain (see Brodwin, 1972; Kosinski, 1979; Swardson, 1976)
- Kurt Vonnegut (see Harris, 1972; Klinkowitz, 1971; May, 1972; Philmus, 2005).

This collection of entirely white, male authors nevertheless represents a sizeable spread of work across the late nineteenth, twentieth and early twenty-first centuries (with a slight emphasis on the post-World War II period of the twentieth century) and includes Irish, German, French, Russian and American writers. Despite its disparate nature, this list also bears a close resemblance to a list of authors most frequently identified as 'absurd' by members of a large community of readers reading within a non-academic context, the reported experiences of whom I will be examining at points throughout this book. As we shall see, fuzzy though the boundaries around scholarly notions of absurd prose fiction may be, they nonetheless do seem to reflect other readers' ideas about absurd texts and their authors formulated in non-academic contexts.

As outlined in Chapter 1, online book discussion websites provide readily accessible, naturalistic and public conversations about literature which can prove enormously helpful in any attempt to broaden our understanding of literary experience beyond the academic domain. I pointed out in Chapter 1 that, although the members of such websites may include academic readers, the sites themselves exist outside the usual physical and social parameters of higher-education discourse, offering participants a separate, and arguably more neutral, space within which to interact with literature and with other readers. Numerous websites allow members from any social or geographical background to communicate with one another, to tag works of literature, to share recommendations, to write reviews and to discuss books in a virtual environment with other readers from around the world. One of the largest such websites is LibraryThing, which claims to have over 1,400,000 members from across the globe (LibraryThing, 2012). Not only do the extended discussions of literary texts which take place on websites such as LibraryThing exist as naturally occurring accounts of literary experience, but even the more minimal activity of tagging texts can be revealing of readers' perceptions of literature. For example, the tag 'absurd' is a popular one on LibraryThing and, at the time of writing, it had been used 1,654 times by 570 different users to describe works of literature. The related tag 'absurdism' had been used 1,174 times by 385 users, while 'absurdist' had 724 uses by 220 members. LibraryThing also enables users to search for particular literary works using combined tags (known as 'tagmashes'), and a search on the website for one or more of the above terms returned the following list of the twenty novels most frequently tagged in this way:

1. *The Outsider* by Albert Camus (first published in 1942)
2. *The Trial* by Franz Kafka (first published in 1925)
3. *The Plague* by Albert Camus (first published in 1947)
4. *Catch-22* by Joseph Heller (first published in 1961)
5. *Incidences* by Daniil Kharms (written between 1933 and 1937 and first published as this collection in 1993)
6. *The Fall* by Albert Camus (first published in 1956)
7. *The Castle* by Franz Kafka (first published in 1930)
8. *Alice's Adventures in Wonderland* by Lewis Carroll (first published in 1865)
9. *Slaughterhouse-Five* by Kurt Vonnegut (first published in 1969)
10. *Exile and the Kingdom* by Albert Camus (first published in 1957)
11. *Metamorphosis* by Franz Kafka (first published in 1915)
12. *The Hitchhiker's Guide to the Galaxy* by Douglas Adams (first published as a novel in 1979)
13. *Molloy, Malone Dies* and *The Unnamable* by Samuel Beckett (first published in French between 1951 and 1953, then in English between 1955 and 1958)
14. *A Confederacy of Dunces* by John Kennedy Toole (written in 1964 and first published in 1980)
15. *The Third Policeman* by Flann O'Brien (written between 1939 and 1940 and first published in 1967)
16. *A Happy Death* by Albert Camus (written between 1936 and 1938 and first published in 1971)

17. *Dirk Gently's Holistic Detective Agency* by Douglas Adams (first published in 1987)
18. *The Master and Margarita* by Mikhail Bulgakov (written between 1928 and 1940 and first published, in a censored version, in 1967)
19. *The First Man* by Albert Camus (written in 1960 and first published, incomplete, in 1994)
20. *The Long Dark Tea-Time of the Soul* by Douglas Adams (first published in 1988).

It is worth noting here the complex publishing histories of many of these texts, as shown by the dates in parentheses. In some cases, these are the result of censorship, particularly in the case of the original works of Russian authors Daniil Kharms (see Cornwell, 1991b) and Mikhail Bulgakov (see Vatulescu, 2010: 55–76), and serve as evidence of a common perception of many absurd texts as socially and/or politically subversive. In other cases, a considerable gap between the dates of writing and publication occurs because of the death of the author, such as that between John Kennedy Toole's suicide in 1969 and the final publication of his novel *A Confederacy of Dunces* in 1980, or between Albert Camus's accidental death in 1960 and the eventual appearance of his last, unfinished work, *The First Man*, in 1994. The challenging nature of absurd stylistic experimentalism is also evidenced here to a degree since, on occasion, even the authors of absurd works themselves have struggled to retain faith in the value of their creations when faced with scepticism or rejection from others: Toole's suicide is widely accepted to have been at least in part the result of the rejection of his manuscript, while Flann O'Brien gave up attempting to have *The Third Policeman* published after its completion, claiming the novel had blown from the backseat of his car while driving from Donegal to Dublin (see Snipe, 1997: 289).

Faced with such a broad-ranging collection of authors and novels, it is illuminating to view the identification of the absurd in literature in both academic and non-academic reading contexts through the single lens of cognitive psychology. From this perspective, the apparently irregular and imprecise categorisation of absurd literary works within both domains can be seen in fact to be functioning in the same way as any other form of human categorisation. According to the theory of prototypes originally developed by psychologist Eleanor Rosch (see Rosch, 1975, 1977, 1978; Rosch and Mervis, 1975; for summaries, see also Lakoff, 1987: 5–153; Murphy, 2004: 41–6), human beings categorise all perceptions and experiences in conceptual configurations which take a radial structure in the mind. At the core of each category are located central examples, the very best or prototypical instances of a particular grouping. One of the most frequently cited examples of such a radial configuration is the way in which human beings commonly categorise different types of fruit (see, for example, Liu, 2006: 338–9; Stockwell, 2002a: 28–9): apples, oranges, pears and bananas can all be considered as typical

examples of the 'fruit' category and have a central position in our understanding of it. Prototype structures also contain less good, or secondary,
examples of categories, as well as the most peripheral members. In the 'fruit'
example, for instance, strawberries, kiwi fruit, lemons and lychees can be
seen as progressively less good examples of the category and are positioned
ever further out in the radial grouping. Crucially, however, the boundaries
between different categories are neither fixed nor impermeable and any one
item may have membership of several different conceptual categories (consider tomatoes, for example, which are included in both the 'vegetable' and
'fruit' categories in many people's minds). Furthermore, the categories we
create are prone to expansion or reduction as the result of new experiences
and the influx of new information, and are also greatly influenced by cultural
and sociological factors: the items I, as a northern European, have included
in my 'fruit' category and their configuration within that conceptual structure
are likely to differ from those included in the 'fruit' category by someone
from, say, China or Brazil.

In terms of our experiences of literary reading, then, our individual notions
of a particular literary category, such as the absurd, will contain a variety of
examples, ranging from those texts which we consider to be prototypically
absurd and those which, for whatever reason, belong only peripherally to
the group. These groupings of texts, of course, form the cognitive basis of
our notions of literary genre. Once again, the permeable boundaries between
categories are of crucial importance when dealing with literary texts, as Steen
explains in his discussion of literary genres as communicative events:

> A particular genre event can be a central or marginal case for the cat-
> egory it exemplifies in that it can display better or worse characteristics
> of the genre it belongs to. Any historical novel, for instance, is (a) a
> novel but (b) less typical since it is not completely fictive. This per-
> spective therefore allows for the inclusion of a particular genre event
> within the class of a genre as more or less typical, or even as a hybrid
> between two genres, without undermining the complete system. This is
> in fact how many language users operate with genres that are in a stage
> of transition or that have ended up on the border between two well-
> defined but mutually exclusive categories.
>
> (Steen, 2011: 30)

The fact that a particular text fits into the conceptual category of 'absurd',
then, does not preclude it from also belonging to other categories, such as
'modernist', 'humorous', 'post-war' or 'existentialist'. Indeed, Steen seems to
be arguing here that an initial conceptualisation of hybridity between genres
is a key factor in how new, more distinct genres eventually develop.

Steen goes on to suggest a detailed framework for the understanding of
genre in cognitive-psychological terms. The framework develops along three

essential planes – context, text and code – and can be summarised as encompassing the following considerations (Steen, 2011: 32–3):

1. An understanding at the level of *context* of the influence of
   - the participants in a discourse, their relationships and roles
   - the goals and functions of the discourse itself
   - the spatio-temporal setting of the discourse
   - the social and cultural domain within which the discourse is positioned (e.g. entertainment, business, law, politics)
   - the role of the medium of the discourse (e.g. newspaper, television, film, prose fiction).
2. An understanding at the level of the *text* of the roles of
   - the content of the text, its themes and topics
   - the type of text it is (e.g. narrative, argument, instruction)
   - the form of the text and its formal superstructures (e.g. the Introduction–Methods–Results–Discussion superstructure for scientific reports)
   - the structure of the text, how it refers and coheres.
3. An understanding at the level of *code* of the possible effects of
   - the modality of the text, its use of language and/or other sign systems (such as sound and image)
   - the significance of the choice of one language over another
   - the register of the text
   - the style of the text
   - the use of rhetorical devices within the text.

What this model proposes is a cognitive, context-sensitive and stylistically driven approach to the examination of all genres of discourse; what it offers literary scholarship specifically is a principled means of comprehending the complex interrelationships between writers, readers, a text and its context, which underpin both the phenomenon of the absurd in literature and all other literary genres. As such, Steen's suggested framework will be followed as a guiding set of analytical principles throughout this book. Over the course of each of the coming chapters, my discussion will examine the social, historical and cultural contexts in which absurd reading and writing takes place, the overarching discourse structures through which the absurd is made manifest in literature, and the specific textuality of that discourse.

Context, community and situated concepts

Of particular interest in the present chapter is Steen's emphasis on the importance of context as a key influencing factor in readers' conceptual configurations of items within a literary genre. Indeed, from some of the most recent research into the human conceptual system there is persuasive empirical evidence that categories are not, in fact, abstract structures distilled from the relevant properties of various exemplars at all. Instead, the 'situated simulation' view (see Barsalou, 1985, 2003, 2009; Barsalou et al., 1998, 1999; Yeh and Barsalou, 2006) recognises that categories are made up of concepts that are necessarily dependent on the particular context to which they are attached and are tailored to the needs of a specific situation. What is more, concepts seem to function as *simulations* of previous experiences involving both the human conceptual system and the sensory-motor system. As Barsalou explains:

> When a category is represented conceptually, the neural systems that processed it during perception and action become active in much the same way as if a category member were present (again, though, not identically). On conceptualising *CAR*, for example, the visual system might become partially active as if a car were present. Similarly the auditory system might reenact states associated with hearing a car, the motor system might reenact states associated with driving a car, and the limbic system might reenact emotional states associated with enjoying the experience of driving (again all at the neural level).
>
> (Barsalou, 2003: 523)

The neuroscientific research that Barsalou summarises here suggests that human beings perform simulations of concepts in order to help them achieve particular goals in particular circumstances. Each concept contains a package of contextualised information about a likely background setting, possible actions an agent could take and possible emotions and other consequences that might arise as a result of those actions (Barsalou, 2003: 552). Barsalou goes on to explain,

> Together these inferences produce the experience of 'being there' with a category member, preparing an agent for situated action in a particular context . . . A given simulator can construct an indefinitely large number of specific simulations to represent the respective category. Rather than a concept being a fixed representation, it is a skill for tailoring representations to the constraints of situated action. Because the same category can take different forms, be encountered in a variety of settings, and serve many goals, a fixed representation would not be optimal. No single representation could possibly serve all of these different situations well. A much better solution arises from having a simulator tailor conceptualisations to particular situations.
>
> (Barsalou, 2003: 552–3)

Our individual notions of a particular literary genre, then, will vary not only according to our personal experiences in the same way that any other category is culturally and experientially dependent, but these variations will further depend on the specific context in which we encounter a text and on our specific goals within those circumstances. This is a view which finds further support in Berkenkotter and Huckin's study of writing within the academic genre, in which the authors conclude that 'genres are inherently dynamic rhetorical structures that can be manipulated according to the conditions of use and that genre knowledge is therefore best conceptualized as a form of situated cognition embedded in disciplinary activities' (Berkenkotter and Huckin, 1993: 477).

This is not to say, however, that literary genres and literary categorisation are entirely individualistic and that study of them is therefore necessarily doomed to relativism. Let us return for a moment to readers' tagging behaviours on literary websites. Examining patterns of tagging across a large number of different readers in this way, reading in different situations and with different goals, can give us a clear picture of *shared* concepts of texts and authors as well as the necessary situatedness of individual responses. Although all the readers in non-academic contexts whose opinions and categorisations are examined in this book are situated in different locations around the world and are of different ages and social backgrounds, they are also defined as a group by the fact that they are all reading the texts in English in the early twenty-first century and have all made a conscious decision to join the literary website of their choice and to share their experiences of literature on it. Similarly, all the readers in academic contexts whose work is considered here are brought together by a shared occupation and a shared interest in literature of a certain period and style. Their critical work can be seen to congregate around the late twentieth century, with the majority of it discussing literature in terms of absurdism appearing from the late 1960s onwards. Sociolinguists talk about such situated and shared language behaviour in terms of 'communities of practice' (see Eckert, 2000; Eckert and McConnell-Ginet, 1992; Wenger, 1998), which are defined as follows:

> An aggregate of people who come together around mutual engagement in an endeavor. Ways of doing things, ways of talking, beliefs, values, power relations – in short – practices – emerge in the course of this mutual endeavor.
>
> (Eckert and McConnell-Ginet, 1992: 464)

As we have seen above, the publication dates of absurd texts collect around the mid to late twentieth century. Although it is impossible to know the extent to which their authors were consciously or deliberately writing with a mutual endeavour in mind, following a properly rigorous stylistic examination of their work, they can nevertheless be defined by the shared patterns of language use they display. Readers who identify texts in terms of the absurd are similarly situated at a specific point in history and defined as a community of practice through their common behaviour.

From this perspective, the literary absurd in both a readerly and a writerly sense can been as a predominantly post-World War II phenomenon occurring across several communities of practice. Furthermore, if we cross-reference the novels most frequently identified as 'absurd' by readers in an academic context writing in English with those similarly identified by readers writing in English on LibraryThing, we can begin to come close to an understanding of how these texts are understood by a population of combined reading communities. It could easily be argued on this evidence alone that Albert Camus, as the author most often described as absurd in both reading contexts, is a prototypical example of an absurd author (the contentious nature of this statement will become apparent in the discussion of Camus's work later this chapter). Following this reasoning, Franz Kafka, Daniil Kharms, Joseph Heller, Samuel Beckett and Kurt Vonnegut would also seem to occupy relatively central positions within the category of absurd authors, occurring, as they do, in both academic and non-academic lists of favourites. Finally, on the periphery of the conceptual structure, come those authors whom the two reading communities appear to agree upon somewhat less: John Barth, Mark Twain, Thomas Pynchon, Joseph Conrad and Herman Melville nominated by academics; Lewis Carroll, Douglas Adams, John Kennedy Toole, Mikhail Bulgakov and Flann O'Brien nominated by readers in a non-academic setting. However, to pursue this argument based on simple frequency data alone would not give a complete picture of how these authors and their literary creations are experienced and perceived by their readers – although Barsalou (1985) has shown that frequency of occurrence within a category does correlate with an item's perceived prototypicality to some extent. Far more detailed scrutiny, along the lines laid out by Steen (2011), must be undertaken in order to grasp fully the positions particular texts and writers occupy in readers' conceptual categories and the contextualised and experiential reasons which underpin this positioning. Therefore readers' identifications of certain authors and their prose-fictional work as 'absurd' are only the starting point of the present endeavour; a fully contextualised, cognitive and stylistically focused account of the experience of reading the absurd is my ultimate objective.

A cline of experimentalism

In Rosch and Mervis's (1975) study of the internal structure of conceptual categories, the authors explore the hypothesis that the members of a category perceived as most typical would be those with the most attributes in common with other members of the category and with the least number of attributes in common with other categories. Rosch and Mervis termed such shared attributes 'family resemblances', building their empirical investigations directly on Wittgenstein's (1953) original formulation of this notion. When approaching the literary absurd as a genre with an assumed radial structure, the notion of family resemblances as a defining feature of conceptual categories is a very useful one. The identification of points of commonality between literary texts should enable both central and more peripheral examples of a literary genre firstly to be recognised and secondly to be understood in terms of their relative typicality compared with other texts. The same principles can also be applied to the authors of those texts, and we have already seen two of the most common features of absurd writers to be white and male. Although Cornwell (2006: 33–64) has argued that the antecedents of the absurd stretch as far back in history as Ancient Greece, another family resemblance between the authors listed earlier in this chapter is their location around the mid to late twentieth century. Those writing after World War II, then, can be considered, from a prototype-theoretical perspective, to be more typical of absurd authors than those writing at other historical moments. Note, too, that, as a result of this, the prototypicality originally assigned to Albert Camus on the basis of his frequent occurrence within readers' 'absurd' categories is somewhat undermined by his slightly peripheral historical position (1913–60).

As a stylistician, the family resemblances which interest me the most in the present study are those which might be found in the linguistic structures and narrative techniques of absurd texts. It is to these crucial points of textual commonality that the least critical attention has been paid over the years, and this has had, in my opinion, the most detrimental effect on our understanding of the literary absurd as a reading experience. In their failure to attend to absurd style in any detail, preceding literary critics have almost entirely disregarded the planes of both text and code, which Steen (2011) outlines as key components, alongside context, in the proper understanding of any genre of discourse. This is not to say that literary critics have not acknowledged the importance of style in the construction of a literary absurd. In fact, numerous tantalising suggestions have been made that the communication of an absurdist thematic is necessarily dependent on the style of a given literary text. Indeed, for Cornwell, style is a crucial component of the absurd:

> [the absurd] may be considered a prominent period style, observable in the second half of the twentieth century, or (given the presence of now recognised practitioners from the 1920s and 1930s) perhaps a period running through the middle quarters of the century, and a little beyond.
> (Cornwell, 2006: 310)

Here, Cornwell correlates style and a historical period (albeit one with limited clarity) as key constituents in his definition of the absurd. His study as a whole, however, focuses more on a historical survey of absurdism, rather than attempting to describe its stylistic techniques or its discoursal structures. As such, it only skirts around the issue of style and offers little in the way of a delineation of the typical linguistic features of absurdist texts.

In his earlier seminal study of absurd drama, Esslin, too, outlines the importance of style in the absurd:

> A term like Theatre of the Absurd is a working hypothesis, a device to make certain fundamental traits which seem to be present in the works of a number of dramatists accessible to discussion by tracing the features they have in common.
>
> (Esslin, 1980: 12)

Unfortunately, Esslin does not specify what these 'fundamental traits' or 'features' are, offering only impressionistic descriptions of the works of each of his chosen dramatists, as well as some discussion of their reception on their first performance, but without reference to the stylistic features the texts may share. However, Esslin does provide more rigorous detail in his differentiation between those writers he considers to be dramatists of the absurd and those, including Jean Giraudoux, Jean-Paul Sartre and Albert Camus, whom he identifies as belonging to an earlier tradition of 'existentialist theatre' (Esslin, 1980: 25). He argues that

> these writers differ from the dramatists of the Absurd in an important respect: they present their sense of the irrationality of the human condition in the form of highly lucid and logically constructed reasoning, while the Theatre of the Absurd strives to express its sense of the senselessness of the human condition and the inadequacy of the rational approach by the open abandonment of rational devices and discursive thought. While Sartre or Camus express the new content in the old convention, the Theatre of the Absurd goes one step further in trying to achieve a unity between its basic assumptions and the form in which these are expressed.
>
> (Esslin, 1980: 24)

As far as Esslin is concerned, Sartre, Camus and their contemporaries can be seen to be expressing the same metaphysical anguish as Samuel Beckett, Harold Pinter and the rest of Esslin's absurd playwrights, only in a more conventional, realist form. Indeed, Esslin goes on to describe Camus's writing as displaying 'the elegantly rationalistic and discursive style of an eighteenth century moralist' (Esslin, 1980: 24), while he claims that Sartre's plays are 'based on brilliantly drawn characters who remain wholly consistent and thus reflect the old convention that each human being has a core of immutable, unchanging essence' (Esslin, 1980: 24).

Esslin argues that the 'Theatre of the Absurd', by contrast, is characterised by its deliberate violation of such literary and dramatic norms, displaying features which can be seen to defy those conventions which had previously defined the qualitative boundaries of the literary canon. As he explains:

If a good play must have a cleverly constructed story, these have no story or plot to speak of; if a good play is judged by subtlety of characterization and motivation, these are often without recognizable character and present the audience with almost mechanical puppets; if a good play has to have a fully explained theme, which is neatly exposed and finally solved, these have neither a beginning nor an end; if a good play is to hold up the mirror to nature and portray the manners and mannerisms of the age in finely observed sketches, these seem to be reflections of dreams and nightmares; if a good play relies on witty repartee and pointed dialogue, these often consist of incoherent babblings.

(Esslin, 1980: 21–2)

However, Esslin is also quick to point out the speed and readiness with which such initially incomprehensible avant-garde work was embraced by its audiences and transformed into the 'all too easily understood modern classic' (Esslin, 1980: 11). Indeed, as outlined in Chapter 1, Esslin's own terminology enjoyed a similar rush of popularity following the publication of *The Theatre of the Absurd*, as the phrase swiftly became a widely used, but often ill-defined, umbrella term applied to numerous disparate plays and playwrights of the mid to late twentieth century, and later to novels, novelists, poets and poetry far beyond this.

As a consequence, Esslin made several attempts, both in the later editions of his initial monograph and in other subsequent studies of absurd drama (e.g. Esslin, 1965), to redraw and re-emphasise the boundaries of his 'Theatre of the Absurd', describing the term as having become a 'catchphrase, much used and much abused' (Esslin, 1965: 7). Elsewhere, he argues that

the term, coined to describe certain features of certain plays in order to bring out certain underlying similarities has been treated as though it corresponded to an organized movement, like a political party or a hockey team, which made its members carry badges and banners . . . The artists of an epoch have certain traits in common, but they are not necessarily conscious of them. Nor does the fact that they have these traits preclude them from being widely different in other respects.

(Esslin, 1980: 12)

Esslin seems torn, then, between the need to demarcate and differentiate the Theatre of the Absurd from other literary forms and the desire to broaden his grouping to encompass numerous stylistically and historically diverse texts in much the same way as many other literary critics. In fact, the latter of these forces ultimately prevailed, as the term 'absurd' continued to be employed as a means of describing a vast array of drama, prose fiction and poetry – see, for only a sample of these accounts, Brodwin (1972) on Mark Twain; Brothers (1977) on Henry Green; Cuthbertson (1974) on Joseph Conrad; Galloway

(1966) on John Updike, William Styron, Saul Bellow and J.D. Salinger; Hauck (1971) on Herman Melville, Mark Twain, William Faulkner and John Barth; Hilfer (1992) on Joseph Heller, Thomas Pynchon, Kurt Vonnegut, John Barth and Vladimir Nabokov; Hinchliffe (1972) on, among others, Samuel Beckett, John Osborne, Tom Stoppard and Edward Albee; Ketterer (1978) on Kurt Vonnegut and Philip K. Dick; Meier (2001) on Ted Hughes; Michel (1961) on Joseph Conrad; Miller (1967) on William Faulkner, Walt Whitman and Emily Dickinson; Mistri (1988) on John Barth; Penner (1978) on Vladimir Nabokov; Safer (1983b, 1989, 1994) on Ken Kesey, John Barth and Thomas Pynchon; Seltzer (1967) on Herman Melville; Silver (1972) on Wallace Stevens; and Spector (1961) on Herman Melville; Waldmeir (1964) on Joseph Heller and Ken Kesey. As this list shows, in many later studies of novels, short stories and poems, the line so carefully drawn by Esslin between existentialist and absurdist forms becomes blurred, with realist texts such as Ken Kesey's *One Flew Over the Cuckoo's Nest* (1962), for example, often being categorised by literary critics as 'absurd' alongside more stylistically experimental works, such as Thomas Pynchon's *V* (1963).

Weinberg (1970), however, offers a useful formalisation of such apparent academic inconsistencies. Like Esslin, she distinguishes between those novels which convey existentialist concerns through a conventional narrative structure and those which strive to achieve a more stylistically innovative expression of the absurdity of the human condition. In the former, realist category she includes Camus's (1942) *The Outsider* and Sartre's (1938) *Nausea*, as well as later works such as J.D. Salinger's (1951) *The Catcher in the Rye* and Bruce Friedman's (1962) *Stern*. Weinberg goes on to explain,

> These novels are informed by a vision of absurdity and have at their centre a passive, rationalistic, or hopelessly ineffectual victim-hero, dominated by his situation rather than creating or acting to change it. They have a more or less realistic surface, with somewhat surrealistic elements. Realism of detail, rather, underscores the madness of the world, its grotesque comedy.
>
> (Weinberg, 1970: 10)

Weinberg claims that, by contrast, in novels like Pynchon's *V*, Joseph Heller's (1962) *Catch-22* and John Barth's (1958) *The End of the Road*, the same philosophical themes that form the focus of the realist texts listed above are made manifest through what she terms a 'stylized absurd surface' (Weinberg, 1970: 11). She goes on to explain,

> The absurd surface exaggerates. Through exaggeration and repetitions; grotesqueries; unique, exotic, bizarre or strange symbols. . . the absurdity found in life is transcribed through surreal descriptions. Special surrealistic situations, too, are created to embody the inexplicable; and

somewhat common situations, such as those of war, are exaggerated and distorted to produce a heightened effect of the sort experienced in dreams.

(Weinberg, 1970: 11)

Weinberg's separation of absurd prose fiction into two distinct categories, one realist and one non-realist, provides a positive development of Esslin's original classification of existentialist and absurdist drama. In particular, Weinberg further differentiates between absurd prose fiction and numerous other twentieth-century novels which may also make use of a non-realist narrative structure. Although many novels of the last 100 years or so may, for example, display a disrupted chronology, or contain surrealistic elements and situations, not all of them communicate the existentialist unease which, according to Weinberg, must be present in order for a text to be considered truly absurd.

Unfortunately, Weinberg's promising summary of different types of absurd literature does not extend beyond the initial sketchy delineation offered above and her notions of a 'realistic surface', 'surrealistic elements' and an 'absurd surface' remain frustratingly undeveloped and, once again, under-specific in stylistic terms. I would also argue that assigning absurd literary texts to one of Weinberg's categories or the other may, in practice, turn out to be a more complicated task than she suggests. As we have seen at the outset of this chapter, categorisation always involves challenging overlaps, fuzzy boundaries and individual, situated variations. It is more helpful, I would further argue, to think of absurd literature as existing along a cline of experimentalism, with realist texts at one extreme of this and stylistically innovative texts at the other. As we shall see in the next section of this chapter, it is important to understand, too, that a particular text's position along this cline of experimentalism does not necessarily correlate with its position within readers' radial categories of the absurd: the most stylistically experimental texts are not necessarily those which readers consider to be the most prototypically absurd. The following section begins the present book's attempt to describe the diversity and stylistic complexity of absurd literature through rigorous and replicable linguistic analysis, starting at the realist end of the cline of absurd experimentalism with an exploration of the work of one of the founding fathers of the absurd, Albert Camus. However, as we shall see, while Camus's pivotal role in the evolution of the literary absurd is indisputable, his frequent categorisation within other literary and philosophical movements has led to considerable controversy surrounding his work, his politics and his personal and social life. Getting to the heart of this controversy will lead us in turn to address some of the most complex questions at the heart of the phenomenon of the literary absurd in general.

Writing on the boundaries of the absurd

We have already seen earlier in this chapter how the writings of Albert Camus
were viewed by one of the most prominent figures in literary criticism of the
absurd, Martin Esslin. The notion that Camus was 'express[ing] the new
content in the old convention' and had 'the elegantly rationalistic and discursive style of an eighteenth century moralist' (Esslin, 1980: 24) is not peculiar
to Esslin. A significant number of other literary critics share Esslin's view and
have similarly categorised Camus as straightforwardly existentialist, writing
within the same philosophical, political and stylistic tradition as Jean-Paul
Sartre (see Baker, 1993; Barnes, 1962; Christensen, 1962; Friedman, 1964;
Killinger, 1961; Kleppner, 1964; McGregor, 1993; Palmer, 1974). As I noted
briefly in Chapter 1, the majority of these critics also regard the absurd as a
component, albeit an important one, of existentialist thought, rather than
as a philosophy or literary phenomenon in its own right. This standpoint is
illustrated most typically as follows:

> a sense of the absurd is a recognition that the world appears to be
> meaningless, yet one continues to live on as if it were not so, like the
> condemned prisoner who asserts his right to live even after the sentence
> is passed. It is the confrontation of our desire for unity and clarity and
> the world's disunity and irrationality. The absurd for the existential-
> ists is a revelation of certain facets of the human condition as revealed
> through the characters, places, events and situations in their novels. It
> is a matter of analyzing the above criteria, making this a mode of dis-
> covery for any critique of the existentialist novel.
>
> (Baker, 1993: 3)

The absurd, from this point of view, then, is a realisation or feeling, a moment
occurring at some point along the journey to existentialism which, although
crucial, is nevertheless only one element of a larger philosophical quest.
According to this view, novelists, such as Camus, who explore or reflect this
realisation are unproblematically expressing existentialist concerns through
the imaginary worlds they construct.

The number of critics who follow this line in relation to Camus may be
significant, but they are nevertheless in the minority within literary criticism
as a whole. A far greater number of critics recognise the subtle but important
difficulties which arise from categorising Camus solely as an existentialist, in
the same vein as Sartre. These difficulties are largely the result of Camus's
own explicit and repeated rejection of the existentialist label and of the
momentous falling out he had with Jean-Paul Sartre over this very issue in
1952 (see Aronson, 2004; Carroll, 2007; Ehrmann, 1960; Forsdick, 2007;
Sagi, 2002; Sefler, 1974; Sprintzen and van den Hoven, 2004). The two men
enjoyed a close personal friendship, beginning in 1943 and lasting almost

a decade, which was originally based on mutual intellectual respect and political allegiance. However, as detailed in Aronson's (2004) comprehensive account of their friendship and its eventual disintegration, nuanced differences between their two separate worldviews, alongside more personal strains and jealousies, began to develop through the latter years of World War II and beyond. As Sartre increasingly came to embrace communism and, with it, reconcile himself to the possibility of violent struggle towards that end, Camus conversely became increasingly disillusioned with political orthodoxy and, above all else, rejected all forms of violence. Following the publication of Camus's *L'Homme revolté* in 1952 (published in English as *The Rebel* in 1956), which was widely seen as a thinly veiled attack on Sartre and his political opinions, the men's friendship ended explosively through an exchange of searing reviews and public letters. The two men did not speak again, with all possibilities of reconciliation cut off by Camus's premature death in a car accident in 1960.

Crucially, at the core of the personal conflict between Camus and Sartre were tangible and important differences between their views on the human condition and its necessary consequences, which had, in fact, been ever-present throughout their friendship. For example, in Sartre's review of Camus's *The Myth of Sisyphus*, as far back as 1943, Forsdick explains that

> With professional overtones, [Sartre] questions Camus's understanding of Jaspers, Heidegger and Kierkegaard, but goes on to celebrate the anti-conventional humanism of the text's absurdist hero, highlighting the success of the style adopted by the author. In Sartre's view, therefore, Camus is successful as a novelist, but not as a philosopher: the triumph of style over intellectual content is an accusation that would surface in the exchanges leading to their rupture a decade later.
>
> (Forsdick, 2007: 120)

Sartre's view that Camus excelled as a novelist but was fundamentally flawed as a philosopher is now a commonly held one, particularly within existential philosophy itself. Camus is frequently included in surveys of existential thought, since his influence on Sartre and his importance within Sartre's social and political group during the war are undeniable. However, his inclusion in such surveys is almost always fleeting and generally accompanied by a caveat, most typically illustrated by Cooper (1990) in his dismissal of Camus from the existentialist camp:

> One reason for excluding Camus is that, unlike the rest of our writers, it is not at all his aim to reduce or overcome a sense of alienation or separateness from the world. In the attitude of Meursault, *The Outsider*, for example, we find a defiant pleasure taken in our alienated condition. Sisyphus, the 'absurd hero', feels a 'silent joy' in living in

a world where 'man feels an alien, a stranger . . . his exile . . . without remedy'. . . Camus was, by his own admission or boast, not interested in the weighty philosophical topics which occupied his Parisian friends, Sartre and Merleau-Ponty – the nature of consciousness and perception, the mind–body relation, the problem of 'other minds' and so on. Existentialism, as treated in this book, is not a mood or a vocabulary, but a relatively simplistic philosophy in which topics like this are duly addressed. I shall have little to say about those, like Camus, who make a virtue out of being neither a philosopher nor systematic.

(Cooper, 1990: 9)

Although the concept of absurdity is a central one in existential philosophy, Cooper is correct to point out that Camus's use of it has different motivations from those of the existentialists and that such terms when used by Camus are, as he puts it, 'terms of art' (Cooper, 1990: 8).

Having said all this, despite the fact that the political and philosophical differences between Sartre and Camus were of eventual life-changing importance to the two men, and regardless of the care with which the majority of philosophers, biographers and literary critics have separated their motivations and core concerns, it is important to acknowledge that for many other readers, both academic and non-academic, these boundaries are either not discernible or not important. Clear evidence of this beyond the realm of literary criticism and history can be found, once again, in the tagging behaviours of participants in online literary discussion websites. We have already seen that Camus tops the list of absurd novelists compiled by members of LibraryThing. However, on the website Shelfari, currently the third largest online book community in the world (Shelfari, 2012a), the text most frequently tagged 'existentialism' is Camus's *The Outsider*. The same is true on LibraryThing as well, where the novel had been tagged 'existentialism' 1,024 times at the point of writing, followed by *The Plague* (457 times), and beating Sartre's *Nausea* and *Being and Nothingness* (originally published in 1943) into a close third (411 times) and fourth place (322 times) respectively. However, from the prototype-theoretical perspective on genre adopted in the present study, Camus's membership of more than one literary category at once does not present the insurmountable problem with which many literary critics have felt themselves to be faced. On the contrary, the fact that Camus's work straddles at least two major genres of the early twentieth century signals that a fuller understanding of the stylistic family resemblances his texts share with the other members of both of these categories is likely to enable us to understand more about their points of commonality and of difference. From this point of view, Camus can be seen, not as a discordant source of controversy and confusion, but as a key access point to a better comprehension of both the absurd and the existential in literature, since his work defines the very boundaries and crossovers between the two. Since the aim of the present study is to make steps towards a fuller and more rigorous definition of absurd style, an account of the defining stylistic features of existential literature lies beyond its parameters. It is possible within these pages, however, at least to begin to understand one side of Camus's generic identity, his absurdism, through the systematic examination of his work's stylistic resemblances to other texts commonly categorised in this way.

Reading on the boundaries of the absurd

The Outsider (also translated as *The Stranger* in some editions of the text) not only figures prominently in existentialist and absurdist folksonomies, it also scores very highly when rated using one of the star- or number-rating systems available on most literary discussion websites. On the site Goodreads (Goodreads, 2012a), for example, the novel scores an average of 3.86 out of 5.00, with 36 per cent of participating readers rating the text 4 and 30 per cent rating it 5. On Shelfari the novel scores 4 out of 5, on LibraryThing 4.01 out of 5.00 and on Amazon 4.5 out of 5.0, with 68 per cent of people giving the novel the maximum of five stars (Amazon, 2012). (To put these ratings in context with one major work of canonical literature, Shakespeare's sonnets score 4.22 out of 5.00 on Goodreads, 4.5 out of 5.0 on Shelfari, 4.3 out of 5.0 on LibraryThing and 4 out of 5 on Amazon.) The ratings systems offered on most literary websites, however, remain somewhat crude and the strong feelings readers have towards *The Outsider* are more fully expressed in extended online discussions, reviews and conversations. The novel features frequently in reader-generated lists and discussion threads bearing titles such 'Top 10 books to read before you die' and 'Novels you can't imagine never having read', with readers often describing the impact of the text on them in terms such as 'thought-provoking' (Shelfari, 2012b), 'astounding' (Goodreads, 2012a) and 'change[d] my view on life' (Shelfari, 2012b). The following is a typical example of a Shelfari reader's more lengthy report of their response to Camus's novel:

[1]
I enjoyed this novel quite a bit. More than that, actually; this man, Meursault – I find him to be a fantastic, wonderful creature. The philosophy of existentialism is something so good and this book is full of such truth. The writing style is something that adds to it – Camus has done an excellent job of giving to the reader Meursault's personality and managing to make everything seem quite so simple. I adore Meursault. I adore this man, and I cannot say so enough. Existentialism is inside of me, devouring my brain, but it's nice to be able to put a name to one's way of thinking.

(nyssa, 2011)

What is particularly interesting about this report is that it centres mainly around the reader's emotional responses to and evaluations of the main character in the novel, Meursault, which are highly positive. The overall positivity exhibited towards *The Outsider* here is shared by many readers in this and other online book communities. However, the specific emotions readers tend to feel towards Meursault are on the whole more subtle and complex than is perhaps reflected in the quotation above. Consider the following report from another Shelfari reader:

[2]
I hate the main character and love him at the same time. It wasn't until the last chapter that I actually liked him. What a genius. And now that I look back, I understand who and what he is. He wasn't a character meant to sympathize with, or relate to. He wasn't even much of a character until the last chapter. He was a montage of existentialism; an indifferent symbol, robotic in attitude. I like to think if I read it backwards, it would be about an existentialist genius who grew more and more mechanical as time went on. Seriously, the last chapter is a god damn literary masterpiece. Only reason I like this book. What *The Stranger* said about God, and what little time we have to dwell on such uncertainties is beautiful. And I completely agree. We waste our lives worrying about the post-life without giving any thought to what's happening in our current life. Regardless of the afterlife – which I personally don't believe in – we should all take the time to appreciate the life we have now; for better or for worse.

(cura, 2012)

In report (2), more ambivalent and conflicting emotions are described in relation to Camus's text. This reader expresses strong negative appraisal of the main character ('I hate the main character', 'It wasn't until the last chapter that I actually liked him', 'He was . . . an indifferent symbol, robotic in attitude') alongside equally clear positive appreciation of both him ('I . . . love him at the same time', 'What a genius', 'an existential genius') and the text as a whole ('the last chapter is a god damn literary masterpiece').

Such wavering emotional and evaluative responses are particularly interesting when considered through the lens of cognitive and phenomenological research into the psychology and emotion of literary experience. This body of research is considerable in size and range (for usefully extensive surveys see Keen, 2006, 2007) and includes numerous studies exploring the phenomena of identification, emotional response and the real-world impact of literary texts through a diversity of empirical and experimental methods. One of the key theories in this area is known as 'transportation theory' (Gerrig, 1993; Green, 2004; Green and Brock, 2000; Green et al., 2002, 2004). Gerrig explains the central analogy of this theory of narrative experience as follows:

Someone (the traveler) is transported, by some means of transportation, as a result of performing certain actions. The traveler goes some distance from his or her world of origin, which makes some aspects of the world of origin inaccessible. The traveler returns to the world of origin, somewhat changed by the journey.

(Gerrig, 1993: 10–11)

Following on from this basic metaphor, Green and Brock (2000) develop a fifteen-point self-report scale (which asks readers, among other things, to score how involved they felt in a text, how distracted from their surroundings they felt and so on) against which the extent of a reader's transportation into a narrative world can be measured. Green et al. (2004) go on to argue that being transported by a narrative is necessary before readers can begin to form identifications with fictional characters. They explain,

Central to the process of identification is the adoption of a character's thoughts, goals, emotions, and behaviors, and such vicarious experience requires the reader or viewer to leave his or her physical, social, and psychological reality behind in favor of the world of the narrative and its inhabitants . . . In essence, to identify with a character means seeing the character's perspective as one's own, to share his or her existence. Achieving such an altered state of awareness relies upon transportation into the story world. Upon reentering the real world, the individual has been transformed as a consequence of merging him- or herself with a story character.

(Green et al., 2004: 318)

Transportation theory, then, recognises the potential of narrative texts not only psychologically to take readers away from their real-world surroundings but to have a longer-term transformative effect on them beyond this initial reading experience. A significant number of extended commentaries made by readers of *The Outsider* online include reports of a transformative as well as transportative experience of the narrative. Interestingly, both types of experience seem possible regardless of any ambivalent feelings readers may have towards the main character himself.

In a separate series of empirical studies, Miall and Kuiken (2002b) (see also Miall and Kuiken, 1994; Kuiken et al., 2004) argue that feelings associated with literary reading occur within four domains, each domain having a different function. The first of these domains they term 'evaluative feelings' and argue that these relate to the overall enjoyment or pleasure derived from reading. They point out that these feelings are not confined to reading alone and may also be experienced watching film or television, for example. Second, 'narrative feelings' are feelings prompted by an event or situation within the fictional world. This category includes feelings of sympathy or empathy with a character. Miall and Kuiken's third category is that of 'aesthetic feelings' and relates to a heightened interest prompted by formal features of a text (see also Miall and Kuiken, 1994). They explain that aesthetic feelings are 'what readers have in mind when they report that passages within a text are so striking that they capture and hold their attention' (Miall and Kuiken, 1994: 224) and that readers tend to slow their reading and report increased uncertainty in response to such foregrounded stylistic and narrative features. Finally, readers may also experience feelings of 'self-modification' during or after reading, described as follows:

> Readers may experience self-modifying feelings that restructure their understanding of the text and, simultaneously, their sense of themselves. Readers commonly recognize settings, characters, or events as familiar (e.g., a story event is reminiscent of something they have directly experienced or have read before). But, at times, they also find themselves participating in an unconventional flow of feelings through which they realize something that they have not previously experienced – or at least not in the form provided by the text. At these times, the imaginary world of the text is not only unfamiliar but disquieting. One aspect of this disquietude is the possibility that the shifting experience of the world of the text may be carried forward as an altered understanding of the reader's own lifeworld.
>
> (Kuiken et al., 2004: 175)

Once again, the final domain of feelings identified in this study recognises the significant potential of literary reading to have a lasting effect on readers' lives beyond their initial interaction with a text.

If we return to readers (1) and (2) above, we can see evidence of all four domains of feelings at play in these self-reports of emotional responses to *The Outsider*. Report (1) contains evidence of evaluative feelings (e.g. 'I enjoyed this novel quite a bit') and aesthetic feelings (e.g. 'The writing style is something that adds to it – Camus has done an excellent job of giving to the reader Meursault's personality and managing to make everything seem quite so simple'). Most strongly in this example, though, the reader expresses uncomplicated identification with Meursault and clear feelings of empathy with him (e.g. 'I find him to be a fantastic, wonderful creature') and possibly with Camus as well (since it is not clear whether the comment 'I adore this man' refers to Meursault or to his creator). Also interesting here is the final comment, 'Existentialism is inside of me, devouring my brain, but it's nice to be able to put a name to one's way of thinking', which seems to suggest that *The Outsider* has confirmed rather than altered this reader's understanding of the real world. It does not seem, then, that the text has been self-modifying for this reader.

Reader (2) also reports experiencing each of the domains of feelings set out by Miall and Kuiken, but with different levels of intensity from reader

(1). For example, evaluative feelings about the text as a whole are described, but with far less of the intensity and uncomplicated positivity that reader (1) seems to have experienced (seen in the ambivalent comment 'Only reason I like this book'). The reader's identification with Meursault appears to have been problematical too and seems to hinge on a love–hate dichotomy (e.g. 'I hate the main character and love him at the same time'). On the whole, this reader seems to have engaged in a more mindful reading of the text, expressed through the overwhelming concentration in the report on aesthetic feelings. The cleverness of the book and of its existential philosophy, for example, is commented upon in various ways and at various points (e.g. 'What a genius', 'What *The Stranger* said about God, and what little time we have to dwell on such uncertainties is beautiful'). The reader also appears to have considered Camus's construction of Meursault's character carefully, as well as his possible motivations for employing particular narrative techniques (e.g. 'I understand who and what he is', 'He wasn't a character meant to sympathize with, or relate to . . . He was a montage of existentialism; an indifferent symbol, robotic in attitude'). Particularly noteworthy is the way in which one section of the book, the last chapter, is singled out for special appreciative commentary ('the last chapter is a god damn literary masterpiece') and how this appears to be directly tied to the reader's overall feelings of self-modification (seen in the closing comments, 'We waste our lives worrying about the post-life without giving any thought to what's happening in our current life . . . we should all take the time to appreciate the life we have now; for better or for worse'). So, while reader (2) reports fewer narrative feelings and a much less straightforward identification with Meursault, this commentary nevertheless contains greater evidence of self-modifying feelings than the report from reader (1).

Building absurd worlds

At this point in the discussion of Camus's novel and its central position within readers' conceptual categories of both literary existentialism and the absurd, it is useful to turn to the text itself and begin to explore the precise stylistic components of the narrative which might give rise to readers' feelings and responses. One of the features of the text most frequently discussed in literary criticism on *The Outsider* is the motif of heat and light which recurs at various key points in the narrative (for typical examples see Feuerlicht, 1963; Frohock, 1949; McCarthy, 1988; Viggiani, 1956). Consider the following extract from near the beginning of the novel, describing a scene soon after the death of Meursault's mother:

It was a rustling sound that woke me. After having my eyes closed, the whiteness of the room seemed even more dazzling than before. There wasn't a shadow to be seen and every object, every angle and

curve stood out so sharply that it was painful to the eyes. It was at that
point that mother's friends came in. There were about ten of them in
all, and they came gliding gently into the blinding light. They sat down
without even a chair creaking. I saw them more clearly than I've ever
seen anyone and not a single detail of either their faces or their clothes
escaped me. And yet I couldn't hear them and I found it hard to believe
that they really existed. Almost all the women were wearing aprons tied
tightly round their waists, which made their swollen bellies stick out
even more. I'd never noticed before what huge paunches old women
can have. The men were almost all very thin and carrying walking-
sticks. What struck me most about their faces was that I couldn't see
their eyes, but only a faint glimmer among a nest of wrinkles. When
they sat down most of them looked at me and nodded awkwardly,
with their lips all sucked into their toothless mouths, and I couldn't tell
whether they were greeting me or whether they just had a twitch.

(Camus, 1982: 15)

The first thing to note about this passage, and indeed the novel as a whole,
is its overall unexperimental narrative style. Camus presents a realistic scene
for his readers here and such mimesis is most often described in cognitive
approaches to literary analysis in terms of the ways in which an immersive
fictional world is constructed through language. One such approach, Text
World Theory (for overviews, see Gavins, 2007; Werth, 1999), provides a
framework for the rigorous and systematic examination of the mental representations created in literary fictional discourse. As I have already explained
in Chapter 1, I will be making use of Text World Theory throughout this
book and introducing individual components of the framework as they
are needed. Under this approach, the mental representations created by
fictional texts are known as 'text-worlds' (see Gavins, 2007: 10), conceptual
spaces constructed in the minds of readers and listeners and initially based
on the deictic markers contained within the text. These markers are known
as 'world-building elements' (see Gavins, 2007: 35–52) and they define the
spatio-temporal setting of a text-world; they specify any characters (referred
to as 'enactors' in Text World Theory) or objects present in the world and
establish social and physical relationships between those entities, as well as
describing time and place more generally. World-building elements, then,
include spatial deictics such as locatives, spatial adverbs and demonstratives,
as well as temporal deictics such as variations in tense and aspect, temporal
locatives and temporal adverbs. The text-worlds readers construct in their
minds based on these deictic foundations have the potential to be as richly
detailed and immersive as the real world, as the information provided by the
text is fleshed out with readers' real-world knowledge and experiences in a
process known as 'inferencing' (Gavins, 2007: 24–5). All text-worlds originate
from a 'discourse-world', the immediate real-world situation surrounding the

participants in any discourse (see Gavins, 2007: 18–34). The discourse-worlds of literary communication are normally split, with the author and the reader occupying separate spatial and temporal locations. This means that the participants must rely even more heavily on their inferencing abilities and it is from their immediate environment, and from the background knowledge and experiences which feed into it, that the participants draw the inferences they make in relation to the language they encounter. The specific knowledge the participants need to understand the discourse at hand is regulated and defined by the text itself, according to what in Text World Theory is known as 'the principle of text-drivenness' (see Gavins, 2007: 29).

Much of the passage above is dedicated to describing in detail the setting in which the narrator finds himself on waking. *The Outsider* remains fixed with a first-person perspective throughout, with the repeated use of the personal pronoun 'I' acting to lock the text-world to the narrator's homodiegetic point of view (see Genette, 1980). From this deictic zero-point, a scene is constructed in which a stark contrast exists between the background of the text-world and other foregrounded world-building elements. Initially, however, the people and objects populating the text-world are not clearly defined at all, as the narrator describes the sensation of being temporarily blinded on opening his eyes. He refers, for example, to 'the whiteness of the room' being 'even more dazzling than before', to the sensation being 'painful to the eyes', and to his mother's friends entering noiselessly 'into the blinding light'. The disorienting feel of these lines is emphasised by the repeated use of specific but indefinite reference (e.g. 'a rustling sound') and yet further by non-specific indefinites such as 'every object, every angle'. Despite the blinding whiteness of the room, the narrator claims to see the main figures in the text-world, his mother's friends, 'more clearly than I've ever seen anyone'. However, it is also worth noting that he also continues to refer to a persistent feeling of disorientation, stating he 'couldn't hear them and . . . found it hard to believe that they really existed'.

The capacity of certain visual or textual figures to attract greater perceiver attention than others is now well documented in neuroscience, cognitive psychology and cognitive poetics (see, for example, Emmott et al., 2006, 2007, 2010; Posner, 2004; Sanford et al., 2006; Stafford, 2007; Styles, 2005, 2006). Discussing how particular elements of a fictional text-world may draw greater reader attention than others, Stockwell (2009: 25) provides an inventory of the typical features of good textual attractors, as follows:

- newness
  (currency: the present moment of reading is more attractive than the previous moment)
- agency
  (noun phrases in active position are better attractors than in passive position)

- topicality
  (subject position confers attraction over object position)
- empathetic recognisability
  (human speaker > human hearer > animal > object > abstraction)
- definiteness
  (definite ('the man') > specific indefinite ('a certain man') > non-specific indefinite ('any man'))
- activeness
  (verbs denoting action, violence, passion, wilfulness, motivation, or strength)
- brightness
  (lightness or vivid colours being denoted over dimness or drabness)
- fullness
  (richness, density, intensity or nutrition being denoted)
- largeness
  (large object being denoted, or a very long elaborated noun phrase being used to denote)
- height
  (objects that are above others, are higher than the perceiver, or which dominate)
- noisiness
  (denoted phenomena which are audibly voluminous)
- aesthetic distance from the norm
  (beautiful or ugly referents, dangerous referents, alien objects denoted, dissonance)

(Stockwell, 2009: 25)

Meursault's mother's friends score very highly as textual attractors according to this inventory. Their first mention gives them newness in the text, but they also have agency, empathetic recognisability, definiteness and activeness. They are large and dominate the narrator in height, as they stand over him and sit around him as he lies on a bed. Although they are not at first described as bright, full or noisy (they are the opposite, in fact, as they sit down 'without even a chair creaking'), their movement against the static white background of the room makes them dissonant in the scene and thus also causes them to hold our attention. As the narrator sketches further detail around these silent figures, they come more sharply into focus as text-world entities. Most notably, the narrator concentrates on the women's aprons, which presumably are at eye level as he lies on the bed. His description of the aprons here gives the women greater volume and fullness, as Meursault notes they 'made their swollen bellies stick out even more. I'd never noticed what huge paunches old women can have', and this again adds to the sense of the physical dominance of the female figures over the narrator. The men, by contrast, are arguably less attractive as text-world figures. Although they are also active, definite and in topical position, they do not dominate the scene in the same way as the women. Where the women's large bellies form the centre of the narrator's attention, the men are 'very thin', their eyes are barely visible and presented as 'a faint glimmer among a nest of wrinkles', and their lips are 'all sucked into their toothless mouths'. Where the women are voluminous and swelling outwards, the men are wizened, cavernous and imploding.

The overall feel of the passage is one of disorientation, and the dwarfed position and general passivity of the narrator are emphasised as the overbearing figures of his mother's friends hover around and above him. Although the novel has a fixed homodiegetic narration throughout, it does not afford the reader easy access to Meursault's inner thoughts and feelings, in either this or any other situation he encounters. Simpson (1993) develops Genette's (1980) categories of heterodiegetic and homodiegetic narration into a more nuanced account of narrative forms, based on the patterns of predominant modality exhibited in fictional texts. Boulomaic modality expresses the wishes of the speaker and includes such modal lexical verbs such as 'wish', 'want' and 'desire', as well as modal adverbs such as 'hopefully' or 'regrettably', and adjectival and participial constructions such as 'it is hoped that' or 'it is regrettable that'. Deontic modality expresses varying degrees of obligation attached to a particular action. This category of modality includes modal auxiliaries such as 'must' and 'may', as well as participial and adjectival constructions such as 'it is required that they inform the authorities' or 'it is forbidden to feed the animals'. Simpson notes that homodiegetic narration in which boulomaic and deontic modality are foregrounded tends to be 'co-operatively oriented towards an implied reader through its clear rationalisation of obligations, duties and desires' (1993: 57). Simpson terms these kinds of narratives 'positively shaded' (1993: 56). By contrast, Meursault employs no boulomaic or deontic modality, but instead makes frequent use of epistemic and perception modality in a narration which typifies Simpson's category of 'negatively shaded' homodiegesis (1993: 58). Epistemic modality expresses varying degrees of commitment to the truth of a particular proposition and includes such modal auxiliaries as 'could', 'might' and 'may', as well as modal lexical verbs such as 'think', 'suppose' and 'believe'. Perception modality is a sub-set of this modal system and includes the sorts of references to the senses which Meursault makes frequently throughout the text (e.g. 'the room seemed even more dazzling', 'I'd never noticed', 'I couldn't tell'). He refers repeatedly to his sight in particular, in order to interpret his situation, suggesting an overall lack of confidence in his assertions. Simpson notes that this type of narration typically tends to create a feeling of 'uncertainty, bewilderment and alienation' (1993: 53).

In Text World Theory terms, modality of any kind causes new mental representations, known as 'modal-worlds' (see Gavins, 2007: 91–125), to be created, through which the speaker's attitude to a proposition can be conceptualised and understood separately from its originating text-world.

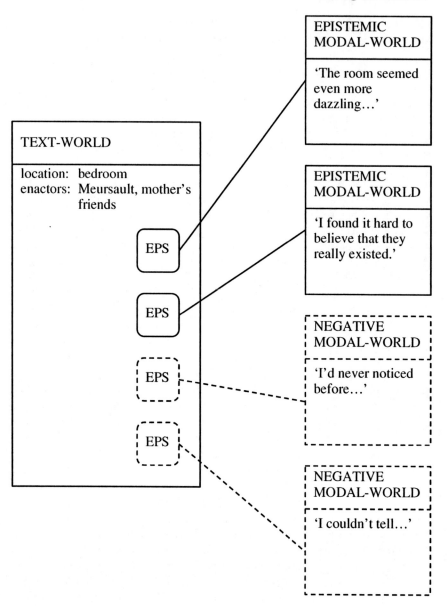

Figure 2.1 Embedded worlds in *The Outsider*

Figure 2.1, which follows standard Text World Theory notation (see, for example, Gavins, 2007; Hidalgo Downing, 2000; Werth, 1999), shows the configuration of such embedded modal-worlds which emerges in the scene from *The Outsider* as Meursault makes use of epistemic and perception modality. The main text-world is shown to the left of the diagram, containing Meursault and his mother's friends as enactors. The top two text-worlds emerging to the right of this main text-world occur when Meursault first uses perception modality to describe how the room *'seemed* even more dazzling' on waking, and secondly when he uses epistemic modality to refer to his difficulty believing in the existence of his mother's friends within the room. Both of these are modal-worlds which relate a particular degree of epistemic commitment on Meursault's part (and they are marked 'EPS' on the diagram to reflect their epistemic quality), both of them relatively weak and existing at an epistemic distance from the main text-world. The other two modal-worlds shown in dotted lines at the bottom of the diagram both result from modalised propositions in the text which also happen to be negated. The first occurs when Meursault comments that he'd *'never* noticed before what huge paunches old women can have' and the second when he says he *'couldn't* tell' whether his mother's friends were greeting him. Negative worlds are represented in this way in Text World Theory in order to reflect the fact that, from a cognitive perspective, negative propositions are foregrounded: they must first be brought into focus in the discourse before then being negated (for a summary see Gavins, 2007: 102; Hidalgo Downing, 2000). Again, these modal-worlds are epistemically remote from the main text-world and draw particular reader attention as a result of their negation. On the whole, the resulting conceptual structure, in which Meursault's weak epistemic commitment is established in a series of separate worlds embedded within the main narration, conveys the uncertainty Simpson (1993: 53) identifies as typical of negatively shaded texts. Most interestingly, Meursault relies on his sight and his senses even when it is clear to the reader that they are obscured or unable to function properly: although he claims to see the figures in the bedroom clearly, for example, his continuing references to the blinding light suggests that even his basic perceptions are not trustworthy.

Text World Theory draws a further distinction between worlds that are 'participant-accessible', created by participants in the discourse-world, and those which are 'enactor-accessible' (see Gavins, 2007: 73–81), created by entities in the text-world. The difference between these two types of world is essentially ontological and can be explained as follows:

> Our mental representations of enactors in the text-world are, of course, based on our experiences of real people in the real world, and we expect both types of entity to have the same emotions, reactions, abilities and general behaviour. However, we also retain our understanding of text-world enactors as entities which exist outside the ontological parameters of our real world. Not only are we unable to question or negotiate directly with enactors who are confined to the text-world level, but our knowledge of their backgrounds and personalities is similarly limited to information provided by the text. When a discourse-world participant creates a text-world, we can assess the reliability of its content based on

discourse-world factors . . . When a text-world enactor creates a text-world, on the other hand, we can only make use of other text-world elements in our evaluation of its reliability.

(Gavins, 2007: 78)

Because Meursault is a text-world enactor, participating in the unfolding story of *The Outsider*, the text-worlds created through his fixed first-person focalisation are only enactor-accessible in nature. They do not have the same ontological status as participant-accessible text-worlds and cannot be assessed for truth and reliability in the same way. However, the reader must accept the content of Meursault's text-worlds if a mental representation of the text is to be constructed at all; as we will see in Chapter 4 of this book, many literary texts rely on lulling the reader into a false sense of security in this way in order to play narrative tricks at a later stage. Meursault is the reader's only point of access to the world of *The Outsider* and, despite accumulating evidence of the possible undependability of his version of events, the reader, in effect, remains stuck with his perspective. We have no choice but to base our mental representations of the text not only on the enactor-accessible text-world but on the further embedded modal-worlds Meursault creates and which exist at yet another ontological remove from the reader's reality.

As argued in preceding literary criticism on the text, heat, too, plays a key role in the construction of the text-world of *The Outsider* and in the presentation of Meursault's character as passive and overwhelmed by his situation. Consider another key moment in the narrative:

The sun was beginning to burn my cheeks and I felt drops of sweat gathering in my eyebrows. It was the same sun as on the day of my mother's funeral and again it was my forehead that was hurting me most and all the veins were throbbing at once beneath the skin. And because I couldn't stand this burning feeling any longer, I moved forward. I knew it was stupid and I wouldn't get out of the sun with one step. But I took a step, just one step forward. And this time, without sitting up, the Arab drew his knife and held it out towards me in the sun. The light leapt up off the steel and it was like a long, flashing sword lunging at my forehead. At the same time all the sweat that had gathered in my eyebrows suddenly ran down over my eyelids, covering them with a dense layer of warm moisture. My eyes were blinded by this veil of salty tears. All I could feel were the cymbals the sun was clashing against my forehead and, distinctly, the dazzling spear still leaping up off the blade in front of me. It was like a red-hot blade gnawing at my eyelashes and gouging out my stinging eyes. That was when everything shook. The sea swept ashore a great breath of fire. The sky seemed to be splitting from end to end and raining down sheets of flame. My whole being went tense and

I tightened my grip on the gun. The trigger gave, I felt the underside of the polished butt and it was there, in that sharp but deafening noise, that it all started.

(Camus, 1982: 59–60)

This section of the novel relates Meursault's arbitrary murder of an Arab on a beach and is one of the most discussed and analysed passages in literary criticism on *The Outsider* (see, for example, Britton, 2010; Davis, 2003, 2007; John, 1955; Morreale, 1967; Solimini, 2001). Once again, the scene is described from the fixed first-person perspective of Meursault. One of the features of the passage most commented upon by literary critics is the fact that Meursault does not narrate any emotional response to the act of murder he commits, before, during or after the incident. Interestingly, this episode is also characterised by an overall lack of modality. Where the earlier scene in the bedroom, discussed above, contains frequent use of epistemic and perception modality and fits perfectly with Simpson's (1993) category of negatively shaded narration, the beach scene contains barely any modality at all. Simpson (1993: 73) categorises narrative such as that used in this episode as having 'neutral shading', lacking both modalisation and evaluative adjectives or adverbs. Compared with the earlier passage and its abundant fluctuating modality, Meursault's report of his murder of the Arab is, as Simpson (1993: 75) puts it, 'flat and unreflective' in a manner typical of neutral shading.

Simpson goes on to note that a reliance on categorical assertion over modalised expression can make neutrally shaded text difficult to distinguish from heterodiegetic narration. However, alongside the repeated use of the first-person pronoun, which serves to remind us that our focaliser is a character participating in the unfolding scene, Meursault also makes frequent reference to physical sensations and to the heat and light which surrounds him in his immediate environment in particular. He talks a great deal here of how things *feel* to him and the predominant sensation described is one of overwhelming physical pain (e.g. 'it was my forehead that was hurting me most', 'I couldn't stand this burning feeling any longer', 'All I could feel were the cymbals the sun was clashing against my forehead'). The theme of impeded sight which we saw in the earlier passage is also present once again in this extract, as Meursault describes how 'all the sweat that had gathered in my eyebrows suddenly ran down over my eyelids . . . My eyes were blinded by this veil of salty tears.' Although the neutral shading means that few embedded modal-worlds are created in this section of the novel, an added conceptual layer is constructed in a different way by Meursault's recurrent use of metaphor to describe his physical experiences. Alongside the description of his sight being obscured by a 'veil of salty tears', Meursault's metaphors occur most frequently around heat and light in the passage. Again, these metaphors often relate overwhelming physical pain and are violent in nature. The sunlight reflecting off the Arab's knife, for example, is first personified as leaping up off the steel of the blade, then depicted as 'a long, flashing sword lunging at my forehead', a 'dazzling spear', and finally 'like a red-hot blade gnawing at my eyelashes and gouging out my stinging eyes'.

Text World Theory's account of the conceptual spaces created by metaphor builds on the foundations laid down in early cognitive linguistics in Conceptual Metaphor Theory (see Lakoff, 1987; Lakoff and Johnson, 1980; Lakoff and Turner, 1989) and later developed in Conceptual Integration Theory (for a summary, see Fauconnier and Turner, 2003). Metaphors create another kind of separate mental representation, adjacent to but also crucially feeding back into the main text-world from which they spring. The various conceptual elements upon which the metaphor is constructed (such as a sword, a spear, a red-hot blade) are blended with our notions of intense sunlight in this metaphor world, resulting in a new and synergistic understanding of the imagery being used. In the examples above, we formulate a mental picture of a blended 'light-spear' or 'light-sword' in a separate conceptual space in order to better understand Meursault's perceptions of his situation in the main text-world. Most importantly, the metaphor world has a structural complexity which is greater than the sum of its component parts: rather than simply bolting two images together, we forge a rich mental representation with what is known in Conceptual Integration Theory as 'emergent structure' (see Fauconnier and Turner, 2003: 41–4; Gavins, 2007: 148).

As further illustration, Figure 2.2 shows the conceptual structure created by the metaphor 'The sea swept ashore a great breath of fire', in particular. The main text-world is once again shown to the left of the diagram. From this text-world three separate mental representations relating to the three key components of the metaphor feed into a blended metaphor world shown to the right of the diagram. These mental representations are known as 'input spaces' in Conceptual Integration Theory's terms (see Fauconnier and Turner, 2003: 40–4) and form the basic conceptual building blocks of the metaphor. Once they are blended together in the metaphor world, however, the resulting mental representation takes on a new complexity and contains elements and relationships inferred from the reader's background knowledge and experience, in addition to those contained within the input spaces themselves. In the metaphor world, then, the sea becomes personified as it performs the action of sweeping its fiery breath towards the shore. Actions and events such this one are known in Text World Theory as 'function-advancing propositions' (see Gavins, 2007: 56; Werth, 1999: 190–202); they are shown in Text World Theory notation by a vertical arrow and are described following the model set out in Systemic Functional Linguistics (see Berry, 1977; Halliday and Matthiesson, 2004; Thompson, 2004; and for an account of the adoption of the model in Text World Theory, see Gavins, 2007: 53–72). This grammar identifies the different kinds of processes represented in discourse and the various participant roles attached to them. In the present example, the sea, normally an inanimate object, becomes personified when it takes the

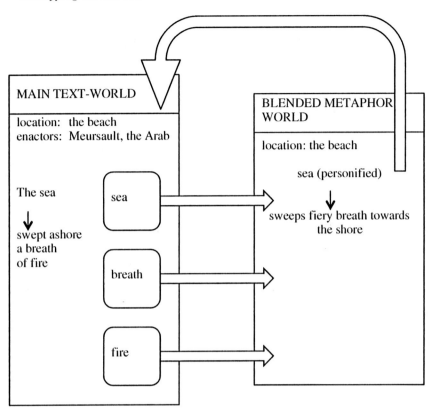

Figure 2.2 Metaphor worlds in *The Outsider*

participant role of ACTOR in a material intention process, which can normally be carried out only by animate entities. Most interestingly, this process in the blended world also contains a reversal of prototypical expectation; the sea in the input space is cold and wet, according to our usual schematic knowledge, but it takes the properties of heat and dryness as the ACTOR in the blended metaphor world. Crucially, the metaphor as a whole feeds back into its originating text-world, extending our understanding of Meursault's experience of the intense and oppressive heat on the beach.

What is particularly noteworthy about these and many other metaphors in *The Outsider* is the way in which natural but inanimate elements, such as the sea and the sun, are frequently given animate properties and often take the role of ACTOR in material processes described in the text. In the passage above, for example, the sun burns and clashes cymbals, sunlight leaps, a sword lunges and the sea sweeps. By contrast, material intention processes by the animate actors in the scene are few: Meursault only moves forwards and tightens his grip on the gun, while the Arab only draws his knife and holds it outwards. The majority of the other processes associated with Meursault relate to cognitive activity and physical sensation (e.g. 'I felt drops of sweat gathering', 'I couldn't stand this', 'I knew it was stupid', 'All I could feel were the cymbals' and so on) rather than deliberate action. At the episode's climax, the murder of the Arab, we are told that 'The trigger gave' and Meursault's actions are transformed into an event process by the inanimate ACTOR (the gun).

It is clear, then, that a number of stylistic patterns exist within *The Outsider* which may be responsible, in part at least, for some of the most common readers' emotional responses to the text. Camus builds an unexperimental and potentially immersive text-world which readers are given access to only through Meursault's fixed, first-person perspective. As we have seen, Meursault is the only means by which we may build a mental representation of the text at all and empathy with him is further encouraged through the repeated portrayal of him as dominated by other characters and natural forces beyond his control and as passive and overwhelmed by his physical surroundings. The metaphorical structures created throughout the novel form a recurring sub-text in which natural elements and inanimate objects are seen as more active than Meursault himself, with heat and light in particular often causing him considerable physical pain. In these ways, Meursault is presented as a victim of his circumstances to a great extent, a prototype of the absurd 'passive, rationalistic, or hopelessly ineffectual victim-hero, dominated by his situation', as Weinberg (1970: 10) puts it. The point at which he acts to change this state of affairs, in his murder of the Arab on the beach, is where many readers report struggling to retain their emotional connection with Meursault. We have seen, however, that it is in this episode where Meursault is apparently in the greatest physical discomfort, where the natural environment is at its most violent and threatening and where he is presented as being at his most passive. Nevertheless, empathetic connections with Meursault are not straightforwardly established by the style of the novel. Throughout the text of *The Outsider* readers are given constant suggestions that Meursault's perceptions, and thus the version of events he describes, are not reliable. Modality, in particular, plays a key role in Camus's construction of a character of questionable mental and moral stability. Meursault's world is alternately populated with multiple contradictory modal-worlds or he is devoid of any insight into his motivations and emotions. It would seem that it may be this key point of textual and conceptual conflict which causes many readers to formulate ambivalent opinions of Meursault and his absurd predicament.

Experimenting with absurd worlds

The above stylistic analysis of the text-worlds of *The Outsider* has provided insight into the textual and conceptual structures at the heart of one of the most renowned novels on one of the boundaries of the absurd. In so doing, it has also offered some possible explanations for readers' responses to and categorisations of the text. However, the reports of fluctuating empathetic connections with characters and authors and the reports of self-modification examined so far are not confined to those texts at the realist end of the cline of absurd experimentalism. These kinds of responses are in fact typical of readers of absurd literature participating in online discussions of absurd narratives and their authors, regardless of the degree of realism the individual texts themselves display. To explore this further, it is useful at this point to turn to an author whose work covers a broad range of narrative styles, from traditional realism to highly experimental multimodality, and who, like Camus, occupies a position within multiple literary categories simultaneously. Donald Barthelme's (1931–89) historical situation, writing in the second half of the twentieth century, has led him to be classed primarily as a postmodernist by literary critics (for just a few examples see Ebert, 1991; Gillen, 1972; Herrero-Olaizola, 1998; Hudgens, 2001; Klinkowitz, 1991; Olsen, 1986; Sloboda, 1996, 1997; Wilde, 1982). Just as a comprehensive definition of existentialist style lies beyond the bounds of the present study, so too must the linguistic characteristics of postmodernist literature remain outside the focus of this book. Indeed, as with the literary absurd, there is little agreement within literary criticism itself as to what postmodern style actually is. For the purposes of the present discussion, however, literary postmodernism can be loosely defined as a playful style associated with certain post-World War II writers and often involving the use of such metafictional narrative features as pastiche, intertextuality and narrative fragmentation (for a comprehensive examination of the techniques of postmodern fiction, see McHale, 1987). What is interesting about Barthelme are the stylistic family resemblances he shares with other authors and works that have been categorised as absurd, elements of his fiction which have received far less attention from academic readers in the past (notable exceptions are Hoffmann, 1986; McCaffery, 1979, 1982; Oberman, 2002; Rother, 1976; Wilde, 1976). However, Barthelme's absurdism does feature prominently in non-academic online discussions and categorisations of his work, with readers on a range of websites frequently tagging Barthelme himself, his individual texts or elements of these works as 'absurd'. Interestingly, readers of the work of Donald Barthelme, just like the readers of Albert Camus, also rate his work very highly in online fora. His story collection *Forty Stories* (Barthelme, 1989, originally published in 1987), for instance, scores 4.09 out of 5 on LibraryThing. Once again, it is worth comparing this score to those given to canonical works of literature, such as Charles Dickens's *Great Expectations* (which scores 4.19) or Jane Austen's *Pride and Prejudice* (which scores 4.67) or, indeed, to less critically acclaimed but nonetheless internationally best-selling works such as Stephanie Meyer's Twilight series (scoring 3.99) or J.K. Rowling's Harry Potter novels (scoring 4.64). According to these crude measures, it would seem that those readers

who read Barthelme regularly value him very highly and, as we will see later
in this chapter, this assumption can be seen to be confirmed further in the
ways Barthelme's readers often speak passionately about their self-modifying
experiences in interactions with his texts.

Below are the opening lines from one of the stories in Barthelme's *Forty
Stories* collection, 'Some of Us Had Been Threatening Our Friend Colby'
(Barthelme, 1989: 167–71):

> Some of us had been threatening our friend Colby for a long time,
> because of the way he had been behaving. And now he had gone too
> far, so we decided to hang him. Colby argued that just because he had
> gone too far (he did not deny he had gone too far) did not mean that
> he should be subjected to hanging. Going too far, he said, was some-
> thing everybody did sometimes. We didn't pay much attention to this
> argument. We asked him what sort of music he would like played at
> the hanging. He said he'd think about it but it would take him a while
> to decide. I pointed out that we would need to know soon, because
> Howard, who is a conductor, would have to hire and rehearse the musi-
> cians and couldn't begin until we knew what the music was going to be.
> Colby said he'd always been fond of Ives's Fourth Symphony. Howard
> said that this was a 'delaying tactic' and that everybody knew that the
> Ives was almost impossible to perform and would involve weeks of
> rehearsal, and that the size of the orchestra and chorus would put us
> way over the music budget. 'Be reasonable', he said to Colby. Colby
> said he'd try to think of something less exacting.
>
> (Barthelme, 1989: 167)

This story is of particular interest in the present discussion because of the
great many stylistic similarities it shares with the extracts from Camus's *The
Outsider* analysed earlier in this chapter. Perhaps the most striking feature of
the text-worlds constructed in the opening sequence of the story is their lack
of definiteness. Note, in particular, the repeated use of non-specific indefinites
in the first four sentences, in the references to 'Some of us', 'a long time' and
to 'something everybody did sometimes', as well as the specific but indefinite
'the way he had been behaving'. Such indefiniteness leaves the spatial and
temporal parameters of the text-worlds created here under-defined and their
deictic configurations are difficult to conceptualise, since no other information is provided about where the story is set or about what Colby has done
to deserve the threatened punishment. In much the same way as we saw
Meursault struggling to piece together a coherent perception of his surroundings in *The Outsider*, so the reader of 'Some of Us Had Been Threatening
Our Friend Colby' is given little help establishing the deictic boundaries of a
mental representation of Barthelme's narrative and must instead rely heavily
on inferences at the level of the discourse-world.

Where Meursault was depicted as threatened and overwhelmed by his physical environment and by natural forces in particular, Barthelme creates a sense of threat in his narrative through the unknown and unrealised. For example, a key feature of the opening of the story is the frequent shifts in time that are represented over a relatively short space. Colby's bad behaviour, for instance, has happened at a point in time prior to the narrating time of the story, indicated by the past perfect tense in 'he had gone too far', compared with the simple past 'we decided to hang him'. At a temporal point even further in the past, the friends had *already* been threatening Colby, yet again in an unspecified manner, because of ongoing but unspecified bad behaviour. Thus, in just the first two sentences of the story, three separate temporal zones are represented and the narrative switches rapidly between them, with none of the resulting text-worlds being developed beyond the point of simply containing Colby and/or his unnamed friends engaged in the minimally detailed activities of threatening, behaving and deciding. In Text World Theory terms, the temporal and spatial shifts between conceptual spaces which exist at the same ontological level are known as 'world-switches' (see Gavins, 2007: 48–50). Crucially, events of central significance to the narrative, i.e. the reasons behind the planned hanging of Colby, are contained in a temporally distant world and are not fully fleshed out. Further information about these events is not provided within the most temporally proximal text-world either. The simple-past text-world in which the main bulk of the narrative action unfolds at no point includes a disclosure about what, precisely, Colby has done to deserve his fate. Instead, the focus remains on the meticulous planning of the finer details of Colby's hanging, in which his friends enthusiastically engage over several pages.

Just as readers of *The Outsider* are given limited access to Meursault's inner thoughts and emotions, Colby's mind, too, remains inaccessible to us, but for different reasons and through different narrative techniques. 'Some of Us Had Been Threatening Our Friend Colby' is narrated in the first person by a homodiegetic narrator, one of Colby's friends, resulting in a narration which is enactor-accessible in much the same way as Camus's text. However, the narrator of Barthelme's story remains unnamed throughout and he chooses to present Colby's emotions only through reports of his speech. For example, in the first paragraph (quoted above) we are told that 'Colby said he'd always been fond of Ives's Fourth Symphony', and later in the story further comments by Colby on certain planned aspects of his hanging are similarly reported in indirect style, such as 'Colby said he thought drinks would be nice but was worried about the expense' (Barthelme, 1989: 168). At no point over the course of the story are we granted direct access to Colby's thoughts and the emotions the narrator infers from Colby's behaviour are greatly downplayed. At one point, for example, the narrator comments, 'Colby began to look a little green, and I didn't blame him, because there is something extremely distasteful in thinking about being hanged by a wire

instead of a rope – it gives you a sort of revulsion, when you think about it'
(Barthelme, 1989: 170). Note here that the focus is more on the narrator's
emotional response (i.e. revulsion at imagining *himself* being hanged by a
wire) rather than on Colby's, and that his overall flippant tone is emphasised
by the use of an informal inclusive second-person address ('when *you* think
about it').

Throughout Barthelme's short story, then, a heightened contrast develops
between the minimally represented actions and emotions of the victim of
the hanging, Colby, and highly detailed descriptions of the plans his friends
concoct for his hanging. Between them, they finalise painstaking schemes for
the musical setting of the hanging, the design of the invitations (down to the
font and the colour of the paper), arrangements for food and drink, and the
architecture of the gibbet. Consider the following extract, which occurs after
the friends decide that hiring a professional hangman would be too expensive:

> Tomás, who is quite modern in outlook and not afraid of innovation,
> proposed that Colby be standing on a large round rubber ball ten feet
> in diameter. This, he said, would afford a sufficient 'drop' and would
> also roll out of the way if Colby suddenly changed his mind after
> jumping off. He reminded us that by not using a regular hangman we
> were placing an awful lot of responsibility for the success of the affair
> on Colby himself, and that although he was sure Colby would perform
> creditably and not disgrace his friends at the last minute, still, men have
> been known to get a little irksome at times like that, and the ten foot
> rubber ball, which could probably be fabricated rather cheaply, would
> insure a 'bang-up' production right down to the wire.
>
>   (Barthelme, 1989: 170)

This is just one example of the many hypothetical situations the friends dream
up over the course of the story and it is characterised, like all the others, by
the way it leads to the creation of multiple modal-worlds. According to Text
World Theory (see Gavins, 2007: 118–23), modal-worlds occur not only as
the result of modalised discourse but whenever a remote or unrealised situation is described. Modal-worlds of this type allow possibilities, conditionals
and hypotheticals to be conceptualised as epistemically remote from their
originating worlds. In the passage above, the first of these is created when
Tomás's proposal that Colby be standing on a rubber ball is put forward; this
world is just an idea at this point in the narrative and exists in an unrealised
moment in the future. A second modal-world is embedded within this one, as
Tomás's initial idea is justified through the use of the further hypothetical of
the ball providing a sufficient drop to kill Colby. Within the same sentence,
the conjoined clause beginning 'and would also roll out of the way . . .' also
contains a subsequent conditional construction ('*if* Colby suddenly changed
his mind after jumping off') and therefore embeds a third modal-world within

the second: the ball rolling away is imagined as happening following another unrealised situation (Colby changing his mind).

Yet further modal-worlds are also created in the passage, as Tomás's opinions of Colby's reliability are related to the reader. The narrator's report of these opinions begins as indirect speech ('He reminded us that . . .'), continuing to the point where we are told that Tomás was '*sure* that Colby would perform creditably'. The epistemic modality here creates another modal-world, which has yet another one embedded within it, since again Colby's possible but unrealised future behaviour ('*would* perform creditably') is being assessed. The narration then slips temporarily into free indirect speech, with the use of 'still' signalling the stronger presence of Tomás's own voice at this point in the passage, further emphasised through the ironic tone of 'a little irksome'. Text World Theory also views free indirect discourse as modal-world forming (see Gavins, 2007: 128), since the dual-voicing of this form of narration adds an extra epistemic filter to the text-world construction. Free indirect forms require readers to conceptualise another character's version of events layered on top of that presented by the narrator. In this case, the free indirect speech contains three embedded epistemic modal-worlds: the first occurs with the epistemic modality in 'men have been *known*' (note that the person doing the knowing here is again unspecified); the second results from the hypothetical construction in '*could* probably be fabricated rather cheaply'; and the final modal-world is created with '*would* insure a "bang-up" production'. It is worth noting in this final example that, because of the free indirect speech here, it is difficult to tell whether the use of inverted commas reflects a shift to direct speech (where the narrator would be directly quoting Tomás), or whether they indicate Tomás himself using direct speech (presumably quoting some other textual entity) within the free indirect discourse.

Humour and the absurd

That Colby, like Meursault, is another 'rationalistic, or hopelessly ineffectual victim-hero, dominated by his situation rather than creating or acting to change it' (Weinberg, 1970: 10) is clear. Colby looks on passively as his executioners calmly debate whether to have limousines transport guests to his hanging, or whether a firing squad would be better, an idea which is quickly dismissed as Colby 'trying to "upstage" everyone with unnecessary theatrics' (Barthelme, 1989: 169). All the various macabre proposals for the manner of Colby's death are held in a kind of conceptual suspended animation, as unrealised possibilities for the future, until the very final paragraph of the story, in which they are suddenly made concrete:

Everything went off smoothly on the day of the event (the music Colby finally picked was standard stuff, Elgar, and it was played very well by

Howard and his boys). It didn't rain and was well attended, and we
didn't run out of Scotch or anything.

(Barthelme, 1989: 171)

Note here how the narration switches from the predominant multiple layering of modal-worlds, resulting from repeated modalisation, hypotheticality
and conditionality, to a complete lack of embedded text-worlds at its close.
Barthelme moves from a negatively shaded narrative (Simpson, 1993: 53)
to a neutrally shaded form (Simpson, 1993: 73) in exactly the same way we
saw Camus's text shift earlier in this chapter. However, the starkest difference between the two texts is, of course, the dark humour which pervades
Barthelme's story, whereas the bleakness of Camus's novel remains unironic
throughout.

The humour inherent in a significant body of absurd prose fiction has been
the focus of numerous literary-critical studies over the last forty years (e.g.
Brodwin, 1972; Cornwell, 2006: 14–18; Hanţiu, 2010; Hauck, 1971; Janoff,
1974; Ketterer, 1978; May, 1972; O'Neill, 1983; Pratt, 1993; Read, 1981;
Safer, 1983a, 1983b, 1994; Winston, 1972). However, as with the majority of
literary criticism on other aspects of the literary absurd, this work makes little
or no reference to the stylistic techniques through which absurd humour is
created, makes no attempt to analyse rigorously how humour might be functioning on a linguistic or discoursal level and does not address the conceptual
effects absurd humour might have on the reader. As I have already noted,
to my knowledge there have been no previous attempts to define the stylistic
parameters of the literary absurd in general and no attempts to examine the
style of absurd prose fiction in particular in a systematic and transparent
manner. A number of preceding linguistic studies have, however, turned their
attention to the humour of absurd drama (see, for example, Burton, 1980:
24–7; Corfariu and Rovenţa-Frumuşani, 1984; Gerzymisch-Arbogast, 1988;
Herman, 1998: 238–9; Sherzer, 1978, 1979; Sikorska, 1994; Simpson, 1998,
2000). Of existing studies of the language of dramatic absurdity, the majority take a pragmatic-stylistic approach, noting the ways in which dialogue in
particular in absurd drama can be seen to violate various linguistic norms
associated with cooperative and coherent intercommunication in everyday
language situations. Such studies have tended to define the absurd in drama
as centring around the formulation of some kind of incongruity between the
discoursal behaviour that is expected in everyday spoken dialogue and that
which is represented between the characters in a dramatic text. Although
I will return to some of these studies at points later in this book, they are
of little help in the present discussion of absurd humour in a non-dialogic
context. Barthelme's story makes use of various forms of the representation
of speech, but does not represent any extended dialogue between its characters. It is nevertheless clear that humour is of central importance in our
experiences of the absurd in literary prose. Indeed, the humorous and playful

quality to much of Barthelme's work appears to be the defining feature which leads many literary critics to categorise his texts as postmodern as well as absurd (for example Hudgens, 2001: 117; Klinkowitz, 1991: 17; Kusnir, 2004; Nealon, 2005; Stengel, 1992).

Far more helpful in an examination of humour in absurd prose fiction, then, are the more cognitively driven theories of humour which have emerged as a dominant approach within the field of humour studies over recent years (for an extensive survey, see Simpson, 2003: 29–46). Chief among these is the General Theory of Verbal Humour (henceforth GTVH) set out in Attardo and Raskin (1991) and further developed in Attardo (1997). GTVH also centres around the key notion that humour arises out of incongruity, but in this approach our notions of the incongruous are seen to be cognitively rather than pragmatically located. It is important to emphasise that GTVH, too, was not developed in relation to narrative fiction but rather as a means of accounting for verbal humour of various kinds. Nevertheless, the cognitive principles it has at its core are more easily generalisable beyond verbal forms than those drawn from face-to-face dialogic interaction. According to the GTVH framework, jokes operate firstly through a 'set up', or the establishment of a neutral context around which a subject is able to make predictions about expected behaviour and outcomes based on previous knowledge and experience of similar situations (Attardo, 1997: 411). Since GTVH draws greatly on schema theory (following Schank and Abelson, 1977), this existing knowledge is understood as being script-based. Schema theory defines scripts as knowledge stores of stereotyped sequences of actions and events which characterise familiar situations and are constructed in the mind as the result of repeated experience. Scripts can be understood as extended prototype structures, containing series of events and actions elaborated far beyond simple core concepts and covering our expectations of such everyday situations as attending a lecture, ordering food in a restaurant or catching a bus. (Within schema theory research, it is conventional for these scripts to be given simplified labels appropriate to their content and for these labels to be represented in small capitals, e.g. the LECTURE script, the RESTAURANT script, the BUS script.) The key to verbal humour, according to GTVH, is the way in which incongruous scripts are opposed, so that expected, normal or plausible behaviours and situations are contrasted with unexpected, abnormal or implausible eventualities (for a critique of this approach in relation to satirical humour, see Simpson, 2003: 37–46). The final critical point in verbal humour is that of 'resolution', when the incongruity established through the opposition of scripts is first identified and then resolved by the reader or listener. Most interestingly, Attardo notes that the degree of resolution achieved in humorous texts can vary and that adequate resolution is least likely to occur in what he terms 'absurd humour' (Attardo, 1997: 409; see also Attardo, 2001: 25).

Returning to 'Some of Us Had Been Threatening Our Friend Colby', it is clear that Barthelme opposes a number of different situational and personal scripts within his short story. The title and the first sentence of the narrative both contain the term 'our friend' in reference to the character Colby, which, under a GTVH approach, can be seen to act as a linguistic header instantiating a FRIENDSHIP script. According to this script, readers might reasonably predict certain stereotypical behaviours from Colby and the other characters in the story. These might include, for example, shared interests and social activities and are likely to be based on a basic assumption of shared affection. As the story progresses, however, this script is quickly opposed with one of EXECUTION, the predicted sequence of which is unlikely to fit with most people's expectations of friendly behaviour, creating the key ingredient of incongruity in the text early in the narrative. As Attardo rightly predicts, however, the absurd flavour of Barthelme's humour comes from the fact that this incongruity is never resolved. 'Some of Us Had Been Threatening Our Friend Colby' comes without a punch-line and, instead, further incongruities and script oppositions develop as the narrative unfolds. Not only does the planned hanging go against our expectations of friendship, but Colby's behaviour as victim is similarly incongruous with the EXECUTION script. Focalised through the perspective of the narrator, Colby appears to participate calmly in the planning of his own death, attempting only a minor and short-lived delay (in his request for the performance of Ives's Fourth Symphony) and only one explicit protestation, which follows a discussion about whether he should be hanged from a gibbet or a tree: 'Colby said that everyone went too far, sometimes, and weren't we being a little Draconian?' (Barthelme, 1989: 169). The meticulous details of the hanging on which the friends eventually agree also oppose most people's notions of what an execution should or might plausibly entail. Both the imagined but unrealised possibilities the friends create over the course of their discussions (which include a gibbet stained in dark walnut, a professional hangman from South America and guests transported in limousines) and the eventual reality of the hanging – plenty of Scotch and Colby hanged from a tree after jumping off a ten-foot rubber ball 'painted a deep green and [which] blended in well with the bucolic setting' (Barthelme, 1989: 171) – are characterised by both their abnormality and implausibility within the setting.

The scripts Barthelme puts together in 'Some of Us Had Been Threatening Our Friend Colby' are extreme in their opposition and the majority of readers giving their responses to this text online focus on the humour this opposition produces. Readers on Goodreads, for example, variously describe the story as 'fun, fun, fun', 'witty and callous' and 'absurd and grotesque', with one reader commenting 'Not only did I love it, but I laughed heartily through the whole thing' (Goodreads, 2012b). However, Barthelme's humour operates in stylistically varied ways across his work and readers' responses to it also vary accordingly. We can usefully compare, for example, the prevailing response of general amusement that most online readers give to 'Some of Us Had Been

Threatening Our Friend Colby' with the apparently more profound emotions
they report in relation to 'The Balloon', a short story which was originally
published in Barthelme's *Sixty Stories* collection in 1982. 'The Balloon'
is Barthelme's most frequently anthologised short story and describes the
appearance one night of a giant balloon over New York and the consequent
responses of the city's inhabitants. The story opens as follows:

> The balloon, beginning at a point on Fourteenth Street, the exact loca-
> tion of which I cannot reveal, expanded northward all one night, while
> people were sleeping, until it reached the Park. There, I stopped it;
> at dawn the northernmost edges lay over the Plaza; the free-hanging
> motion was frivolous and gentle. But experiencing a faint irritation at
> stopping, even to protect the trees, and seeing no reason the balloon
> should be allowed to expand upward, over the parts of the city it was
> already covering, into the 'air space' to be found there, I asked the engi-
> neers to see to it. This expansion took place throughout the morning,
> soft imperceptible sighing of gas through the valves. The balloon then
> covered forty-five blocks north–south and an irregular area east–west,
> as many as six crosstown blocks on either side of the Avenue in some
> places. This was the situation, then.
>
> (Barthelme, 1982: 53)

As in 'Some of Us Had Been Threatening Our Friend Colby', Barthelme
constructs a coherent and potentially immersive text-world in these opening
lines, but one in which certain deictic oddities are nevertheless immediately
apparent. Although New York is not explicitly named as the setting of the
narrative, it is likely that any regular reader of Barthelme's fiction would infer
this detail from previous discourse-world knowledge of the author and his
works, as well as from the proper nouns 'Fourteenth Street', 'the Park', 'the
Plaza' and 'the Avenue'. Indeed, although I have never visited New York, my
own assumption on my first reading of the text that this was the story's background was confirmed when I consulted a map of New York: Central Park
is exactly forty-five blocks north of Fourteenth Street; the Plaza is located at
the south-eastern corner of the park and is bordered on its eastern side by
Fifth Avenue. Given this geographical precision, as well as that added by
the further information that the balloon covered 'as many as six crosstown
blocks on either side of the Avenue in some places', the narrator of the story
seems oddly coy about the 'precise location' on Fourteenth Street at which
the balloon originated. It is also clear from the opening paragraph that the
first-person narrator of the story is responsible for the appearance of the
balloon, since he states 'I stopped it' and 'I asked the engineers to see to it',
but he withholds the reasons for its creation for many pages to come.

The narrator also does not reveal any other details about himself and, in
contrast with the precise world-building of the city setting in the opening

lines, the enactors populating the text-world remain under-defined throughout the narrative. For example, 'the engineers' above are given no further
detail than this definite but non-specific reference and no proper names are
used elsewhere in the story. As the reactions to the balloon of the population of New York are documented over the coming pages, these people are
referred to only in the most general terms as 'some people', 'daring children',
'one man' and so on. The imbalance between the detail given to the balloon
and its physical location and that given to the enactors in the text-world
continues throughout. Consider this extract from the second paragraph of
the text:

> ... there were no situations, simply the balloon hanging there – muted
> heavy grays and browns for the most part, contrasting with the walnut
> and soft yellows. A deliberate lack of finish, enhanced by skillful instal-
> lation, gave the surface a rough, forgotten quality; sliding weights on
> the inside, carefully adjusted, anchored the great, vari-shaped mass at
> a number of points.
>
> (Barthelme, 1982: 53–4)

Not only is this description highly detailed, but it also contains some odd
deleted agency: note that the person who is responsible for the 'deliberate lack of finish', the 'skillful installation' and who presumably 'carefully
adjusted' the weights is never named.

Although the narrator seems keen to play down his responsibility for the
balloon's appearance, he is nevertheless a highly opinionated presence in the
story. As he relates to the reader the multitude of responses to the balloon
given by the city's inhabitants, not only are these opinions each represented
in separate enactor-accessible modal-worlds, but they are frequently followed
up with the narrator's own judgements layered on top of other people's
judgements:

> There were reactions. Some people found the balloon 'interesting'. As
> a response, this seemed inadequate to the immensity of the balloon,
> the suddenness of its appearance over the city; on the other hand, in
> the absence of hysteria or other societally-induced anxiety, it must be
> judged a calm, 'mature' one.
>
> (Barthelme, 1982: 54)

Note here the occurrence first of an epistemic modal-world relating to some
people finding the balloon 'interesting' (the epistemic remoteness of which
is further emphasised by its inclusion as a piece of reported speech within
inverted commas), then of a second modal-world containing the narrator's
reaction, which is modalised using epistemic perception modality ('this
seemed inadequate'). These worlds are then balanced by a further contras-

tive opinion ('on the other hand'), which itself contains deontic modality ('it *must* be judged') as well as further inverted commas ('a calm, "mature" one') which seem to distance the narrator from his own initial assertion. Such multiple layering and embedding of worlds quickly emerges as the predominant pattern in 'The Balloon', as the majority of the narrative becomes dedicated to the construction of modalised opinions and assessments, while the basic particulars of their originating text-world – who created the balloon and why – drift ever further out of focus.

The embedded worlds Barthelme creates in 'The Balloon', then, begin as multitudinous and contradictory and eventually become incoherent and nonsensical as the story progresses. Barthelme's more experimental style in 'The Balloon' is most extreme in the following section of the story:

> It was also argued that what was important was what you felt when you stood under the balloon, some people claimed they felt sheltered, warmed as never before, while enemies of the balloon felt, or reported feeling, constrained, a 'heavy feeling'. Critical opinion was divided: 'monstrous pourings'
>
>   'harp'
>
> XXXXXXX 'certain contrasts with darker portions'
>   'inner joy'
> 'large, square corners'...
>   ::::::: 'abnormal vigor'
>   'warm, soft lazy passages'
> 'Has unity been sacrificed for a sprawling quality?'
>   '*Quelle catastrophe*'
>   'munching'
>
>   (Barthelme, 1982: 56–7)

Parts of this section of the narrative seem to be snippets of direct speech (e.g. 'large, square corners'), while others appear to be extracts from written 'critical opinion' (e.g. 'Has unity been sacrificed for a sprawling quality?'). The typography of the paragraph is less easily comprehended, however, as are those isolated words which do not appear to have any relation to the balloon or its appearance at all (e.g. 'munching', 'harp'). At this point in the text, Barthelme's experimentalism makes the construction of a text-world practically impossible. It is also, however, another example of script incongruity, since it is the only paragraph in the story to take this experimental form and is thus in opposition to the rest of the narrative, which is relatively coherent and conventional. It is crucial, too, that this paragraph relates to 'critical opinion' of the balloon, the discourse of which Barthelme satirises throughout the story. The coherent world-building through which the New Yorkers' acceptance and enjoyment of the balloon are narrated (as they meet beneath it, touch it, hang lanterns on it and run and dance on it) is contrasted with the interspersed inclusion of incongruously opaque discourse relating critical responses from unnamed sources, most often in a passive form, for example 'Ideas of "bloat" and "float" were introduced, as well as concepts of dream and responsibility' (Barthelme, 1982: 56).

As I have already briefly noted above, responses to 'The Balloon' from readers in non-academic online environments differ from those given to 'Some of Us Had Been Threatening Our Friend Colby' in one key way: they include frequent reports of more profound emotional reactions than simple amusement. For example, readers in a discussion thread about *Sixty Stories* on the Amazon website describe the story collection variously as 'my favourite book', 'ironic . . . but also heartfelt', 'beautiful . . . disturbing . . . confusing', 'a perfect collection of wonderfully absurd literature', and as 'well-crafted creations show[ing] the master at his absurdly best'. Consider, also, the following extended commentary from the same discussion thread:

> One thing is for certain: if you do not have a taste for the absurd you are probably not going to like Barthelme. His stories are filled with absurdist/surrealist elements. But for me, what separates him from other 'experimental' writers is his ability to elicit emotion from the reader. For example, when I first read the ending of 'The Balloon', I felt like I had been punched in the stomach. And I couldn't say exactly why.
>
> (mingus, 2006)

Like many others, this reader reports a strong emotional response to 'The Balloon' in particular, which he describes in highly physical terms. He also locates this response very clearly at the ending of the story, which runs as follows:

> I met you under the balloon, on the occasion of your return from Norway; you asked it if was mine, I said it was. The balloon, I said, is a spontaneous autobiographical disclosure, having to do with the unease I felt at your absence, and with sexual deprivation, but now that your visit to Bergen has been terminated, it is no longer necessary or appropriate. Removal of the balloon was easy, trailer trucks carried away the depleted fabric, which is now stored in West Virginia, awaiting some other time of unhappiness, some time, perhaps, when we are angry with one another.
>
> (Barthelme, 1982: 58)

This closing paragraph produces a stark and sudden contrast to the rest of the narrative in a number of ways. First, specific proper names are used for the first time in the entire story ('Norway', 'Bergen', 'West Virginia'), anchoring the text-world in a material deixis, compared with the less concrete details the reader has had to infer from background discourse-world knowledge throughout the rest of the text. Most importantly, and just as we have seen both in Barthelme's other short story and in Camus's novel, there is a sudden disappearance of modalisation and our focus returns abruptly to the matrix text-world. As noted earlier in this discussion, this text-world, from which the whole of the rest of the elaborate conceptual structure of 'The Balloon' originates, remains under-defined and redundant in the narrative up to this point. The sudden collapse of all its surrounding worlds brings the reader swiftly back to a much closer ontological point. Although still only enactor-accessible, the text-world containing the narrator and his second-person addressee has almost no embedding, no distant opinions, no attitudes and judgements. It is likely that it is this sudden switch to a less remote, more intimate, more tangible text-world which causes readers to feel 'punched in the stomach', as 'mingus' reports above. The only deviation from its unmodalised texture comes in the final sentence, where a possible future world is imagined where the balloon may reappear 'some time, perhaps, when we are angry with one another'. However, this epistemic modal-world remains as unrealised, remote and inaccessible as all the other worlds embedded throughout the story, while in the text-world of their reunion only the narrator and his lover remain materially present – and the balloon, of course.

The literary absurd, so far

This chapter began the present attempt to clarify our understanding of the absurd reading experience by first examining readers' identification of the absurd within two different domains of literary interaction: academic criticism and literary discussions in non-academic online environments. Although existing scholarly definitions of the literary absurd were shown to be ill-defined on the whole, it was also noted that they nevertheless accurately reflect a substantial population of readers' perceptions of the phenomenon in non-academic contexts in terms of the breadth of works they encompass. Recent research in cognitive psychology allows the nebulousness of both academically situated and non-academically situated notions of the absurd to be explained as indicative both of the prototype structures underlying readers' concepts of genre and of the family resemblances shared across permeable conceptual boundaries. I have also made an argument in this chapter for this essential situatedness of concepts to be borne in mind and, in particular, the fact that our perceptions of categories and their members will depend greatly on our cultural and individual contexts, as well as on our goals within specific reading situations.

In order to explore these ideas further, Albert Camus's novel *The Outsider* was selected for analysis as the text most frequently identified as 'absurd' by readers participating in online discussions of literature. Camus's position on the borderline between two literary categories – the absurd and the existential

– also facilitated a discussion of the cline of experimentalism along which all absurd prose fiction can be situated. My analysis of *The Outsider* was rooted in the analytical framework of Text World Theory, a cognitive-linguistic model of the mental representations human beings create during discourse, which offers a systematic means of analysing textual style, its context of production and reception, and the conceptual structures it entails. From this perspective, the stylistic means were uncovered by which Camus builds a text-world in which the narrator, Meursault, is presented as dominated by his circumstances and by the natural environment in particular. Alongside the predominant metaphorical structures to be found at crucial moments in the narrative, the use of epistemic modality and the embedded modal-worlds it creates were shown to contribute greatly to Meursault's victim status. I further suggested that this complex of enactor-accessible worlds, and more crucially their sudden disappearance at a key point in the narrative, may be at the heart of many readers' ambivalent empathetic connections with the narrator.

Donald Barthelme's short fiction also exists on the boundaries of the absurd and so provides an interesting counterpoint to Camus. Furthermore, Barthelme's work displays a range of narrative styles which can be positioned at various points along the cline of absurd experimentalism and to which Barthelme's readers respond in varied ways. My analysis of 'Some of Us Had Been Threatening Our Friend Colby' drew out some of the stylistic family resemblances to be found between Barthelme's and Camus's writing, including the occurrence of multiple embedded modal-worlds and an identical sudden switch to neutrally shaded narration at a key plot moment. The deictic construction of Barthelme's text-worlds, however, was shown to be more experimental and therefore more challenging than that in *The Outsider*. Under-defined spatial and temporal parameters emerged as key characteristics of Barthelme's style in this text, requiring greater inferencing effort from readers. Humour, too, was shown to play an important role in 'Some of Us Were Threatening Our Friend Colby', which opposes the scripts of FRIEND-SHIP and EXECUTION to comic effect. By contrast, a more subtle form of absurd humour was found to underpin Barthelme's short story 'The Balloon', one of his most widely read and best-loved texts. In this story script oppositions are both less dominant in the narrative and less extreme in nature. Consequently, readers' responses to 'The Balloon' tend to focus more on the emotional impact of the story than on its humorous content. Once again, I put forward an argument that these powerful emotional responses may to a great extent be the result of the same sudden collapse of multiple modal-worlds at a significant narrative moment, which has been identified operating in the other absurd texts examined over the course of the chapter.

As a whole, this chapter has shown that readers can form profound and self-modifying connections with authors and characters regardless of the position the text concerned occupies within the radial conceptual structure of the category of the literary absurd. The degree of stylistic experimentalism exhibited by the text has also been shown to have little bearing on its emotional effect, with readers of experimental absurdism reporting equally strong emotions in relation to these texts as readers of more conventional narratives. In the next chapter, the empathetic link between reader and text is explored in more depth, as the minds of absurd characters form the focus of the discussion.

3 Absurd Minds

The preceding chapter examined the ways in which different reading communities identify and discuss the absurd in prose fiction, exploring these patterns of categorisation in terms of the conceptual structures which underpin our notions of literary genre. The text-worlds created in three texts positioned on the boundaries of the absurd were explored and, among other stylistic features, varying uses of focalisation in these works were found to be of crucial importance in the construction of absurd characters. The different stylistic choices made by different authors were shown to affect the degree to which readers are able to gain access to particular characters' minds. I also made a further suggestion that this varying accessibility may in turn affect the extent to which readers are able to form emotional connections with textual entities. The present chapter continues the exploration of characterisation in the literary absurd, building on the discussion of focalisation in Chapter 2 with a more detailed analysis of textual representations of fictional minds. Of particular interest over the coming pages are the various stylistic techniques through which the perspectives of characters are constructed in fictional narrative in order to present absurd predicaments and character emotions. The chapter takes the form of three case studies: Saul Bellow's *The Victim* (originally published in 1947); Mordecai Richler's *Barney's Version* (1997); and Tom McCarthy's *Remainder* (2007). Through the stylistic analysis of each of these texts, the examination of absurd characterisation begun in the previous chapter continues here in greater investigative depth.

A singularly masculine phenomenon?

It has already been noted in Chapter 2 that the majority of authors whose works are identified as 'absurd' by readers in both academic and non-academic contexts are white and male and writing towards the second half of the twentieth century. Although we have seen that the boundaries of the absurd can stretch far beyond these parameters, those texts and authors occupying a position at the centre of the 'absurd' prototype shared by a broad spectrum of readers tend to have these core characteristics in common. It can further be noted that the main characters of such prototypically absurd novels are also, in the main, white and male and most often occupy text-worlds that take the twentieth century as their temporal setting too. This would suggest that the key philosophical questions which are commonly explored through the literary absurd align with the preoccupations of Western post-World War II white men. That war, of course, underscored the senselessness of the human condition for a widespread population and literary evidence would also suggest that it produced a discernible cluster of existential crises in the men who survived. Indeed, substantial support can be found within gender and masculinity studies for the notion that questions of identity and authenticity, in particular, became fundamental anxieties for men in the late twentieth century and beyond, and that these anxieties can be found reflected in an array of fictional forms (for extensive surveys, see Baker, 2006; Brod and Kaufman, 1994; Ferrebe, 2006; Lea and Schoene-Harwood, 2003). Even if women authors have been responsible for absurd novels, evidence drawn from literary criticism and from the online literary discussions examined so far in this book would suggest that readers on the whole tend not to attribute absurdism to women.

In one rare exception to this rule, Geherin (1964) presents an analysis of Joan Didion's novel *Play It As It Lays* as an absurdist text, in which he nevertheless suggests that the female experience of the absurdity of the human condition may be necessarily different from male encounters with similar crises. Discussing Didion's main character, Maria, who undergoes, among other things, the breakdown of her marriage, the incarceration of her daughter and an abortion over the course of the novel, Geherin argues,

> What distinguishes Maria's experience from that of most heroes of existential novels is that hers is uniquely feminine, not that Didion has written a blatantly feminist tract, nor that Maria's encounter with nothingness is ultimately qualitatively different from a man's. However, one must understand her experiences as a woman to appreciate fully the nature of her crisis ... By having a woman protagonist, Didion adds a heightened sensitivity and emotional impact to the encounter with nothingness.
>
> (Geherin, 1964: 68–9)

It is impossible to tell whether the absence of women writers from literary criticism on the absurd and from non-academic readers' categorisations of absurd literary texts is due to similar, questionable perceptions that women's 'heightened sensitivity' somehow gives them a peculiar perspective on the human condition that is 'uniquely feminine', precisely because so little is said about women and the absurd in any domain of reading. It is clear, however, that for some reason women are not in general considered to be prototypical writers or experiencers of the absurd by the majority of readers who choose to offer commentary on the phenomenon. Cornwell (2006: back cover) claims to 'offer a comprehensive account of the absurd in prose fiction' but is able to dedicate only two pages of his 350-page study to a brief survey of women absurd writers, all of them playwrights, commenting,

> There seem to have been very few women absurdist writers . . . While, to an extent at least, employing absurdist linguistic techniques, women writers are seen as avoiding, or rejecting, the pessimistic and abstract philosophies entailed in absurdism.
>
> (Cornwell, 2006: 292)

Similarly, although Derksen (2002) argues for an interpretation of the work of Margaret Hollingsworth as absurdist, she notes that male exclusivity is 'a defining feature of absurdism' (Derksen, 2002: 209). It would seem, then, that a consideration of the fictional minds represented in absurd narratives must necessarily be confined mainly to the examination of male characters and their male authors. This is not to say, however, that the fictional conscious-nesses portrayed within absurd prose fiction are entirely homogenous. The limitations of my own expertise, and of my language abilities in particular, mean that I am able to offer within this book an accurate stylistic analysis only of absurd texts written in English. However, even within these con-straints, an array of styles and different linguistic techniques for constructing character in the absurd can be found.

Character-building

Chapter 2 looked at two authors, Albert Camus and Donald Barthelme, whose work occupies a position within two literary categories simultane-ously: the absurd and the existential in Camus's case; and the absurd and the postmodern in Barthelme's case. Similarly, different literary critics have focused on different facets of the work of Saul Bellow (1915–2005), depending on their critical objectives. Bellow was awarded the Nobel Prize in Literature in 1976 and is widely considered to be one of the most important American novelists of the twentieth century. Literary criticism on his fiction can be roughly divided into that concerned mainly with Bellow's identity as a Jewish American writer (see, for example, Aarons, 2011; Cronshaw, 2001; Gordon, 1979; Lee, 2002; Nilsen, 1979; Rosenberg, 2009; Wade, 1999) and that which focuses on the more universal existential and absurdist themes to be found in his fiction (see, for example, Fuchs, 1974; Galloway, 1964; Gilmore, 1982; Lehan, 1959; Newton, 1996; Pifer, 1991; Rebein, 2011; Shulman, 1968). However, these two approaches to Bellow's work need not be seen as opposi-tional. In her study of Elie Wiesel's novel *The Accident*, Knopp (1974) states, the world of orthodox Judaism would appear to allow no place in it for notions of the absurd in the contemporary, existential sense. For the traditional Jewish view holds that life's structure and meaning are fully explained and indeed derive from the divinely granted Torah.

(Knopp, 1974: 212)

However, Knopp goes on to argue that the Holocaust presented Jews with a particular crisis of faith, calling into serious question the Jewish people's covenant with God and leaving 'the theologically serious Jew isolated, to struggle in an unaccustomed loneliness with an indifferent, or worse, hostile universe' (Knopp, 1974: 213). Knopp then elaborates:

> Against this background the reality of Auschwitz confronts the Jew with a dilemma, an 'absurdity' which cannot be dismissed easily and which stubbornly refuses to dissipate of its own accord ... After Auschwitz, he is joined to the French existentialists in being confronted with the absurdity of the universe, an absurdity engendered and given substance by the Holocaust and signaling the breakdown of the covenant. The only possible response that remains within the framework of Judaism is denunciation of God and a demand that He fulfill His contractual obligations.

(Knopp, 1974: 213)

It would seem, then, that the momentous existential crisis World War II caused across a large population of its male survivors may have been particularly acute in the survivors of the Holocaust, and that post-war Jewish identity and post-war absurdism may in fact be closely interconnected.

One thing that all literary critics are agreed upon is that Bellow is a master of characterisation and that many of the key themes of his work are communicated in his construction of keenly portrayed human minds. Indeed, Bellow's Nobel Prize was given in recognition of 'the human understanding and subtle analysis of contemporary culture that are combined in his work' and Bellow dedicated his Nobel lecture to a discussion of the demise of characterisation in the contemporary novel (see Nobelprize.org, 2012). As Rebein argues,

> Bellow balances a closely observed representation of the social world (particularly the world of the modern city) with an equally compelling rendering of his characters' interior states. He is interested in character as it is revealed under pressure or strain, isolated from others, frustrated, on the verge of financial ruin or emotional collapse. Male and middle-aged, the typical Bellow protagonist soon descends into a slough of despair; the physical world, with its demands and entanglements, blankets him; the mistakes of the past haunt him; and his relations with other people become frayed or completely undone.

(Rebein, 2011: 32)

Bellow's novel *The Victim* is one of his earliest works but is widely considered to be exemplary of Bellow's core concerns with characterisation.
The novel follows Asa Leventhal, a middle-aged magazine editor living
in New York, who is haunted by a former acquaintance, Kirby Allbee,
while his wife is away from the city visiting family during a hot summer.
Allbee is an alcoholic and homeless after losing his job and spending all of
his inheritance from his dead wife's estate. He first approaches Leventhal
in a city park and goes on to pursue him many more times at his home,
at work and in public, as it is revealed that he blames Leventhal for the
loss of his job and the subsequent down-turn in his fortunes. Several years
before the novel opens, Allbee secured Leventhal an interview with his
boss, Mr Rudiger, and, for reasons which remain unclear throughout the
novel, Rudiger launched a verbal attack on Leventhal during the interview.
Leventhal, in turn, lost his temper with Rudiger and Allbee lost his job
soon afterwards. Over several weeks, Leventhal has a series of increasingly
disturbing confrontations with Allbee while also struggling to deal with the
illness and eventual death of his young nephew. The novel tracks his fluctuating emotions towards Allbee and his shifting feelings of responsibility
and guilt.

The passage below can be seen as a typical example of the predominant
narrative style of *The Victim* and in particular of the many sections of the
novel in which Leventhal broods over previous encounters and conversations
with other characters. Here Leventhal is first described going for breakfast at
a restaurant near his home and then mulling over a recent conversation about
Allbee with his close friend Harkavy as he walks through uptown New York.
Leventhal is trying to decide whether to call another old acquaintance of all
three men, Williston, for advice:

> Leventhal bathed, dressed and went down for breakfast. In the restau-
> rant he took a booth instead of sitting at the counter as he did on week-
> days. He found a copy of the *Tribune* on the seat and read, propping the
> paper on the sugar shaker while he drank his coffee. Afterward he took
> a walk uptown, enjoying the weather and looking in shopwindows . . .
> He had not seen Williston for three years or more and to ask him,
> out of a clear sky, about something so difficult and obscure, perhaps
> forgotten, might appear strange. Besides, if Williston was capable of
> believing he had injured Allbee on purpose, he would be cold to him.
> And perhaps Harkavy was right. Perhaps he would be trying to get
> Williston to assure him that he still liked him, to demand that assurance
> of him more than fairness. He pictured Williston sitting before him in
> an habitual pose, at ease in his chair, his fingers in the pockets of his
> vest, red-cheeked, his blue eyes seeming to say, 'So much frankness and
> no more', the exact account remaining in doubt.
>
> (Bellow, 2008: 84–5)

At the beginning of this episode, a coherent and potentially immersive text-world is built from a perspective external to Leventhal; the whole of *The Victim* is narrated in the third person by a heterodiegetic narrator, in Genette's (1980) terms. The narrative in the first four sentences of the extract above is unmodalised and the focus remains on the world-building details of the restaurant, most of which are given using definite reference ('the counter', 'the seat', 'the sugar shaker' and so on), and on Leventhal's physical movement within the scene. However, the third-person perspective in *The Victim* does not leave the reader without access to Leventhal's thoughts and motivations. The omniscient narrator not only has a view of Leventhal at the present moment in the restaurant, but also seems familiar with his more long-term habits, as we are told that Leventhal took a booth rather than 'sitting at the counter as he did on weekdays'. The present participle 'sitting' here expresses a continual aspect and creates a brief world-switch (see Gavins, 2007: 48–50) to the habitual text-world in which all Leventhal's previous weekday visits to the restaurant are compressed (see Fauconnier and Turner, 2003) into one mental representation. Furthermore, the spatial deixis in 'went *down* for breakfast' suggests that the narrator is occupying a viewpoint that is proximal to Leventhal as he leaves his apartment to go to the restaurant. We are also given a brief glimpse into Leventhal's inner thoughts in the first few lines as we are told that he was 'enjoying the weather'. Soon afterwards, the narrative slips further into Leventhal's point of view, as his ruminations about Allbee, Harkavy and Williston are represented using free indirect thought.

As already outlined in Chapter 2, Simpson (1993) offers a more fine-grained set of distinctions between the different forms external narrators can take and their consequent stylistic effects. He firstly labels homodiegetic narratives as 'Category A' and heterodiegetic narratives as 'Category B', before going on to examine the various patterns of modal shading to be found in Category A narratives, which are summarised in Chapter 2 of this book. Simpson further notes that all heterodiegetic Category B narratives are either situated with a perspective outside the consciousness of the characters participating in the text-world, or are mediated through the point of view of a particular character; Simpson terms the former type of narrative 'B in Narratorial mode' and the latter 'B in Reflector mode' (Simpson, 1993: 62). Once again, Simpson goes on to analyse patterns of modality in Category B texts and further divides his Narratorial mode and Reflector mode categories according to the modal shading they display, resulting in a total of six possible forms of heterodiegetic narration. Simpson's typology of heterodiegetic narration is summarised in Figure 3.1. As illustrated here, heterodiegetic narratives that are in either Narratorial or Reflector mode may be positively, negatively or neutrally shaded in the same way as Category A homodiegetic narratives.

According to Simpson's typology, then, the passage from *The Victim* above begins as a Category B narrative in Narratorial mode. The opening lines of the episode are further characterised by their lack of modality, which

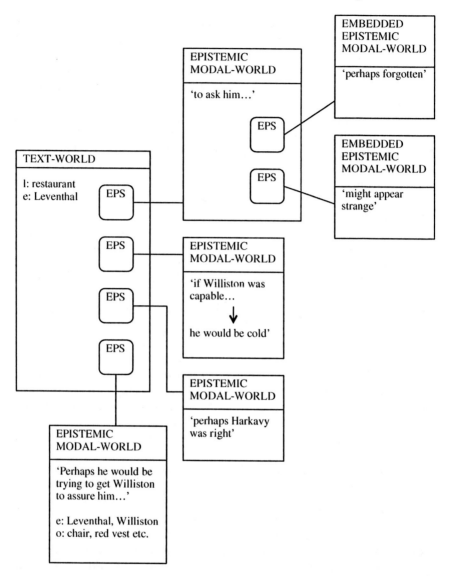

Figure 3.2 Embedded worlds in *The Victim*

the 'apodosis' component defines a situation which is consequent on the protasis, such as the imagined outcome 'he would be cold to him' in the above example. From a text-world point of view, the protasis establishes an epistemic modal-world which has its status as a remote possibility made linguistically evident, while the apodosis takes this hypothetical situation to a further point or conclusion (see Gavins, 2007: 121). The use of the infinitive in 'to ask him' operates conceptually in the same way as 'if Williston was capable', marking the imagined scenario, and its corollaries, as a distant and unrealised epistemic modal-world. Both of these worlds are shown emerging from the main text-world at the top of Figure 3.2. Note, however, that the conditional construction through which Leventhal first imagines asking Williston about Allbee contains an added conceptual complexity. Once the protasis, 'to ask him', has established a distant possibility, the apodosis component of the conditional is made up of two further remote worlds. In the first of these embedded epistemic worlds, Leventhal speculates that Williston may have forgotten the incident he wants to ask him about, using epistemic modality, as already noted above ('*perhaps* forgotten'). In the second embedded modal-world, Leventhal projects himself into Williston's perspective and predicts that his behaviour, in the imagined circumstance, 'might appear strange'. In this case, he is referring to Williston's possible view of an unrealised situation rather than his own, giving the apodosis element of the conditional an additional epistemic filter. Leventhal goes on to create another two epistemic modal-worlds in this episode of the narrative, shown in the bottom half of Figure 3.2. The first is fleeting and relates to his brief admission that 'perhaps Harkavy was right', but the final hypothetical world is markedly more developed than the others. Leventhal describes an imagined scenario involving a conversation with Williston, detailed down to his friend's likely posture, his colouring and the position of his hands. Just as in Barthelme's short story, all the worlds that are created from Leventhal's perspective in *The Victim* are only enactor-accessible, having been filtered through a participating character's mind. What makes the hypothetical worlds in *The Victim* different from those in 'Some of Us Had Been Threatening Our Friend Colby', however, is their central concern with the perceptions and emotions of other characters, rather than simply with the description of possible future events and actions.

Reading other people's minds

Throughout his considerable body of research into the construction of fictional minds in narrative, Palmer (see, for example, 2002, 2004, 2005, 2007a, 2007b, 2010, 2011) argues that it is not possible to achieve a full understanding of the complexity of fictional consciousness through the application to a text of simple categories of speech and thought representation alone. He argues that the key motivation of readers for reading narrative fictions is to follow the fictional minds created within them and that we understand and respond to the characters of literary texts in the same way we understand and respond to real people; we use the same cognitive and psychological processes to comprehend a fictional world and its inhabitants as we use to comprehend the real world. As Palmer explains:

Fictional narrative is, in essence, the presentation of mental functioning. The term *plot* is generally defined as a chain of causally connected
events in a story. But what are these causal connections in practice?
Generally, events in the storyworld are of little importance unless they
become the *experiences* of characters. Events can occur independently
of characters, but they will, on the whole, only have a significance
for the narrative because of their effect on those characters' minds.
Descriptions of novels by actual readers tend to focus less on events
themselves than on characters' reactions to those events, what they
were thinking and feeling, their beliefs and desires, and so on.

(Palmer, 2011: 202)

Palmer further argues that readers are able to read characters' minds as
embedded narratives by constructing what he calls a 'continuing consciousness frame' (see Palmer, 2004: 175–83), collecting together all the isolated
references made to a particular proper name in the text and building an
understanding of that consciousness that continues in the spaces between
individual mentions of the character. Palmer makes use of the concept of
'Theory of Mind' (henceforth ToM) to explain the processes by which we
reconstruct the minds of fictional entities. ToM is a term used by psychologists to refer to the awareness of other people's minds and the ability to
attribute thought processes to them (see, for example, Apperly, 2011; Baron-
Cohen, 1995; Carruthers, 2000; Carruthers and Smith, 1996; Goldman, 1992;
Leslie, 1991). Within this discipline, there are two main theories about how
ToM works: the so-called 'theory-theory', which posits that all human beings
hold a general theory of how states of mind work and that we attribute this
to other humans; and the 'simulation theory', which argues that we simulate
the mental states of others in order to form an understanding of their feelings
and motivations (for a useful summary, see Carruthers and Smith, 1996).
As Belmonte (2008) points out, the focus of psychologists working on ToM
has, in the main, always been on the development of the concept as 'a vehicle
for understanding evolutionary differences between human and non-human
social cognition, clinical differences between normal human cognition and
abnormal states such as autism and schizophrenia, and developmental differences between different states of cognitive maturation' (Belmonte, 2008: 192).
By contrast, in literary studies ToM has gained popularity over recent years
as a far broader concept used to discuss relationships between fictional characters, between characters and readers and so on – see the work of Zunshine
(2003, 2006, 2008) in particular.

In his own use of ToM, Palmer (2004) argues that readers are able to
construct continuing consciousness frames by attributing states of mind to
characters based not just on explicit representations of the character's own
thoughts (such as in the use of free indirect thought in the passage from *The
Victim* above) but also on a wide variety of other textual cues. These cues

might include a character's reported physical actions, such as laughing or scowling, as well as other characters' behaviour towards them and speech and thought about them. Readers make constant inferences about the minds of fictional entities based on these cues and derive their overall understanding of a character from them, a process which has also been termed 'mindreading' by other theorists (see Malle and Hodges, 2005; Whiteley, 2010). Stockwell (2009: 137–44) responds to Belmonte's concerns that the specific psychological meaning of ToM has been reduced by literary critics 'to a special case of narrative processing' (Belmonte, 2008: 199) and argues for an alternative term of 'mind-modelling'. This term, he argues, distinguishes the literary-specific activity through which readers build a mental representation of a character, which includes the beliefs, desires and emotions of that textual entity, often over the course of an entire text. Stockwell argues, using a Text World Theory approach, that the construction of our complex notions of character is not simply a matter of passively reading textual cues but that it is an active and imaginative process of serial inferencing, which builds up over an extended text into a detailed model of a character's mind and personality.

As an illustration of all of these ideas, consider the following episode, towards the end of *The Victim*, which takes place at the vigil for Leventhal's nephew, held in the boy's mother's Roman Catholic church:

> He gazed at Max's burly back and his sunburnt neck, and, as his glance moved across the polished rows of benches, he saw Elena sitting between Villani and a priest. The look she gave him was one of bitter anger. Though the light was poor, there was no mistaking it. Her face was white and straining. 'What have I done?' he thought; his panic was as great as if he had never foreseen this. He was afraid to let her catch his eye and did not return her look. Helping Max up the aisle, he sat down beside him, still holding his arm. What would he do if then and there – imagining the worst – she began to scream at him, accusing him? Once more she turned her face to him over her shoulder; it seemed to be blazing in its whiteness. She must be mad.
>
> (Bellow, 2008: 162)

Although Leventhal is the reflector of the fiction here in Simpson's (1993) terms, there are a number of other fictional minds represented in the text. The first of these to be mentioned in the extract is Max, Leventhal's brother, who has returned from working away in Texas to attend his son's funeral. Even this fleeting first mention of him, in which Max's back is described from Leventhal's point of view as 'burly' and his neck as 'sunburnt', adds to the reader's continuing consciousness frame of Max as a physically strong and hardworking man who has been emotionally devastated by the death of his young son, a frame which is further added to by the description of Leventhal 'Helping Max up the aisle'. The second other fictional mind represented in the paragraph is that of Max's wife, Elena. Earlier in the novel, the reader has seen Leventhal paying regular visits to Elena and has witnessed her increasing distress at her son's deteriorating health. We also know from other scenes in the novel that Leventhal blames himself both for not insisting that Elena take his nephew to the hospital sooner and for not insisting that Max return from Texas earlier; instead, he chose to give in to Elena's fear of hospitals and delayed contacting his brother. Leventhal's mind-modelling of his sister-in-law's state of mind is clearly depicted in the description of her face as showing 'bitter anger', as 'white and straining' and as 'blazing in its whiteness'. However, the reader's understanding of Elena's feelings towards Leventhal is built from a wider complex of mind-modelling moments than this instance alone. The continuing consciousness frame readers are able to construct for Elena over many chapters is also one which includes her irrational fear of hospitals and her refusal to call a doctor to her son because of this for many days of his illness. When Elena turns to look at Leventhal in anger during the vigil, then, readers of the entire novel are able to comprehend that she blames him for insisting his nephew be admitted to hospital (which from her previous behaviour we can infer she is convinced killed him), while Leventhal blames himself for not acting against her wishes much sooner. The conflict between the two characters' perceptions of one another is confirmed in Leventhal's incredulous direct thought, 'What have I done?' and in his final mind-modelling assertion 'She must be mad'. His continuing guilt over his nephew's death, however, is indicated in 'his panic' and his attempts not to meet Elena's gaze, as well as in the representation through free indirect thought of his imagining Elena screaming at him ('What would he do if then and there – imagining the worst – she began to scream at him, accusing him?').

Palmer's cognitively based, whole-text approach to the analysis of fictional minds is of further help in understanding characterisation in *The Victim*, in that Palmer insists that too much emphasis has been placed in preceding narratological accounts of character consciousness on 'private, passive, solitary and highly verbalized inner thought at the expense of all other types of mental functioning' (Palmer, 2011: 202). In his most recent research, Palmer has argued in particular for a proper consideration of how *intermental*, as well as *intramental*, thought functions in narrative fiction. As he explains:

> such thinking is joint, group, shared or collective, as opposed to intramental, or individual or private thought. It is also known as *socially distributed*, *situated*, or *extended cognition*, and also as *intersubjectivity*. Intermental thought is a crucially important component of fictional narrative because, just as in real life, where much of our thinking is done in groups, much of the mental functioning that occurs in novels is done by large organizations, small groups, work colleagues, friends, families, couples and other intermental units.
>
> (Palmer, 2011: 213)

Palmer argues, for example, that it is possible to identify a 'Middlemarch mind' (Palmer, 2005) in Eliot's novel based on the same sorts of textual cues as those noted in *The Victim* above; through this intermental consciousness the shared opinions and values of the population of Middlemarch can be understood as a collective and coherent whole. Palmer goes on to argue, in relation to this novel,

> Studying the Middlemarch mind is like looking at a painting by Turner, Seurat or Cezanne. Close up, all you see is a mass of apparently incoherent brushstrokes; move away and you are aware of shapes emerging and the subject of the whole picture materializes. Close up, the subjects that comprise this large intermental unit are unique and all have slightly different perspectives on their storyworld. The thought of them collectively swallowing Lydgate makes no sense at all. Move away, however, and the consensus emerges, and it then feels absolutely right to say that Middlemarch intends to swallow Lydgate whole.
>
> (Palmer, 2011: 232)

Palmer's claims about intermental thought in fiction seem to go against much existing and accepted thought in cognitive science (although this statement in itself is, of course, evidence that he may be right!). As Herman (2011) points out, both ToM and Palmer's use of it grow out of a Cartesian dualism which the majority of cognitively framed cultural studies has sought to disprove over the last thirty years or so. Stockwell (2011) also raises the question: if Palmer accepts the central cognitive-scientific argument that all minds are embodied, in which body is the 'social mind' situated that Palmer identifies as responsible for intermental thought?

Nevertheless, Palmer presents convincing textual evidence for the gradual accumulation of shared values and opinions into a tangible and coherent mass across the course of a whole narrative. Indeed, it is possible to identify a number of intermental units in *The Victim* against which Leventhal's actions and opinions become framed. Perhaps the most important of these units is made up of Leventhal's friends and acquaintances, the men of a similar age and social background to him with whom he spends most of his social and working time. Leventhal's close friend Harkavy is one part of this unit, as is Williston. It is clear that Allbee also once formed part of the group, until his loss of social status and his subsequent overall bad behaviour led him to be excluded. Many of Leventhal's thoughts in the novel are dedicated to what this intermental unit as a collective thinks of him and of his actions. Their opinions and assessments are of crucial importance to Leventhal and much of the anxiety he expresses over the course of the text centres around his desire for acceptance within this social group. However, Leventhal's need for approval from his contemporaries is complicated by the fact that he often suspects individual gentiles among the group of harbouring anti-Semitic prejudices against him and against other Jewish members of the same unit. Because of this, Leventhal struggles throughout the novel to come to terms with the fact that he desires to be an accepted part of a social and intermental unit the judgements of which he neither trusts nor wholly approves.

The following extract provides a useful example of the ways in which the intermental unit of Leventhal's contemporaries is represented in the novel:

> It was for Williston, even if he was [Allbee's] benefactor, to explain why he was ready to believe such a thing. And when you said that someone was your benefactor, what did it actually mean? You might help a man because he was a bother to you and you wanted to get rid of him. You might do it because you disliked him unfairly and wanted to pay for your prejudice and then, feeling that you had paid, you were free and even entitled to detest him.
>
> (Bellow, 2008: 85)

This passage is once again made up of Leventhal's free indirect thought as he here ponders the possibility that Williston might think he deliberately made life difficult for Allbee for some reason. The passage starts with a clear focus on Williston as an individual, referred to both by his proper name and by the singular third-person pronoun 'he'. However, the shift to the second person indicates that Leventhal is reflecting no longer just on Williston's behaviour, but on the norms of behaviour accepted across a wider social group. His repeated use of this generalised 'you', to use Herman's (1994) term, throughout the rest of the extract brings his own opinions and those of the rest of his friends and acquaintances together under one address form. The general and inclusive nature of 'you' in this instance is further underlined in the indefinite references which accompany it in, for example, 'when you said that *someone*', 'You might help *a man*' or 'he was *a bother*'. Leventhal is here laying out the values of an intermental unit of which he considers himself a part and using it to assess Williston's actions and his own reactions to them.

It is important to remember, however, that, in the passage above, the text-world is filtered through Leventhal's point of view: these are *his* perceptions of the collective opinions of a group of men whom *he* considers to share a certain outlook. It is not necessary that the reader will share his point of view or will accept Leventhal's assessments of Williston's behaviour. Indeed, a number of other stylistic features of the text operate throughout the novel to suggest that Leventhal's increasingly paranoid state of mind may lead to his judgements being unstable and untrustworthy. The abundance of hypothetical, but ultimately unrealised, worlds which are constructed from within Leventhal's perspective as reflector of the fiction accumulate over the course of the novel to paint a portrait of their creator as misguided in his opinions most of the time. The enactor-accessible imagined scenarios he constructs involving his colleagues and friends through various linguistic means throughout the text rarely materialise as actual occurrences. As we have already seen, in particular the predominant pattern of weak epistemic commitment which is expressed through the negative modal shading of Leventhal's perspective also shows him to be uncertain of his own opinions and judgements.

Furthermore, in another marked similarity to Camus's *The Outsider*, Leventhal's physical environment is described in terms of physical oppression at frequent points throughout the novel. Note, for example, the similarities between Leventhal's perception of Elena's rage in the vigil scene above, which is described in terms of 'blazing' whiteness and light, and the descriptions of blinding light in the key scenes in *The Outsider* examined in Chapter 2. The heat of the New York summer in *The Victim*, too, although it does not obscure Leventhal's senses to the same degree as Camus's narrator experiences, has a direct influence on his perceptions of other people:

> After getting off the subway he delayed going home. He stopped in the park. The crowd was extraordinarily thick tonight. The same band of revivalists was on the curb. A woman was singing. Her voice and the accompaniment of the organ were very dim, only a few notes emerging from the immense interminable mutter. He searched for a long time before he found a seat near the pond where a few half-naked children were splashing. The trees were swathed in stifling dust, and the stars were faint and sparse through the pall. The benches formed a dense, double human wheel; the paths were thronged. There was an overwhelming human closeness and thickness, and Leventhal was penetrated by a sense not merely of the crowd in this park but of innumerable millions, crossing, touching, pressing. What was that story he had once read about Hell cracking open on account of the rage of the god of the sea, and all the souls, crammed together, looking out? But these were alive, this young couple with bare arms, this woman in late pregnancy, sauntering, this bootblack hauling his box along by the strap.
> (Bellow, 2008: 164)

Here, Leventhal is on his way home from the vigil for his nephew and the city park in which he pauses is described as overwhelmingly hot, but also crushingly overcrowded. As with the scene in the restaurant analysed earlier in this chapter, the episode begins in Narratorial mode, with no modalisation and little access granted to Leventhal's thoughts and feelings. The slip into Reflector mode once again begins gradually, with brief indications of Leventhal's point of view, for example in the evaluative adjective in 'interminable mutter', as well as the explicit reference to the character's view of the scene in 'He searched for a long time'. The shift in focalisation is complete when the deictic zero point of the text-world becomes locked with Leventhal, with the proximity of people *to him* described as an 'overwhelming human closeness and thickness'. Just as in *The Outsider*, the use of metaphor to convey the suffocating nature of the experience here is particularly interesting. Although it is not clear whether any of the people in the park are actually touching Leventhal, the representation of their number as 'an overwhelming closeness and thickness' is highly physical and material. The description creates a metaphor world in which the people in the park are blended with the notion of a thick liquid. The subsequent description of Leventhal being 'penetrated' by a sudden awareness of the world's population adds to the blend, as his body is represented as somehow permeable. The material penetrating Leventhal's body is, of course, another metaphor through which ideas are being presented as physical objects which Leventhal (in his permeable state) is unable to resist. Leventhal then goes on to make a comparison through free indirect thought between a fantastical story of hell splitting open and the scene in the park. Although far-fetched, this analogy is brought much closer to Leventhal's reality through the use of proximal deixis in this focalised section of the narrative: note the shift from 'the god of the sea' and 'all the souls' to 'these', 'this young couple', 'this woman' and 'this bootblack', all of which add to the sense of suffocating closeness in the section of the text.

Such stifling scenes are repeated frequently throughout *The Victim* and the overpowering heat of the city forms a constant backdrop to Leventhal's harassment by Allbee, his increasingly distressing family circumstances and his mounting paranoia. Bellow couples finely detailed text-world building in Narratorial mode with the creation of multiple hypothetical worlds in a highly modalised Reflector mode to establish a clear-cut characterisation of Leventhal as physically overwhelmed, paranoid, uncertain and unreliable. In particular, the third-person omniscient narrator at no point intervenes in the narrative to confirm or deny any of Leventhal's speculations or ruminations. In the sections of the novel where the text-world is not filtered through Leventhal's perspective, the narrator offers no modalisation of his own, nor any explicit evaluation of either Leventhal or any of the other characters in the novel (for an analysis of the same technique at work elsewhere see Gavins, 2010). As Leventhal staggers through the New York summer, fighting to make sense of the bewildering predicament in which he finds himself, he remains isolated and insecure, and neither he nor the reader is offered any clear moral guidance from an omniscient source.

Versions of unreliability

Having examined the stylistic techniques through which Saul Bellow shapes the paranoid mind of Asa Leventhal, it is useful now to turn to a contrasting text by an author who has had direct comparisons drawn between his work and Bellow's but who makes use of focalisation in his absurdist writing in noticeably different ways. Mordecai Richler (1931–2001) is a Jewish

Canadian writer who, like Bellow, provides critics with a range of different identities and different viewpoints from which to approach his work (for a representative spread, see Darling, 1986). Richler and Bellow were both born in Montreal (although Bellow's family moved to Chicago when he was eight years old), which perhaps particularly encourages critics to make connections between the two authors (for indicative examples, see Cohen, 1981; Craniford, 2006; Golden, 1981). However, their fiction also bears stylistic and thematic similarities which give substance to these comparisons. As well as being noted for his humorous explorations of Canadian, and specifically Jewish Canadian, identity (see, for example, Antor, 2005; Kramer, 2008; Quennet, 2002; Spergel, 2005), Richler's concerns with the broader theme of the absurdity of the human condition have also been the focus of literary critical responses to his work (see, for example, Gadhi, 1989; Kramer, 2008; Moss, 1983; New and New, 2003: 197). The pivotal role played by the absurd in Richler's last novel, *Barney's Version*, published in 1997, is made explicit in the closing paragraphs of the text. Here, the core beliefs of the novel's narrator, Barney Panofsky, are summarised by his son: 'Life was absurd, and nobody ever truly understood anybody else' (Richler, 1997: 406).

Barney Panofsky is an ageing television producer living alone in Quebec. He is the first-person narrator of *Barney's Version*, which is presented to the reader as an autobiography, the title page reading 'BARNEY'S VERSION With Footnotes and an Afterword by Michael Panofsky'. As the novel progresses, we learn that Michael Panofsky is Barney's eldest son by his third wife, Miriam, and 'a militant socialist . . . sinfully rich and married to an aristo' (Richler, 1997: 66), as Barney puts it. Barney's first marriage was to Clara Charnofsky, a beautiful and enigmatic poet who committed suicide while she and Barney were living in Paris in 1952. 'The Second Mrs. Panofsky' is referred to only using this term throughout the novel and is described by Barney as 'a member of that much maligned group, the Jewish American Princesses' (Richler, 1997: 189). Barney goes on to add,

> The Second Mrs. Panofsky was not a bad person. Had she not fallen into my hands but instead married a real, rather than a pretend, straight arrow, she would be a model wife and mother today. She would not be an embittered, grossly overweight hag, given to diddling with New Age crystals and consulting trance-channellers.
>
> (Richler, 1997: 189)

At the point of Barney's writing, Barney and his third wife, Miriam, are also separated. Miriam is living with Blair Hopper, a former friend of the couple, but continues to form the most regular focus of Barney's thoughts as he reminisces about their past and ruminates on the causes of their separation. Barney and Miriam have another son, Saul, whom Barney describes as 'a born again neo-conservative . . . dirt poor and liv[ing] in squalor in New

York, in an East Village loft, where the infatuated girls come and go, cooking and sewing and boiling his underwear' (Richler, 1997: 66); and a daughter, Kate, who teaches English literature, and about whom Barney offers little in the way of his usual acerbic commentary, noting instead that 'Kate is my darling' (Richler, 1997: 78). Barney claims that the novel is 'the true story of my wasted life' (Richler, 1997: 3), the production of which is motivated by the looming publication of a second autobiography by Barney's nemesis, author Terry McIver. Barney and McIver first met in Paris in the 1950s and Barney fears that McIver's new autobiography will contain fresh accusations and revelations about him, particularly regarding his relationship with his best friend, Bernard 'Boogie' Moscovitch. Barney was charged with Boogie's murder in 1960, after Boogie went missing from Barney's lakeside cottage, but was found not guilty at his trial after the police failed to find Boogie's body. Barney maintains throughout the novel that he and Boogie had been drinking on the day of Boogie's disappearance and that his best friend must have drowned in the lake while Barney was sleeping off the effects of the alcohol.

Since *Barney's Version* is a first-person narrative, readers are given full access to Barney's inner thoughts and have abundant information upon which to build a continuing consciousness frame for him. Barney, as we have already seen, also describes a multitude of other characters in the novel and offers forthright opinions on them, again allowing the reader to formulate their own mental representations of these textual entities, their values and beliefs. Consider the following example (with footnote reference, discussed below) of a description Barney gives of a woman he and Boogie encounter while visiting Cannes in 1952:

> The woman with the gleaming hair seated alone two tables to our left appeared to be in her late twenties. Somebody's gift package. Her fine arms were bare, her linen shift elegant, long bare legs crossed. She was sipping white wine and smoking a Gitane, and when she caught us sneaking glances at her, she lowered her eyes, pouted, and reached for the book in her straw shoulder bag, *Bonjour tristesse*,[2] by Françoise Sagan, and began to read.
>
> (Richler, 1997: 31)

From his perspective as a participating character in this scene, Barney provides a detailed portrait of this woman, giving a description not only of her physical appearance but also his own judgements and assumptions about her. The noun phrases in the passage are predominantly pre-modified with evaluative adjectives, as in 'gleaming hair', 'fine arms', 'long bare legs', allowing the reader to build a clear mental picture not only of the woman, but also of Barney's obvious attraction to her. The novel at this point seems similar to Simpson's (1993) Category A positively shaded narration. Such narratives are characterised by their homodiegesis, which is most often accompanied with abundant *verba sentiendi*, in Fowler's (1986) terms, words denoting thoughts, feelings and perceptions. Barney's narration certainly appears cooperative, as Simpson also notes is typical of such texts, but it does not contain the deontic and boulomaic modality which would also normally feature heavily in a positively shaded fiction. Instead, Barney's subjective point of view is foregrounded in his use of epistemic modality, in '*appeared* to be in her late twenties', which makes a suggestion that Barney may be wrong in this assumption. However, the overall reliability of the description is most seriously undermined by the footnote which accompanies the title of the book which Barney says the woman was reading. This footnote at the bottom of the page is provided by Barney's son and editor, Michael, and reads: '2 It had to be some other book, as *Bonjour tristesse* wasn't published until 1954'.

Footnotes such as this one appear at intervals throughout the text of *Barney's Version* and both the content and the tone of this one can be seen as typical of their overall style. Their presence adds to the impression of the novel as an edited autobiography, although, of course, the editor is just as fictional as the main narrator of the novel. Even in the footnoted text, then, the story remains focalised through a homodiegetic narrator, another textual entity participating in a fictional text-world. It is interesting to note here, however, that the 'Michael' who is supposedly editing the text is a different version of the 'Michael' Barney describes in the main narrative. It is precisely because of such textual phenomena as this that Text World Theory adopts Emmott's (1997) terminology and refers to textual entities as 'enactors' rather than 'characters' (see Gavins, 2007: 41–2). Barney's version of Michael is constructed from a father's perspective; it contains information put together only from his external observations and mind-modelling of his son and constitutes only one textual enactor of a more complex character. The enactor presented as responsible for the editing of the novel is a later version of the same character, Michael, who presents himself to the reader through his footnotes and without the added filter of his father's opinions of him. The notion that we construct our sense of a character from the behaviour and insights of a series of different enactors over an extended text is one which fits neatly with Palmer's (2004) notions of a continuing consciousness frame; our understanding of the character of Michael is built not just from his father's representations of his fictional mind, but also from the direct access we are granted to that mind through Michael's own, albeit brief, focalisations of the text.

It is further interesting to observe that there is a strong contrast between the modal shading of Michael Panofsky's notes on his father's memoirs and that of the main narrative. Note in the example above the use of deontic modality ('it *had* to be some other book'), through which Michael expresses far greater confidence in his assertions than his father seems to have in his memories of the woman in Cannes. The effect of this contrast, and of the contradiction Michael's note presents to Barney's version of events, is to draw

attention to Barney's status as a fictional narrator and to suggest that he
may not be reliable in this role. In Text World Theory, the notion of 'world-
repair' (Gavins, 2007: 141–3) has been developed, once again from the work
of Emmott (1997), to describe instances where new information in a discourse
can cause readers and listeners to make changes to an established text-world
should that information indicate that components have been erroneously
added to the mental representation. This may occur as the result of mishear-
ing or misreading a text or, in fictional narrative, can often be a consequence
of deliberately misleading information being provided by a narrator or character. Some fictional plot twists and revelations can be so radical that they
cause 'world-replacement' (Gavins, 2007: 142), or the complete rebuilding of
a text-world based on newly acquired information. In narratology, the same
process is often discussed in terms of 'denarration' (see Richardson, 2006:
87–9). As Richardson explains,

> [By denarration] I am referring to a kind of negative narration in which
> a narrator denies significant aspects of his or her narrative that had
> earlier been presented as given . . . The effect of this unusual strategy is
> variable: it can play a relatively minor role in the overall text, or it can
> fundamentally alter the nature and reception of the story. The effect it
> produces is nearly always arresting, and to many readers it can be quite
> disconcerting.
>
> (Richardson, 2006: 87)

Richardson goes on to analyse Samuel Beckett's use of denarration in particular, focusing on the way the narrator of *Molloy* often gives information
which he later admits he may be confused about or may be misrepresenting.
It is clear, however, that Richler's use of the technique in *Barney's Version*
differs somewhat from that which Richardson describes above. First of all,
it is not the main narrator of the text, Barney, who undermines the version
of events he has already provided. Rather, Barney's reliability is destabilised
by a secondary narrator who disagrees with him. It is also questionable to
what extent the detail which Michael's footnote corrects (the name of the
book the woman in Cannes was carrying) can be seen as a 'significant aspect'
of the narrative. Instead, I would argue that it is the regularity of Michael's
interjections, and their general aim at disputing Barney's version of history,
which acts in a cumulative manner to destabilise Barney's narrative as whole.

   In the example above, although the positive shading of Michael's footnote
expresses a greater degree of confidence than the epistemic modality his
father uses, it is of little help in repairing the erroneous information already
contained in the text-world of the woman in Cannes. Although Michael
points out that the publishing date of *Bonjour tristesse* does not fit with
the scene in 1952 France, the only other information provided in his footnote is that it must have been 'some other book'. The general effect of the

footnote, then, is to draw attention to the title of the book and to Barney's inaccuracy, rather than to replace the world-building elements with anything more precise. Elsewhere, Michael is able to be more extensive in the world-building, or rather world-repairing, information he gives in his notes:

> 1951. Quemoy and Matsu,[1] if anybody can find those pimples on the China Sea now, were being shelled by the Commies, a prelude, according to some, to an invasion of what was then still called Formosa. Back in America everybody was still scared by The Bomb . . .
>
> [1] Quemoy and Matsu are in the Taiwan Straits, and the mainland Communists did not begin shelling until August 1958. Threatened by the American Secretary of State, John Foster Dulles, they suddenly confined the bombardments to only odd days of the month. Then, in March 1959, the bombardments ceased altogether, without explanation.
>
> (Richler, 1997: 53)

In this example, Barney is recounting a particular period in post-World War II history and his son directly meets his challenge to his reader to 'find those pimples on the China Sea' by giving the precise location of the islands of Quemoy and Matsu. Barney also embarks on some mind-modelling of an unspecified intermental unit here, commenting on a shared view ('according to some') that the shelling of the islands in 1951 was a prelude to another attack. Michael's footnote not only corrects Barney's dates, but also offers a further detail on the lead-up to the actual bombing of Quemoy and Matsu and its sudden cessation. In this case, then, the reader is able to use this information, once again presented in confident manner through categorical assertions, to repair the text-world constructed from Barney's discourse with Michael's version of these historical events.

While Michael's footnotes to his father's autobiography might at first appear more confident and trustworthy than the main text he corrects, after a while their pedantic tone starts to work against the authority they seem to be seeking to establish. Michael's comments and objections are often so minor as to raise the question of his own reliability as a narrating textual entity. Immediately following the footnote on Taiwanese history above, for example, Michael adds a further footnote to his father's comment that, at the same time as the misdated bombings, 'Rotarians were digging A-bomb fall-out shelters in their backyards, laying in supplies of bottled water, dehydrated soups, sacks of rice, and their collection of *Reader's Digest* condensed books and Pat Boone[2] records' (Richler, 1997: 53); here, Michael notes that Pat Boone did not have his first hit single until 1955. Elsewhere, Michael corrects Barney's confusion of Norway with Denmark as a Quisling country (Richler, 1997: 320), he notes that Barney's description of himself rewinding a video-tape clockwise should read 'counter-clockwise' (Richler, 1997: 304) and even interjects in the text when he does not have missing evidence to hand, for example commenting, 'I have been unable to trace this quote' after his father quotes a comment made by a baseball pitcher about his mother (Richler, 1997: 308).

It becomes increasingly clear as *Barney's Version* progresses that Barney is frequently misreporting certain details and events in his textual universe, not only from the evidence given in Michael's corrections but also through Barney's own honesty about his unreliability:

> Hold the phone. I'm stuck. I'm trying to remember the name of the author of *The Man in the Grey Flannel Shirt*. Or was it *The Man in the Brooks Brothers Shirt*? No, that was written by the fibber. Lillian what's-her-name? Come on. I know it. Like the mayonnaise. Lillian Kraft? No. *Hellman. Lillian Hellman.* The name of the author of *The Man in the Grey Flannel Suit* doesn't matter. It's of no importance. But now that it's started I won't sleep tonight. These increasingly frequent bouts of memory loss are driving me crazy.
>
> Last night, sailing off to sleep at last, I couldn't remember the name of that thing you use to strain spaghetti. Imagine that. I've used it thousands of times. I could visualize it. But I couldn't remember what the bloody thing was called.
>
> (Richler, 1997: 12)

This episode comes only a few pages into the novel, but has already been preceded by six corrective footnotes from Barney's son. Michael, surprisingly, does not interject during this passage. Instead, the reader witnesses Barney's confusion and memory loss first-hand and without additional commentary as he denarrates here in precisely the same manner Richardson (2006) identifies in Beckett's text. Barney first replaces one novel title with another, then suggests the possible name of an actress before replacing that too, and finally admitting to being unable to remember the name of an everyday household object. Similar instances populate the entire narrative and elsewhere in the text, among many examples, Barney fails to recount the names of the seven dwarves, refers to his children as 'Michael, Kate, and the other boy' (Richler, 1997: 87), forgets where he parked his car, refuses to give the number of his apartment and eventually forgets even Miriam's phone number.

While Barney's untrustworthiness is apparent from the very start of the novel to the point, in the final chapters, where he is diagnosed with Alzheimer's disease, the homodiegetic structure of the text ensures that the empathetic relationship between the reader and Barney is maintained. Despite Michael's frequent destabilising interjections and Barney's obvious confusion, he remains the source of the vast majority of world-building information from which readers must construct their understanding of the text.

Phelan (1996, 2007a, 2007b) provides a useful differentiation between different types of unreliable narration and their consequent effects. Following Rabinowitz (1977), Phelan first explains the difference between the 'narrative audience' and the 'authorial audience' as follows:

> the narrative audience is the one implicitly addressed by the narrator; it takes on the beliefs and values that the narrator ascribes to it, and in most cases it responds to the characters and events as if they were real. Joining the narrative audience is crucial for our experience of the mimetic component of the text and sometimes for the thematic and synthetic components as well. The authorial audience takes on the beliefs and knowledge that the author assumes it has, including the knowledge that it is reading a constructed text. Joining the authorial audience is crucial for our experience of all the invitations offered by the different components of the text.
>
> (Phelan, 1996: 93)

In more simple terms, the authorial audience is the 'author's ideal audience' (Phelan, 2007b: 210) assumed in his or her creation of the text; the narrative audience is 'the observer position within the narrative world which the flesh-and-blood reader assumes' (Phelan, 2007b: 210). Phelan goes on to argue that engaging with a text involves entering both of these audiences simultaneously, while also bringing our individual subjectivities to bear on that experience. He points out that the authorial audience role, in particular, may not be successfully filled by the flesh-and-blood reader, but that an effort to occupy this position is at least made by the reader in any engagement with a fiction (for a development of these ideas in relation to reader alienation in second-person fictions, see Whiteley, 2010: 141–6).

In *Barney's Version*, then, the form of fictionalised autobiography Richler chooses for his novel, and Michael's footnotes within this in particular, act to draw readers' attention to the text as a fictional construct from their position within the authorial audience. Richler plays other intertextual tricks in the novel which serve to heighten this effect, such as the inclusion of a character named Duddy Kravitz, which was also the name of the main character of one of Richler's most celebrated early novels, *The Apprenticeship of Duddy Kravitz* (originally published in 1958). Through such metafictional and intertextual techniques Richler makes his presence as implied author particularly strongly felt. However, Phelan (1996) points out that our understanding of a fiction is centrally located in the gap between our position as a reader within the authorial audience and our position within the narrative audience. Using the example of *Jane Eyre*, he explains:

> Most obviously – and importantly – in the authorial audience we know that Jane is a fictional character narrating fictional events, whereas in

the narrative audience we assume that a historical personage is recounting her autobiography. Furthermore, it is arguable that each audience
has a different view of the narrative's supernatural events, for example,
Jane's hearing Rochester calling her name, despite being miles away
from him. In the authorial audience, we recognize that this event is only
possible in fiction. In the narrative audience, we accept the event as Jane
does – wonderful and strange, but true.

(Phelan, 1996: 140)

Although readers of *Barney's Version* do not have to assess the truth of
fantastical events such as those presented by the narrator in *Jane Eyre*, they
are faced with a narrative predominantly made up of Barney's forthright
evaluations of other people, of politics, of history and culture, his defence of
his behaviour in each of his marriages and his ongoing protestations of his
innocence of Boogie's murder. The reader must adopt an ethical position on
each of these subjects, which involves recognising the differences between
the authorial audience and the narrative audience in the same way as Phelan
describes above.

Phelan develops this distinction further to provide a nuanced account of
unreliability in fiction and its consequent effects. He draws a line between
unreliability which is 'estranging' and increases the distance between the narrator and the authorial audience, and that which is 'bonding', reducing the
distance between the narrator and the authorial audience (Phelan, 2007a).
He explains,

> in estranging unreliability, the authorial audience recognizes that
> adopting the narrator's perspective would mean moving far away from
> the implied author's, and in that sense, the adoption would be a net loss
> for the author–audience relationship . . . In bonding unreliability, the
> discrepancies between the narrator's reports, interpretations, or evalu-
> ations and the inferences of the authorial audience have the paradoxical
> result of reducing the interpretive, affective, or ethical distance between
> the narrator and the authorial audience. In other words, although the
> authorial audience recognizes the narrator's unreliability, that unreli-
> ability includes some communication that the implied author – and
> thus the authorial audience – endorses.

(Phelan, 2007a: 225)

Phelan argues that narrators can show their unreliability in a number of
ways: by misreporting or underreporting facts and events; by misreading
or misinterpreting; or by misregarding or misevaluating. As I have already
noted above, it becomes clear in *Barney's Version* that Barney is misreporting a lot of the time and that the world-building details he imparts cannot
be relied upon as truthful and accurate. However, his unreliability on this

plane does not lead to an increased distance between the narrator and the authorial audience. Instead, Richler uses a number of stylistic techniques to encourage a close empathetic connection between reader and narrator in spite of his untrustworthiness, ensuring that Barney's unreliability is of the bonding type. Many of these techniques are amply illustrated in the extract from Barney's narrative above. Note, for example, the use of the present tense in the opening lines (e.g. 'Hold the phone. I'm stuck. I'm trying to remember . . .'), creating a highly proximal and involving feel to the passage: this gives the illusion that we are not simply reading Barney's autobiography but that, in parts such as these, we are witness to his writing of it as it happens. The present tense here also gives the illusion of face-to-face conversation, which is further emphasised by Barney's use of rhetorical questions (e.g. 'Or was it *The Man in the Brooks Brothers Shirt?*', 'Lillian what's-her-name?', 'Lillian Kraft?'). Barney also uses a number of imperatives ('Hold the phone', 'Come on', 'Imagine that') and although it is unclear whether these are addressed at the narrative audience or whether Barney is simply talking to himself, the use of the generalised second person later in the passage ('that thing *you* use to strain spaghetti') encourages an interpretation of these choices as inclusive of the implied reader.

Such inclusivity can be found throughout Barney's narrative and the reader is encouraged to occupy the role of narrative audience not only through his frequent direct addresses to that audience and use of rhetorical questions, but also as a result of his consistent openness about his lack of memory about the circumstances surrounding Boogie's disappearance:

> I have wakened more than once recently no longer certain of what really happened that day on the lake. Wondering if I had corrected the events of that day even as I have embellished other incidents in my life, enabling me to appear in a more favourable light. To come to the point, what if O'Hearne was right? What if, just as that bastard suspects, I did shoot Boogie through the heart? I need to think I am incapable of such brutality, but what if I were in fact a murderer?
>
> (Richler, 1997: 310)

Not only does Barney admit his unreliability in numerous examples such as this one, but his misreporting of facts tends to occur only around events of minor importance (such as the date of Pat Boone's first hit). Barney is open about the murder accusation made against him from the start, as well as about his own possible motives, namely the infidelity which took place between Boogie and the Second Mrs Panofsky shortly before Boogie's disappearance.

The character O'Hearne, mentioned in the extract above, is the detective who investigates the case and is convinced of Barney's guilt, dedicating much of his career to proving his guilt. Interestingly, however, it is in great part his behaviour towards Barney which further safeguards the bonding nature of Barney's unreliability. Consider the following lengthy tirade of abuse the detective levels at Barney having already knocked him to the floor the day after Boogie's disappearance:

> 'Panofsky, do yourself a favour', he said, 'We know you did it and sooner or later we'll find where you buried the poor bastard. Asparagus bed my ass. So save us time and effort. Show some *rachmones* for hard-working officers of the law. That means pity in your lingo, which I'm willing to bet I speak better than you. Come clean. Lead us to the body. We give points for that. I'll swear in court you were a real sweetheart, coopera- tive, filled with remorse. You hire yourself a smart Jew lawyer and you are charged with manslaughter, or some shit like that, because there was a struggle and the gun went off by accident. Or it was self-defence. Or, good heavens, you didn't even know it was loaded. Judge and jury will be understanding. Your wife. Your best friend. Holy mackerel it has to be temporary insanity. Worse case you get three years and you're home- free after eighteen months. Hey, you might even get off with a suspended sentence. A poor, deceived husband like you. But if you insist upon that *bobbe-myseh* you're spinning us, and I testify in court that you hit me, nobody will believe your story and maybe you get life, which is at least ten years, and while you're rotting in jail eating dog food, getting the shit beat out of you by bad guys who don't like Jews, your hot number in Toronto will be spreading her legs for somebody else, eh? I mean you finally get out you'll be a broken old man. So what do you say?'
>
> (Richler, 1997: 329–30)

Phelan identifies six different forms of bonding unreliability in total, among which is one he terms 'bonding through optimistic comparison' (Phelan, 2007a: 232). This form of bonding unreliability operates by juxtaposing a potentially estranging narrative (i.e. that of an unreliable man accused, but not proven guilty, of murder) against one which is far more estranging (i.e. that of a violent and anti-Semitic bully). Through this technique, Phelan argues, 'implied authors can guide audiences to recognize one example of unreliability as "better" than another' (Phelan, 2007a: 232).

Michael Panofsky's commentary on his father's memoirs act in a similar way to guide the reader to adopt the narrative audience position and remain bonded with Barney. Not only does O'Hearne's anti-Semitic and violent behaviour make it ethically preferable to opt for Barney's version of Boogie's disappearance over O'Hearne's, but the reader is similarly guided to prefer Barney's flawed but highly involving view of history over his son's pedantry. Furthermore, while Michael's footnotes serve to outline Barney's misreporting when they occur, when they fail to occur at key points in the narrative they serve an opposite function of silently confirming his story by their absence. Of course, Barney's description of his encounter with O'Hearne above includes no other witnesses, so one might argue that Michael would be unable to refute or verify its accuracy anyway. However, Michael does make interjections into accounts of events that are similarly unverifiable elsewhere in the book. For example, in one episode Barney recounts a phone call from a director with whom he is working, which he received at home alone after an evening watching the results of the second Canadian referendum on the future of Quebec. At this point Michael provides a footnote: '[1]I fear that by this juncture my father's memory was unreliable, even somewhat scrambled, and that pages of this manuscript were put together in a haphazard fashion. The referendum was on October 30, 1995, but what follows happened months later' (Richler, 1997: 378). In so doing, he highlights his own inability to judge the truthfulness of his father's report of a private conversation.

The 'Afterword', which forms the final chapter of *Barney's Version*, is narrated entirely by Michael and contains two significant moments of world-repair, the first of which underlines Michael's untrustworthiness as a narrator. Michael describes, again for the most part in the form of categorical assertion, the events which followed Barney's Alzheimer's diagnosis. He narrates in a predominantly neutrally shaded style the final discovery in 1996 of Boogie's remains on top of a mountain some miles from Barney's cottage and O'Hearne's joy at the discovery. He also describes the struggles of Barney's family to come to terms with the apparent fact that Barney was in fact a murderer and liar (only Kate holds on to her belief in his innocence), the rapid deterioration of Barney's health, his eventual death and the contents of his will. He then makes the following remarks on the publication of his father's manuscript:

> After protracted negotiations with the publisher, it was agreed that I could add footnotes, correcting the most egregious factual errors, a chore that obliged me to do a good deal of reading. I was also granted two other privileges. I was allowed to rewrite the incoherent, faltering chapters, dealing with Barney's discovery that he was suffering from Alzheimer's . . . I was also authorized to add this Afterword, subject to the approval of Saul and Kate. But they were not pleased. We quarrelled.
>
> (Richler, 1997: 404–5)

Thus the reader discovers that several of the preceding chapters were 'written' by a different character, although Michael does not give any details beyond the above about which ones, to what extent or in which places. The reader also learns that Barney's other two children disapprove of Michael's rewriting and his overall editing of the book, resulting in the further destabilisation of Michael's version of events.

The second instance of world-repair, which closes the final chapter, is even more momentous than the first, shifting both our understanding of Michael's unreliability and our understanding of his father's absurd predicament throughout the entire novel. Michael describes watching a water-bomber from the porch of his father's cottage as he waits for the estate agent who is to sell the house following Barney's death. The bomber scoops up 'who knows how many tons of water' (Richler, 1997: 406) and dumps it on the nearby mountain. Michael's realisation that this, in fact, must be how Boogie's remains ended up in the same location comes as he drives away to meet his family. He slams on his brakes, pulls over to the side of the road, contemplates calling Saul and offering Kate an apology too. He finally remarks, 'But, oh God, it's too late for Barney. He's beyond understanding now. Damn damn damn' (Richler, 1997: 407). This dramatic confirmation that Barney's protestations of his innocence were true all along finally seals the bond between Barney and the reader, in spite of all Barney's other misreportings throughout the novel. Elsewhere in the final chapter, the ethical position of the reader has already been forced by Michael's comment that his father's view on the fundamental absurdity of existence was 'Not a comforting philosophy, and one I certainly don't subscribe to' (Richler, 1997: 406). The structure of *Barney's Version*, and specifically the stylistic techniques through which a close empathetic link is maintained between Barney and the reader, ensures that readers are more likely to adopt the position of the authorial audience towards which they are guided throughout the text and recognise the absurd nature of the human condition in the manner Barney represents it.

Estranging minds

Chapter 2 of this book explored the important role played by readers' emotions in readings of the absurd made in non-academic contexts and, among other things, looked at some of the varying levels of empathy expressed in online reports towards Albert Camus's genre-defining absurd man, Meursault. So far in this chapter, texts which encourage a close alignment between narrator and reader have formed the focus of the investigation of the stylistic techniques by which readers' emotions might be manipulated. Both Mordecai Richler's *Barney's Version* and Saul Bellow's *The Victim* have been shown to foster strong empathetic bonds with their narrators, despite the reliability of these textual entities remaining in question throughout the novels. Such texts have been shown to fit neatly with Phelan's (2007a) notions of bonding unreliability. It has also been briefly noted, however, that Phelan's typology of unreliability and its effects includes an opposite concept of estranging unreliability: although unreliable narrators are one of the most common features of absurd prose fiction, not all of them operate by the same stylistic means nor do they have the same effects on the reader. It is clear, for example, from the readers' responses to *The Outsider* examined in Chapter 2 that the unreliability of narrating characters is equally likely to cause emotional responses in readers ranging from empathy to ambivalence to aversion.

To enable the further exploration of different types of absurd unreliability, Tom McCarthy's novel *Remainder*, first published in 2005, provides an interesting narrative which can be seen to exemplify Phelan's (2007a) category of estranging unreliability. The text is of additional interest since it bears points of both stylistic similarity to and difference from Camus's *The Outsider*. McCarthy's text is narrated in the first person by an enactor who remains unnamed throughout the novel. From the very beginning of the text the reader is informed about this narrator's recent recovery from a serious brain injury. The injury, we are told, was sustained as a result of an accident which 'involved something falling from the sky', although the narrator also says that this is 'all I can divulge' (McCarthy, 2007: 5). Although he does not give any further detail about the nature of his accident, the narrator does say that it left him in a coma and with temporary memory loss and goes on to describe the rehabilitation programme he underwent in hospital after he regained consciousness. More specifically, he explains in detail the process of 'rerouting' used by his physiotherapists to help him recover the use of his limbs and begin to perform basic tasks such as grasping, lifting, walking and so on. The process as he describes it is based on visualisation techniques through which the patient must imagine the many separate and minute physical movements involved in even the most simple of tasks. The following extract, for example, relates an exercise in which the narrator was told by his therapist to lift a carrot from his lap:

> I closed my fingers round the carrot. It felt – well, it *felt*: that was enough to start short-circuiting the whole operation. It had texture. It had mass. The whole week I'd been gearing up to lift it, I'd thought of my hand, my fingers, my rerouted brain as active agents, and the carrot as a no-thing – a hollow, a carved space for me to grasp and move. This carrot, though, was more active than me: the way it bumped and wrinkled, how it crawled with grit. It was cold. I grasped it and went into Phase Two, the hoist, but even as I did I felt the surge of active carrot input scrambling the communication between brain and arm, firing off false contractions, locking muscles at the very moment it was vital they relax and expand, twisting fulcral joints the wrong directions.
>
> (McCarthy, 2007: 20–1)

This account gives a clear indication of the extent of the damage which has been inflicted on the narrator's brain. The necessity for him to imagine in detail every physical action he performs before he can actually perform it becomes of central importance in the novel as a whole. As the narrator goes on to explain following the extract above, the brain damage he has suffered means there can be 'No Doing without Understanding' (McCarthy, 2007: 21) for him ever again; he must imagine and understand even the smallest movement before he can make his body carry it out.

From the outset of *Remainder*, then, the reader is aware that the central fictional mind being represented in the text is unusual. The narrator's peculiarity is further underlined when it becomes clear that his need to imagine and reimagine events and actions extends beyond what is necessary simply to be able to carry out everyday tasks. Consider the extract from the novel below, in which the narrator describes his relationship with a woman named Catherine. He and Catherine had become friends before the accident and corresponded afterwards. The narrator has just described how their letters began to acquire a sexual undertone and how he began to construct various sexual fantasies involving him and Catherine:

> In another version, we were somewhere in the country. I'd driven her out in my Fiesta, then drawn up and parked beside a field or wood. I'd have her standing in profile, because she looked better this way, with curly hair half-hiding her cheek. I'd move up close beside her, she'd turn to me, we'd kiss and then we'd end up making love in the Fiesta while treetops full of birds chirped and shrieked in ecstasy.
>
> I never got this second sequence quite down, though, due to the difficulty of manoeuvring us both into the car without bumping our heads or tripping on the belts that always hung out from the doors. And then I'd worry about where I'd parked it, and whether someone might speed round a bend and crash into it like the drive-off guy from Peckham.
>
> (McCarthy, 2007: 26)

The fantasy world the narrator constructs at the beginning of this passage is an epistemic modal-world, in Text World Theory terms (Gavins, 2007: 109–25), an unrealised and idealised possibility which exists at a remove from the textual reality. However, although the narrator does seem to recognise the distinction between reality and non-reality, as he discusses the imagined scenario as a fantasy, he seems unable or unwilling to apply the more flexible rules of fictionality to his mental representations. He becomes as frustrated with the minute practicalities of his imaginary worlds as he is with his physical and mental difficulties in his real world. His ability to fantasise freely seems to be somehow limited by the necessity for imagining and reimagining the smallest physical details in his everyday life. Particularly interesting in the above example is that the narrator does not seem fully to understand his ability to control his own mental life: he worries here about another car crashing into his own without seemingly recognising that this is a product of his imagination and subject to his own volition.

Despite such apparent quirks of personality, the full extent of the narrator's unreliability as a source of world-building information does not become apparent until a scene which occurs at the end of the third chapter of the novel. The reader has just been told that the narrator was awarded £8 million as compensation for his accident, news that the narrator has been digesting in a café near his solicitor's offices. He describes watching a group of homeless people opposite the café and feeling deeply envious of the unrestricted and unpredictable nature of their movements. He comments, 'I started thinking that *these* people, finally, were genuine. That they weren't interlopers' (McCarthy, 2007: 52), and decides to approach them. What follows is a detailed description of a resulting conversation with one of the homeless men. The narrator offers to take the man for lunch in a nearby Greek restaurant and describes giving one of the waitresses a £20 note to allow his companion in. He also describes the wine he goes on to order, the appearance of a second waitress (detailed right down to the way her shirt exposes her breasts as she leans over to pour the wine), the homeless man's way of eating his food and so on. The episode also includes a lengthy sequence of direct speech through which the narrator's attempts to explain his situation and his fascination with the homeless man and his friends are related. The narrator then also describes knocking over his wine in a failed attempt to take the homeless man's hand and the reappearance of a member of waiting staff to clear up the resulting mess:

> The waiter came back over. He was . . . She was young, with large dark glasses, an Italian woman. Large breasts. Small.
> 'What do you want to know?', my homeless person asked.
> 'I want to know . . .' I started, but the waiter leant across me as he took the tablecloth away. She took the table away too. There wasn't any table. The truth is, I've been making all this up – the stuff about the homeless person. He existed all right, sitting camouflaged against the shop fronts and the dustbins – but I didn't go across to him.
> (McCarthy, 2007: 56)

The first threat to the stability of the text-world the reader has constructed of the encounter with the homeless man comes with the narrator's correction of the gender of the waiter. He states that the waiter 'came back' when the only waiting staff introduced into the text-world so far have all been female. His subsequent switch to a female personal pronoun ('He was . . . She was') confirms our initial sense that something had gone awry either with our world-building or with the narrator's narrating, in this scene. This is not denarration in Richardson's (2006) sense, but a kind of *renarration* which requires a repair of the text-world. This repair, however, does not simply entail correcting a minor world-building detail. The narrator's misreporting of even this trivial element of our mental representation indicates his fundamental untrustworthiness and has more far-reaching conceptual consequences as a result. As the paragraph continues, the narrator goes on to

admit that the entire sequence, from the moment he approached the homeless man, has been a fabrication, another unrealised epistemic modal-world
masquerading as a more accessible text-world. At this point, we are faced
with a denarration entirely in keeping with Richardson's (2006) notion of
such techniques and readers must consequently not only repair their immediate mental representation of the restaurant scene but also re-evaluate the
dependability of the narrator's entire version of events up to this point in the
novel. Furthermore, as well as causing a re-evaluation of the preceding text,
the narrator's admission has a knock-on effect on the narrative which follows
the episode; readers now proceed under the new knowledge that their only
access point to the text-world is liable to misreport essential world-building
information and cannot be trusted. Most importantly, the manner in which
the narrator reveals his misreporting can be seen to shape the estranging
nature of his unreliability to a great extent. Up until this point in the narrative, the fact that the narrator is a recovering brain injury patient has
encouraged a close and sympathetic alignment between the narrator and the
authorial audience. At the end of the fabricated restaurant scene, however,
the narrator suddenly increases the distance between himself and the authorial audience through his casual and cold-hearted confession: 'I didn't go and
talk to him. I didn't want to, didn't have a thing to learn from him. Besides, I
hate dogs, always have' (McCarthy, 2007: 56).

The renarration and denarration episode above is all the more pertinent
to the narrative as a whole because of the connections it invites the reader
to draw between the narrator's need to imagine and reimagine events, his
apparent tendency to apply the inflexible logical and practical rules of reality
to such imaginary worlds, and his unreliability in the role as the main fiction-
making narrator of the text as a whole. It becomes ever clearer as the text
progresses that the boundaries between reality and fiction are subject to
manipulation and misrepresentation throughout *Remainder* and that the narrator himself is often testing this ontological divide. Not long after the restaurant scene examined above, he describes an incident at a party at the house
of a friend. During the party, the narrator visits the bathroom and describes
experiencing a sudden sense of déjà-vu while looking into the mirror:

> The sense of déjà-vu was very strong. I'd been in a space like this before,
> a place just like this, looking at the crack, a crack that had jutted and
> meandered in the same way as the one beside the mirror. There'd been
> that same crack, and a bathtub also, and a window directly above the
> taps just like there was in this room – only the window had been slightly
> bigger and the taps older, different. Out of the window there'd been
> roofs with cats on them. Red roof, black cats. It had been high up,
> much higher than I was now: the fifth or sixth or maybe even seventh
> floor of an old tenement-style building, a large block.
>
> (McCarthy, 2007: 60)

The narrator goes on to provide a wealth of world-building detail about the scene from the past that he remembers, from the accompanying smell and sound of liver cooking in a frying pan, to the faint sound of a piano playing in another apartment. He claims, 'I remembered all this clearly – crystal-clear, as clear as in a vision' (McCarthy, 2007: 61). However, there are a number of stylistic features of this section of the narrative which continue to blur the boundaries between the narrator's imagination and his perception or memory of events within his own reality. First, although he claims to have been in 'a place just like this' at another point in time, the narrator also admits that he cannot place where or when this memory originated and comments that it does not fit with any of the details of his life until now. There is also an interesting slippage in the way he refers to the crack in the bathroom wall in his friend's apartment: note how he begins by stating, that in the remembered world, he was 'looking at *the* crack', but that this definite reference immediately shifts to the indefinite '*a* crack'. He shifts again to a definite form, in '*that* same crack', before then going on to list numerous ways in which the remembered apartment was actually *different* from his friend's: a bathtub, a bigger window, different taps, higher up the building, roofs with cats on visible from the window. The manner in which he then posits three separate possibilities for the height of the remembered apartment, 'the fifth or sixth or maybe even seventh floor', is reminiscent of his rapid adjustment of minor world-building details in the restaurant scene he made up earlier in the narrative. Each of these stylistic elements not only makes it difficult for the reader to conceptualise the remembered apartment and to understand how closely related it is to the narrator's real world, but also strongly suggests that he may be making up this memory too. Note, also, that even the comparison of the clarity of the memory with 'a vision' is in itself a comparison with another version of unreality.

The narrator, however, goes on to claim that his clearest memory of the past apartment was that all his movements around the space he describes in such detail were 'fluent and unforced' (McCarthy, 2007: 62). The moment he realised this while standing in his friend's apartment, he says, he decided what to do with the £8 million compensation he received after his accident: 'I wanted to recreate that space and enter it so I could feel real again. I wanted to; I had to; I would' (McCarthy, 2007: 62). The middle section of *Remainder* is then dedicated to the narrator's account of how he went about the reconstruction of what may or may not be an authentic memory in order to experience some degree of authenticity in his real life. He hires a 'facilitator', Naz, who acquires a suitable building and oversees the highly complex and expensive process of recreating the remembered apartment as precisely as the narrator describes it. Teams of architects, builders, actors and make-up artists are employed to reconstruct the scene, which includes, among other details, an encounter on the stairs between the narrator and an old woman putting out her rubbish, the distant piano music from another apartment, the smell and sound of cooking liver, and the cats on the rooftops outside. Hours and hours of rehearsals are undertaken to ensure that every detail of the re-enactment fits his specifications precisely. It is during these demanding rehearsals that the narrator's callousness and self-obsession once again reveal themselves and seal the estranging quality of the narration. The narrator insists that his performers are on hand twenty-four hours a day, so that he can switch the building to 'on' mode and enter the re-enactment seamlessly whenever he requires it; the performers must practise their movements over and over again, first in rehearsals and then in the continuous 'loop' of re-enactment; and the narrator also divulges that several dozen cats bought to walk along the rooftops outside the apartment's bathroom window fell to their deaths during the rehearsals in the pursuit of the perfection of the scene.

During the first re-enactment of his memory of the apartment, the narrator says that he experienced several moments of 'weightlessness' and a sensation of 'zinging and intensity' (McCarthy, 2007: 139) at the points at which the recreated scene most closely fitted with his memory. However, on the whole he remains unsatisfied with the project and goes on with further relentless repetitions of the re-enacted memory, attempting to perfect the illusion it has cost him hundreds of thousands of pounds to create. He becomes particularly concerned with perfecting the smells of the apartment and specifically an elusive cooking smell which he describes as being similar to cordite. The sense of authentic existence he seeks, however, continues to evade him and eventually he leaves the set in frustration. He takes a drive in his old Ford Fiesta and visits a repair garage, where a group of mechanics try to mend a blocked windscreen washer in the car but end up soaking his trousers with screenwash. This incident becomes the narrator's new obsession and he instructs Naz to create another re-enactment, once again spending thousands of pounds in an attempt to reproduce the scene precisely. As the novel progresses, the narrator's fixations on certain scenes and experiences become more and more bizarre and the re-enactments he orders of them become increasingly dangerous. He experiments with running the re-enactments at the apartment building and the repair garage at half speed, which seems to increase the physical sensation of authenticity he experiences. He then decides to recreate a local shooting, the aftermath of which he witnesses one day after leaving the repair garage re-enactment, and takes the role of one of the fatalities himself. Lying on the floor at the end of the slow-motion re-enactment of this scene, he suffers some form of relapse and slips into unconsciousness. For several days afterwards he exists in what he describes as 'trances', short periods of semi-consciousness which become gradually less frequent but nevertheless underscore the fragility of the narrator's physical and mental state. By now, he lives full-time in the recreated apartment building and is planning a further re-enactment of another local violent crime with Naz when it occurs to him that the only obstacle to a true sensation of authenticity is the hired teams carrying out the reproductions themselves. He describes Naz at this point in the narrative as follows: 'He looked unhealthy, sick through lack of sleep. His cheeks were pale and jaundiced. Like me, he had become an addict' (McCarthy, 2007: 243). When he suggests to Naz that they create an armed bank robbery, this time rehearsing with actors but substituting them for real people at the point of 're-enactment', Naz enthusiastically agrees.

The boundaries between reality and fiction, then, become completely imperceptible for the narrator by the end of *Remainder*, as he and Naz arrange another precisely rehearsed scene in which all the performers except those playing the narrator's accomplices in the armed robbery are switched with real people in a real bank at the last moment. The five men playing the parts of 'Robber Redactors' are unaware of the switch and their shock and panic when the robbery goes wrong and people start being killed is very real indeed. The narrator's reaction to the deaths, however, is startlingly different from those of the Redactors:

> I stood still on the floor behind him. The only thing that moved was a deep red flow coming from Four's chest. It emerged from his chest and advanced onto the carpet.
> 'Beautiful', I whispered.
>
> (McCarthy, 2007: 269)

Not only are the authorial audience at this moment made finally and disturbingly aware of the narrator's complete lack of empathy, but their estrangement from him is further fostered by ongoing suggestions within the narrative that his entire account may be a fabrication. In a conversation just before the bank robbery, for example, Naz casually asks the narrator when he first came into contact with cordite, the smell he has been trying so painstakingly to recreate in the apartment building. He receives the reply, '"Cordite? . . . I don't think I've ever been near cordite"' (McCarthy, 2007: 258). Furthermore, the narrator's account of the robbery itself begins, 'The day came, finally. Then again, perhaps it didn't' (McCarthy, 2007: 259). At this point, the narrator's use of the epistemic modal 'perhaps' once again relegates the world which has been presented to the reader as a faithful account of the narrator's reality to a mere possibility, an epistemic modal-world the reliability of which is completely unverifiable by the authorial audience.

Indeed, the end of the novel confirms that the whole of *Remainder* has been what Alber (2009: 79; see also Alber et al., 2012) has termed an 'unnatural' storyworld. The novel concludes with Naz and the narrator on board a private jet, fleeing the scene of the fatal robbery. The narrator holds the pilot at gunpoint and tells him to '"Just keep on. The same pattern. It will all be fine"' (McCarthy, 2007: 284), leaving the reader with two possible conclusions:

> Eventually the sun would set forever – burn out, *pop*, extinguish – and the universe would run down like a Fisher Price toy whose spring has

unwound to the very end. Then there'd be no more music, no more loops. Or maybe, before that, we'd just run out of fuel. For now, though, the clouds tilted and the weightlessness set in once more as we banked, turning, heading back, again.

(McCarthy, 2007: 284)

Whichever of the end-points the narrator imagines above is reached – whether the flight continues into eternity or the plane crashes when it runs out of fuel – the narrator himself must as a consequence have been dead from the beginning of *Remainder*. All of the events within the novel have happened at a point in time which precedes the narrating time, a situation which can be seen to fit Alber's description of an unnatural narrative as one which 'denotes physically impossible scenarios and events, that is, impossible by the known laws governing the physical world' (Alber, 2009: 80). Alber further notes that all such unnatural narratives have an estranging effect on their readers, and goes on to explain,

> Most of my examples are impossible scenarios at the level of story and achieve their estranging effect by deliberately impeding the constitution of storyworlds. More specifically, they radically deconstruct the anthropomorphic narrator, the traditional human character, or real-world notions of time and space.

(Alber, 2009: 80)

The narrator of *Remainder*, then, not only impedes the construction of a coherent text-world through the revelation of his own death at the very end of the novel, but also through the multitude of both minor and major world-repairs he requires his readers to make throughout the text. Alber goes on to argue, however, that unnatural narratives are not necessarily unreadable narratives and that readers may adopt any of a number of possible strategies for 'naturalizing' (Alber, 2009: 81) the challenges such texts pose. Alber insists that however odd the textual structure of a narrative may be, it is nevertheless part of a purposeful communicative act which readers will naturally attempt to make sense of, a position which is supported in Text World Theory (see Gavins, 2007: 18–34). Alber proposes that one possible reading strategy is for readers to explain the oddities of a particular text or narrator as 'an internal state' (Alber, 2009: 84). According to this principle, then, the unreliability of the narrator of *Remainder*, his disturbing behaviour and his perplexing manipulations of reality and fiction, can easily be naturalised and explained as the product of his brain injury. He shows himself to be so untrustworthy in the novel, in fact, that many readers may assume that the scenario on the plane is just as likely to be an imagined possibility as any of the other episodes recounted elsewhere in the novel. To return to Palmer's (2004) terms, however unusual and uncooperative the narrator may be, his troublesome narrating behaviour becomes that through which we construct an understanding of his fictional mind.

The literary absurd, so far

The three case studies of absurd novels which have made up this chapter have been presented as a means of exploring in greater analytical depth some of the stylistic techniques through which authors represent the minds of absurd characters. In terms of Steen's (2011) framework for the analysis of genre, discussed in Chapter 2, the focus here has been on deepening understanding of the literary absurd at the levels of text and code in particular. In the first of this chapter's case studies, Saul Bellow's novel *The Victim* was shown to fit Simpson's (1993) description of a Category B narrative with predominantly negative modal shading. Bellow's text has an external narrator but the fiction is reflected through the perspective of the main character, Asa Leventhal, and also exhibits a high density of epistemic modality, typical of negatively shaded heterodiegetic narration. Alongside the multitude of modal-worlds created by this modal shading, however, sit equally numerous hypothetical modal-worlds, through which Leventhal's speculations about other characters' motives and opinions are represented. Indeed, Leventhal has been shown to be fixated on the evaluations made of his actions by a group of his peers which he perceives as functioning as an intermental unit, in Palmer's terms (see, for example, Palmer, 2005, 2010, 2011). This intermental unit has an important influence on Leventhal's decision making as he struggles to reconcile his need for social acceptance by the group with his own contrasting moral principles. Leventhal's concern with the opinions of others has been shown to reach obsessive levels in the novel as he becomes ever more isolated and persecuted by Allbee; the suffocating nature of his paranoia is further emphasised through metaphorical and material representations of the stifling heat of the New York summer in which the novel is set.

As a novel with a homodiegetic narrator, Mordecai Richler's *Barney's Version* stands in stylistic contrast with Bellow's text to some extent. However, the novels share a pattern of predominant epistemic modality which, in the case of Richler's text, is atypical in an otherwise cooperative Category A narration. Furthermore, despite the ease with which the internal perspective of the novel allows the reader access to the narrator's thoughts and feelings, Barney reveals himself to be an unreliable source of world-building information through his frequent misreporting of events. This misreporting is made evident through the footnotes of the novel's fictional editor, Barney's eldest son Michael, whose regular interjections in the narrative expose the inaccuracy of Barney's version of events and destabilise many of the text-worlds the reader builds on the basis of this information. However, Michael's pernickety behaviour acts to subvert his own reliability as a narrator, ultimately strengthening the bond between Barney and the reader instead of weakening it. Richler's novel has been shown to fit neatly with Phelan's (2007a) notions of bonding unreliability, according to which certain novels can be seen to encourage a close connection between reader and narrator in spite of considerable evidence of untrustworthy behaviour on the latter's part. In *Barney's Version*, Barney's narrative is inclusive and empathetic, and alignment with his ethical position is framed in the novel to be greatly preferable to adopting the views either of his son or of any of the other even more objectionable characters in the text. This ethical alignment is fostered in spite of the fact that the reader is presented with a picture of a Barney as a forgetful, cantankerous, possible murderer from the start of the novel.

Because of its very recent publication, little scholarly criticism exists on Tom McCarthy's *Remainder* to add support to a reading of the novel as absurd in nature. However, the text bears so many points of stylistic and thematic resemblance to other novels examined in this book that I have no hesitation in daring potentially to be the first critic to categorise it as an absurdist work. Like Richler's *Barney's Version*, McCarthy's text is narrated in the first person by a participating character who is deeply unreliable. The narrator of *Remainder* has a severely damaged brain and an eccentric view of the world and its ontology: he is a fantasist unable to grasp the basic laws of the fantasies he creates. He lacks empathy and is obsessive in the extreme, determined to secure some sense of authenticity in his radically distorted existence no matter what the cost to others. Most importantly, this narrator is another serial misreporter, but this time his unreliability is highly estranging, in Phelan's (2007a) terms. Not only does his callous disregard for other human beings make it difficult for readers to form an empathetic bond with him but the narrator's misrepresentation of key world-building information demands radical world-repair on numerous occasions throughout the text. Indeed, the narrator's volatile behaviour causes such severe destabilisation of the narrative of *Remainder* that, as Alber (2009) argues, this behaviour is likely to be naturalised by the reader as an internal state, the result of his brain injury.

The most obvious unifying feature running through each of these case studies, then, is the unreliability of the narrators of the fictions, an unreliability which has been shown to take different stylistic forms and to have different effects. Unreliable narrators are by no means confined to absurd prose fiction, of course, but the minds represented in absurd texts can be seen to share unreliability as a common attribute. Of equal importance in the understanding of absurd characterisation is a recognition of the overwhelming and pervasive sense of isolation and uncertainty that each of the narrators examined in this chapter also share. Rather than narratorial unreliability being a defining characteristic of absurdist texts in itself, it can be seen as just one, albeit centrally important, stylistic means through which an absurd sensitivity can be expressed in literature. The next chapter of this book explores other narrative techniques through which the same sensitivity can also be articulated and returns to a consideration of readers' reactions to such devices.

4 Absurd Fictions

This chapter continues the stylistic analysis of absurd prose fiction begun in Chapter 2 and developed with particular reference to characterisation in Chapter 3. Here, the discussion is broadened to consider a further selection of absurdist novels and I examine a more extensive spectrum of narrative techniques through which the absurd may be expressed in literary fiction. The chapter revisits notions of genre and categorisation, and takes another look at the phenomenon of world-repair in absurd texts. It also encompasses a variety of other stylistic features which might be considered characteristic of experimental literary absurdism, including the distortion of spatio-temporal deixis, the metafictional manipulation of ontological boundaries, genre-mixing and the use of multimodality. The aim of the discussion is to add further stylistic detail to Weinberg's (1970: 11) notion of an 'absurd surface' in literary prose fiction and to develop the argument put forward in Chapter 2 of this book that all absurd texts can be seen to exist along a cline of stylistic experimentalism. The focus of the chapter is on the narrative techniques and features which characterise that absurd experimentalism and also on readers' reactions to the challenges with which non-realist texts confront them. The chapter begins with another case study of absurdist narrative – an analysis of Rudolph Wurlitzer's novel *Nog* – before moving on to consider a range of other absurd fictions and readers' responses to them.

Absurd world-building revisited

At various points throughout the discussion so far, texts have been described in terms of their relative immersive qualities. In Chapter 2, in particular, we saw how Albert Camus constructs a realistic and potentially immersive text-world for readers of his novel *The Outsider* and how this realism was argued by Esslin (1980: 24) to be one of the main reasons why Camus is so frequently categorised as an existentialist writer in the same vein as Jean-Paul Sartre. In texts situated farther along the cline of experimentalism, at a greater stylistic distance from the boundaries with rationalistic existentialism, the spatial and temporal parameters of text-worlds are often more difficult for readers to conceptualise. In order to explore such contrasting methods of world-building, consider the following opening lines:

> Yesterday afternoon, a girl walked by the window and stopped for sea shells. I was wrenched out of two months of calm. Nothing more than that, certainly, nothing ecstatic or even interesting, but very silent and even, as those periods have become for me. I had been breathing in and out, out and in, calmly, grateful for once to do just that, staring at the waves plopping in, successful at thinking almost nothing, handling easily the three memories I have manufactured, when that girl stooped for sea shells.
>
> (Wurlitzer, 2009: 11)

These lines begin Rudolph Wurlitzer's novel *Nog*, originally published in 1968. In Gavins (2012), I noted that *Nog* retains a fixed homodiegetic narration throughout and that the reader's only access to the world of the fiction is through the first-person perspective described in the extract above. This perspective is stylistically unremarkable to begin with: it describes a realistic beach scene in, for the most part, conventional simple past-tense narrative. Sufficient deictic information is provided for readers to construct a text-world in which the event time (the point at which the girl walks past the window) is situated one day before the narrating time (the narrator's temporal location as he recounts the incident as happening 'yesterday afternoon'). This event time text-world contains the enactor of the girl and the enactor of the narrator as he watches her collect shells from a beach. There is also a brief world-switch, through which the narrator also tells us what he had been doing prior to the girl's arrival in past-perfect tense ('I had been breathing in and out, out and in, calmly'), before the narration switches back to the scene including the girl ('when that girl stooped for sea shells'). *Nog*, then, is initially unchallenging in its style, save, perhaps, for the puzzling mention in the extract above of three memories which have been 'manufactured'. As the novel progresses, however, it becomes more and more clear that the narrator of *Nog*, like so many other absurd narrators and focalisers, may not be entirely reliable.

The narrator does not approach the girl on the beach, but instead relates his desire to move on from the unnamed Californian town in which he lives, before creating another world-switch in which he describes his memories of a character called Nog, whom he once met in a bar in Oregon. Nog is described as 'one of those semi-religious lunatics you see wandering around the Sierras on bread and tea' (Wurlitzer, 2009: 12) and as being of Finnish extraction. The narrator says Nog sold him a giant rubber octopus, housed in a water-filled bathysphere, balanced on the back of a truck. Over the course of the first chapter, it becomes apparent that the narrator has been travelling around the countryside for a year, showing the octopus at fairs. Along with the bizarre image of the octopus itself, there are a number of other elements of the narrative which suggest that the narrator's version of events may not be trustworthy. For example, in the middle of an otherwise straightforward account of a conversation between Nog and the narrator about the octopus, the narrator tells us that Nog has 'a yellow light that had lately been streaming out of his chest from a spot the size of a half dollar' (Wurlitzer, 2009: 12). Later on in the same scene, the narrator interrupts his detailed description of the octopus itself, saying 'Nog is not quite clear enough. I have to invent more. It always comes down to that. I never get a chance to rest' (Wurlitzer, 2009: 13–14). This self-reflective interjection is reminiscent of the denarrations and renarrations presented by the narrator of Tom McCarthy's novel *Remainder* and analysed in Chapter 3. In a similar fashion here, the clear indication given by *Nog*'s narrator that he is inventing aspects of the story destabilises the text-world and has a knock-on effect on the reader's perception of the rest of his narrative.

The fixed focalisation of *Nog*, however, means that the reader must persevere with the narrator's version of events in order to form an understanding of the narrative world. Over the course of the rest of the opening chapter, the narrator's behaviour becomes increasingly erratic as he goes on to describe a second encounter with the girl on the beach, who takes him to a party where there is a storm and where, yet more bizarrely, he meets an old colonel attempting to build a sea wall from driftwood to keep back the encroaching tide. *Nog*'s narrator is the epitome of Weinberg's 'hopelessly ineffectual victim-hero' (1970: 10) throughout these pages, as he stumbles without apparent motivation from one disorienting episode to another: he aids the colonel's Sisyphean quest for a while; he stumbles back to the party and misunderstands the hospitality of the female host, Sarah, and undresses completely in front of her; he fills a bath with a selection of drugs from a medicine cabinet and mixes them with water, which he says is 'a very reviving thing to do' (Wurlitzer, 2009: 21); he gets into Sarah's bed and goes to sleep; he is woken by Sarah's boyfriend, with whom he plays table tennis for a while before flinging a basket of table-tennis balls at him and tipping over the table, all without explanation. The first chapter of *Nog* closes with the following paragraph:

> What I should have done was get rid of the octopus, what I have been trying to do is get rid of the octopus, what I am beginning just now to remember is that I did get rid of the octopus. I see it now for the first time. I either took it back to the party and put it in the bathtub or danced with it on the beach. No, I did bring it back to the beach but not to dance with. I took off my terrycloth bathrobe and ran down to the truck and got the octopus out of the bathysphere, its tentacles waving all over me. Struggling in the rain and wind, I dragged it back and pulled it up on the sea wall. Such a spectacle gave the colonel enough of

a jolt to finish the sea wall. Then together we threw it in the sea, and I
went home and went to bed. It was something like that, I can remember
something like that, a storm, a party and then the octopus. There was
an octopus, although I know deep down that the octopus is still up on
blocks. I know too that nothing happened and I haven't traveled with
the octopus. But I shall move on anyway, perhaps to New York. I
remember great things about New York.

(Wurlitzer, 2009: 25)

The key stylistic feature through which the narrator's bewilderment and
general unreliability are expressed here is, once again, the use of modality.
The stability of key deictic elements (e.g. the octopus) and story events (e.g.
building the sea wall) is undermined through the use of modalisation in precisely the same way we have seen important world-building details subverted
in Camus, Barthelme, Beckett, Richler, Bellow and McCarthy in the preceding chapters of this book. Once again, it is possible to identify an abundance
of epistemic modality in Wurlitzer's text. These destabilise the unmodalised
propositions that have preceded the paragraph above as the narrator reveals
his uncertainty through the repetition of modal verbs such as 'remember' in
the closing lines. Where earlier in the chapter unmodalised forms predomi-
nated, such as '*I bought* the octopus, and for a year *I traveled* through the
country with it' (Wurlitzer, 2009: 13), from here onwards, and with increasing regularity through the rest of the novel, contradictory degrees of belief
are expressed: 'what I am beginning just now *to remember* is that I did get rid
of the octopus' (Wurlitzer, 2009: 25). The narrator of *Nog* makes recurrent
use of perception modality in particular, and also emphasises the instability
of his narrative through the creation of multiple hypothetical alternatives to
the events he describes, such as 'I either took it back to the party and put it in
the bathtub or danced with it on the beach' in the extract above. Although he
often eventually assigns reality to one of the alternatives he constructs – for
example, 'No, I did bring it back to the beach but not to dance with' – the
faltering modality in the rest of the text once again undermines the dependability of this epistemic commitment.

   These by now familiar patterns of disruptive modalisation, many of
which are typical of Simpson's (1993) category of negatively shaded narration, are by no means the only stylistic feature through which the absurdity
of *Nog* is communicated. As the novel continues, the style of the text as a
whole becomes increasingly experimental. The narrator hitch-hikes to San
Francisco and meets a woman named Meridith in a supermarket. He follows
her to a nearby house, which she appears to share with several other people,
including her husband, Lockett. The narrator has sex with both Meridith and
Lockett and then the three of them drive to a hospital, where they pretend to
be visiting a patient in order to steal a black medical bag full of drugs. Each
of these episodes is narrated in a highly experimental form through which the

world-building elements of the text-world, and the enactors in particular, are frequently muddled or not fully delineated. The extract below is taken from the narrator's description of the time he spends in Meridith's house:

> Lockett needs my mattress more than I need his cabinet. He has to have an oasis, a place to rest and hear what's happening. I encourage him. I roll my sock into a ball and let it roll out. Over the past two days the mattress has become crowded. Someone just sat down and put his legs against the wall. Although my eyes have gotten used to the dark, I try not to notice anyone too closely. Another man sat down and put his legs against the wall. This has begun to happen lately.
>
> (Wurlitzer, 2009: 44)

It is extremely difficult here to build a coherent mental representation of the scene in Meridith's bedroom. It is not clear how many people are on the mattress or who they are and the present tense of the passage adds to the overall disorienting effect. Lockett is nominated as an enactor present in the text-world along with the narrator, but the additional bodies in the room are described only in indefinite terms such as 'someone' and 'Another man'. The narrator's physical position in the scene is also not made fully clear and, once again, no explanation is offered by the narrator for his own actions (such as rolling his sock into a ball and then rolling it out again) or for the actions of others around him.

This confusing spatial and temporal deixis becomes typical of the narrative style of *Nog*. Fleeing through the desert from the hospital theft, the narrator, Meridith and Lockett meet another character, called Bench, who approaches their camp in the middle of the night. When he asks the narrator his name, we are told that he scratches it into the dirt with his knife and that Bench says "'Nog. Well, everyone has a right to their own name'" (Wurlitzer, 2009: 86). It appears here, then, that Nog and the narrator are actually the same person, or at least that the narrator is using Nog's name, a revelation which becomes even more bewildering following an incident which occurs soon afterwards, in a nearby town. The narrator describes being in some sort of bar in the town, although it is unclear how he got there, and the description of the bar is highly reminiscent of a saloon from an old Western film, with dusty shelves holding shot glasses and candles, an old washtub, and a giant cactus extending through a hole in the ceiling. Lockett and Meridith are present, although again their relative physical positions within the space are not fully defined, when the following takes place:

> She strokes my ankle. Two figures rise from a mattress and walk slowly toward the door. Nog has disappeared. I said that before. But I need a memory. I need two memories. With two working for me, I might be able to make a move, even if it's back, toward the ledge. I can always

fake going back. But I've forgotten what is needed, what it will take to push me forward.

The rifle fired.

Lockett's arms spread straight out from the gown. They stiffen and reach toward the ceiling before clutching at the hole in his stomach.

                                                                                    (Wurlitzer, 2009: 101)

Once again, there are several odd switches of tense in this passage: the description begins in the present tense ('She strokes my ankle'), but shifts to the simple past ('The rifle fired') following the narrator's brief departure into an imagined hypothetical world ('I might be able to make a move'), before Lockett's reaction is then narrated in the present tense again ('Lockett's arms spread straight out . . . They stiffen and reach'). Although the shooting itself is presented in passive form with the agent responsible for the action deleted, it would seem reasonable in context to assume that the narrator is the enactor doing the shooting. However, such assumptions are called into question soon afterwards in a conversation between Meridith and the narrator:

> 'Nog is shot,' she said.
> 'Lockett was shot.'
> My voice won't come out. I haven't spoken in so long. I tried to push words out, but nothing happened.
> 'Don't cry,' Meridith said. 'It was Lockett. He was calling himself Nog for a while. I get confused. It was Lockett.'
> Another shot rang out. Glass shattered.
> 'We have to get shut of here,' Meridith said matter-of-factly. She is crying.
> 'It was Bench,' I said.
> 'You said Lockett.'
> 'Bench did in Lockett.'

                                                                                    (Wurlitzer, 2009: 102)

This baffling exchange requires some significant world-repair, although this is not easily accomplished: if the reader has already assumed that the narrator is Nog and Meridith reveals that Nog is Lockett, does this mean that the narrator is also Lockett and that he has been shot? If we also infer that the narrator shot Lockett, did he shoot himself or did Bench shoot him? If we infer that the narrator was responsible for the shooting and here he says that Bench did it, does this also mean that Bench and the narrator are the same person? At least one of these conflicting possibilities is confirmed when, from this point on in the novel, Meridith refers to the narrator consistently as Lockett.

Other world-building elements in *Nog* also lose their integrity as the narrative progresses, not least the black medical bag, which the narrator guards fiercely but also refers to as the octopus several times. The interchangeability of the black bag with the octopus, as well as of the narrator with Lockett, is confirmed in the extract below, from the final paragraph of the novel. Here, the narrator and Meridith are on board a ship which is heading for an unnamed canal on the Hudson River and which seems to be sinking:

> What I should have done was get rid of the black bag, what I am begin- ning to remember is that I did get rid of the black bag. I put it under the bunk. I remember something like that. There was a black bag, although I know too that nothing happened and I haven't traveled around with a black bag. I touched the knob again. There was a quickness, cer- tainly, as if I were about to be sure of something. But it's out of my depth to know what has happened, to touch a doorknob and make a report. I'm not up to that. There have been events, of a sort, and they have occurred quickly, one after the other. The Canal wasn't invented. I'm sure of that. And the rain was cool enough. That was several days ago. And there is Lockett now. I'm lighter. I haven't eaten. This day is lighter than the last. I barked. That's not true. I have to watch that.
>
> (Wurlitzer, 2009: 141)

This passage replicates almost directly the earlier description of the octopus and the building of the sea wall with the colonel, analysed above. The only substantial changes are that the octopus has become the bag and the narra- tor has become Lockett. The passage contains the same fluctuating modality as the earlier sequence, as well as moments of denarration (e.g. 'I know too that nothing happened and I haven't traveled around with a black bag' and 'That's not true'), and the narrator also openly admits here to not being able to make a reliable report on even the most basic of actions.

Nog clearly occupies a position at the extreme end of the cline of absurd experimentalism, since it contains a range of stylistic features which on occasion make it difficult for readers to construct a coherent mental rep- resentation of the narrative at all. Indeed, the text can be seen to exist as a concentration of all the experimental stylistic techniques examined so far in this book into one text: the narrator's bewilderment is communicated through the use of fluctuating epistemic modality and the construction of multiple hypothetical worlds; his unreliability is further emphasised through episodes of denarration and renarration and through the consequent need for world-repair; frequent shifts in tense and the confusion of key spatial world-building elements result in a disorienting effect throughout the novel and impair the construction of a mental representation entirely in some places. Crucially, however, what prevents *Nog* from losing all coherence is the absurd quest of its central character, which underpins the narrative and forms a consistent thread running throughout the novel. The construction of text-worlds which are, at times, incomprehensible and perplexing through an entirely unreliable perspective is not done for the sake of mere ornamentation in this text. Rather, the experimental texture of Wurlitzer's novel facilitates an exploration of identity and perception which the reader experiences first-hand through the narrator's point of view as he stumbles, alienated and confused, from one absurd situation to another.

Absurd landscapes and emotional resonance

The distortion of spatial and temporal deixis in the literary absurd is certainly not confined to *Nog*, but can be seen to be a recurrent feature of many other absurd novels. Whiteley (2010), for example, presents an analysis of the text-worlds of Kazuo Ishiguro's (1995) novel *The Unconsoled*, a text which is frequently identified as absurd or compared with other absurdist novels by readers in both academic and non-academic contexts (see, for example, Lemon, 2011; Shaffer, 2008; Villar Flor, 2000; and, for an account of non-academic responses, Whiteley, 2010: 181–226). Whiteley (2010: 196–204) analyses a number of episodes within the text in which the spatial and temporal parameters of the text-world of the novel present a challenge to readers' schemas of the basic laws of physics. In one such instance, the main character of the novel, Ryder, has a conversation with a hotel porter in an elevator on the way up to his room which lasts for four pages, with the elevator ride itself occupying a further two and a half pages. Towards the end of the same episode, in a further challenge to readers' understanding of the normal physical dimensions of such spaces, the characters suddenly realise that another character has been in the elevator with them throughout the journey but has somehow remained unnoticed until this point. Alongside the schema disruption such spatial and temporal distortions lead to, Whiteley also identifies the same negative modal shading at work in *The Unconsoled* as that examined in other absurd texts in this book, as well as some highly unusual slippages between different focalisers and reflectors at various points in the fiction. In spite of its challenging narrative style, however, Whiteley (2010: 185, 215–16) also points out that readers engaging with the text in non-academic contexts frequently report having highly emotional and 'resonant' experiences of *The Unconsoled*, to use Stockwell's (2009: 17–55) term. Such readers often describe Ishiguro's text as bewildering or disorienting, but also as dream-like and haunting, and as having affected them emotionally for a considerable period after their initial reading. These reports match Stockwell's definition of literary resonance as 'an atmosphere in the mind that seems to persist long after the pages have been put down' (Stockwell, 2009: 17).

Very similar experiences are reported by readers participating in several online reading communities in relation to Flann O'Brien's novel *The Third Policeman*, originally published in 1967. O'Brien's text, as we saw in Chapter 2, features within the top twenty books most frequently tagged as 'absurd' on LibraryThing and has been discussed in terms of its absurdity by a range of literary critics (see, for example, Booker, 1991; Clissmann and Clune, 1975; Cornwell, 2006: 251–78; Doherty, 1989; Hopper, 1995; Kearney, 2006: 200–1; O'Connell, 2009; Snipe, 1997; Tigges, 1988: 205–16). The novel is narrated in the first person by an unnamed narrator, who dedicates the first few pages of the novel to an explanation of his family background. These pages are relatively unremarkable in terms of their style, as the narrator's current circumstances and previous history are related in a realistic and unproblematic manner. The reader is told that the narrator's father was a farmer and his mother owned the public house where they lived during his early childhood. During his boarding school education, the narrator became a scholar of the work of de Selby, a scientist and philosopher, and devoted himself to the study of his work on his return to the family farm following the death of his parents. The narrator also mentions that he has been fitted with a wooden leg following a vaguely described incident in 'one of the places I was broadening my mind' (O'Brien, 1993: 10). He leaves a man named John Divney to run the farm and pub on his behalf while he writes what he considers to be the definitive work on the life and accomplishments of de Selby.

Interestingly, in a similar style to Mordecai Richler's *Barney's Version*, the narrative of *The Third Policeman* contains numerous footnotes which give further details about de Selby's work wherever the narrator deems them to be pertinent to the unfolding story. Unlike in Richler's text, however, these footnotes appear to have been written by the same narrator responsible for the main body of the text. Where Michael's footnotes in *Barney's Version* seek to question and undermine his father's account of events, the narrator's footnotes in *The Third Policeman* serve to elucidate certain elements of his own story. However, this is not to say that the footnotes on de Selby increase the perceived reliability of the narrator. Consider the following example:

The long and unprecedented conversation I had with Policeman MacCruiskeen after I went in to him on my mission with the cigarette brought to my mind afterwards several of the more delicate speculations of de Selby, notably his investigation of the nature of time and eternity by a system of mirrors.[1]

[1] Hatchjaw remarks (unconfirmed, however, by Bassett) that throughout the whole ten years that went into the writing of *The Country Album* de Selby was obsessed with mirrors and had recourse to them so frequently that he claimed to have two left hands and to be living in a world arbitrarily bounded by a wooden frame.

(O'Brien, 1993: 66)

Despite the fact that the footnotes perfectly mimic the format and style of those commonly used in academic discourse, from their layout in smaller font at the bottom of the page to the surname-only references, they most often contain descriptions of de Selby's outlandish experiments and theories. Although the narrator himself is not responsible for these theories, he rarely offers any negative evaluation of de Selby's methods or his arguments, but treats them with the same seriousness afforded any other form of respected science, also giving over his life's work to the study of his ideas. It is evident from the outset, therefore, that the narrator of *The Third Policeman* is guilty of questionable academic judgement at the very least.

Indeed, when it becomes apparent to the narrator that he may not have enough money to finish his account of de Selby's life, he makes plans with John Divney to rob and murder a local retired cattle-trader named Mathers. They wait for the old man at the side of a country road near his home, hit him over the head and steal his black money box. As the narrator finishes Mathers off with a spade, however, Divney makes off with the box, telling his co-conspirator that he has hidden it under the floorboards in Mathers's own home. It is during the narrator's later return to that scene, to recover his new fortune, that the nature of his narration undergoes a dramatic transformation:

> Without stopping to light another match I thrust my hand bodily into the opening and just when it should be closing about the box, something happened.
>
> I cannot hope to describe what it was but it had frightened me very much long before I had understood it even slightly. It was some change which came upon me or upon the room, indescribably subtle, yet momentous, ineffable. It was as if the daylight had changed with unnatural suddenness, as if the temperature of the evening had altered greatly in an instant or as if the air had become twice as rare or twice as dense as it had been in the twinkling of an eye; perhaps all of these and other things happened together for all my senses were bewildered all at once and could give me no explanation.
>
> (O'Brien, 1993: 24)

In Gavins (2000) I noted that the declarative tone which has characterised the storytelling up to this point is suddenly replaced with one of confusion and uncertainty, articulated through an array of epistemic modalities. There is a marked shift here from the predominantly positive modal shading with which the narrative began to the now negatively shaded modal texture. With no clear idea of what has happened to him, the narrator relies on perceived changes in his physical environment to describe his bewildering predicament, creating multiple hypothetical worlds through such phrases as '*as if* the daylight had changed', '*as if* the temperature . . . had altered' and '*as if* the air had become twice as rare'. Furthermore, the narrator shows little trust in what his senses are telling him, adding '*perhaps* all of these and other things happened' and admitting 'all my senses were bewildered all at once and could give me no explanation'.

From the episode in Mathers's house onwards, the narrative of *The Third Policeman* takes on a clear absurdist style, not only in terms of its modal structure but also in terms of the landscape through which the narrator finds himself wandering. Several literary critics have described O'Brien's text as a depiction of hellish terrain (see, for example, Doherty, 1989; Hunt, 1989; Mazzullo, 1995). However, the majority of the descriptions the narrator provides of the countryside through which he travels are, on first impression, coherent portrayals of picturesque rural Ireland:

> I looked carefully around me. Brown bogs and black bogs were arranged neatly on each side of the road with rectangular boxes carved out of them here and there, each with a filling of yellow-brown brown-yellow water. Far away near the sky tiny people were stooped at their turfwork, cutting out precisely-shaped sods with their patent spades and building them into a tall memorial twice the height of a horse and cart . . . Nearer, a house stood attended by three trees and surrounded by the happiness of a coterie of fowls, all of them picking and rooting and disputating loudly in the unrelenting manufacture of their eggs. The house was quiet in itself and silent but a canopy of lazy smoke had been erected over the chimney to indicate that people were within engaged on tasks.
>
> (O'Brien, 1993: 88)

There is little in this passage alone that can be identified as reminiscent of hell. It is, rather, the unchangeable and unremitting nature of the landscape, along with the narrator's repeated insistence that he cannot wait to escape it, which gives rise to the sense of his tortured entrapment throughout *The Third Policeman*. Furthermore, within the overall idyllic setting of the novel, there are also several individual world-building elements which appear highly distorted or unusual. Among them is the police station the narrator happens upon as he wanders away from Mathers's house:

> As I came round the bend of the road an extraordinary spectacle was presented to me. About a hundred yards away on the left-hand side was a house which astonished me. It looked as if it were painted like an advertisement on a board on the roadside and indeed very poorly painted. It looked completely false and unconvincing. It did not seem to have any depth or breadth and looked as if it would not deceive a child . . . I had never seen with my eyes ever in my life before anything so unnatural and appalling and my gaze faltered about the thing uncomprehendingly as if at least one of the customary dimensions was missing, leaving no meaning in the remainder.
>
> (O'Brien, 1993: 55)

The oddly two-dimensional police station, then, is greatly at odds with the surrounding pastoral landscape. According to Stockwell's (2009) typology of textual attraction, discussed in Chapter 2 of this book, the house draws particular attention because of its newness, its topicality and its size, but perhaps most notably because of its 'aesthetic distance from the norm', as Stockwell (2009: 25) puts it.

Many readers giving their responses to *The Third Policeman* in online fora also note the 'netherworldly' qualities of the text-world in which the narrator finds himself, but most often they link this to the other characters he encounters over the course of the novel. As typical examples of some of the extended commentary given by readers on LibraryThing, for instance, consider the following reaction to the text:

[1]
This is an exaggerated world of a band of wooden legged men and half man half bicycle policemen, and yet there is a straightforward robbery and murder plot underpinning the strangeness. The story has moments of horror, comedy, and tenderness, and segments which exercise the mind with intriguing possibilities of what lies beyond our worldly perceptions of normality. The plot leaves plenty of scope to wander and wonder ahead the various twists and turns. The dreamlike quality of the narrative reflects a stream of unconsciousness which becomes clear in a beautifully crafted finale.

(DekeDastardly, 2011)

This reader refers specifically to the existence of 'half men half bicycle policemen' in the novel as characteristic of the strangeness of the text-world. The narrator first encounters one of these policemen, Sergeant Pluck, at the police station described in the extract from the novel above. Very much like the police station itself, the sergeant's appearance is described as ugly and unnerving: he is 'an enormous policeman', who somehow creates 'a very disquieting impression of unnaturalness, amounting almost to what was horrible and monstrous' (O'Brien, 1993: 56).

The conversations the narrator has with Sergeant Pluck following this first meeting have been identified by Simpson (1997, 2000) as frequently 'comprised of recursive strings of exchanges which are often triggered in the opening phase of interaction and which have no obvious end-points' (Simpson, 2000: 263). Simpson analyses, for example, an exchange between Pluck and the narrator in which Pluck tries to establish the narrator's name. Pluck ignores the narrator's insistence that he cannot remember his name and lists, instead, one apparently randomly selected name after another, as follows:

'Are you completely doubtless that you are nameless?' he asked.
'Positively certain.'

'Would it be Mick Barry?'
'No.'
'Charlemagne O'Keeffe?'
'No.'
'Sir Justin Spens?'
'Not that.'
'Kimberley?'
'No.'

(O'Brien, 1993: 103)

This exchange continues for a further thirty-four lines of the novel before the sergeant finally gives up. Simpson (2000: 252) notes that the incongruous schematic structure of the conversation displays the same 'low resolvability' which Attardo (1997: 409) identifies as a key characteristic of all absurd verbal humour (for an account of similar discourse features in Irish absurd drama, see also Simpson, 1998). Other conversations in the text can also be seen to have incongruity at their heart, but often for different reasons. In one exchange, for example, Sergeant Pluck explains 'the Atomic Theory' to the narrator, by which he reasons that several local people who spend a good deal of time riding bicycles may have in some way exchanged atomic particles with their bicycles and become part bicycle themselves. (The definite article attached to this fantastic theory is also worth noting!) A consistent pattern of behaviour on the narrator's part can be seen to be emerging at this point in the novel: just as the narrator fails to take issue with the outlandish theories of de Selby that he recounts in his footnotes, he similarly fails to assert himself in the conversation with Sergeant Pluck about his name, and he once again fails to take issue with the sergeant's bizarre Atomic Theory here. Throughout the sergeant's invective, in fact, the narrator only ever interjects with polite and supportive phatic tokens, such as 'To say the truth I did not think of that', 'That is a hard question' and 'That is well known' (O'Brien, 1993: 87–8). Indeed, Simpson (1998) argues that a marker of 'classic absurdism' is the way in which characters within a represented world rarely appear surprised by the improbable or the unexpected.

In spite of the oddness of the text-world of *The Third Policeman*, the apparent compliance of the narrator in its absurdity and the consequent questions raised about his reliability, many readers report emotional and resonant experiences of the text in their discussions in non-academic online fora. The following extracts provide useful further examples of such responses to the fiction:

[2]
The Third Policeman is a shining example of how powerful an absurdist, surreal plot can be. This novel concerns a murderous man and his accomplice, and the dream-like ways that he is subsequently pursued

by three policemen. There are passages that are really hilarious, and others that are downright disturbing. The writing is a pleasure to read, with the language bordering on the poetic in places. But essentially this is a book about ideas – dizzying, disjointed ideas admittedly, but no less fascinating and gripping for that. I went through the novel assuming that the ideas made the novel a little stilted and even, on occasion, trivial – until I reached the end. I don't want to give it away, but the end of the novel completely transforms how you perceive the rest of the novel. It made me want to reread the whole thing, as it does show the novel is far deeper and richer than it at first appears.

(RachDan, 2009)

[3]

Our protagonist seems to have slipped down the rabbit hole and, as is always the case in such alternate worlds, everyone except our rather poor choice of hero seems to find this world perfectly normal . . . There is a continuous sense of being lost when reading this story, but never so lost that you can't imagine finding a familiar path just around the next corner . . . One could see how the world our narrator finds himself in could be, in some ways, the world that de Selby posits as the real word in his writings. But it's curious that the narrator has such a high regard for de Selby, while noting in each citation just one more of de Selby's theories that don't hold water. The narrator seems to be convinced that de Selby must be brilliant partly because de Selby is difficult to comprehend, and partly because his ideas don't seem to align with reality . . . I'm uncertain about the way the running commentary on de Selby fits in. It seems to suit the tone and point of view of the novel, but it's significance, beyond the observations made above, escapes me . . . the workings of this strange world are fascinating to contemplate; and our hero's situation and attempt to extricate himself from it succeeds in gaining our support (not bad for a murderer and robber).

(Osbaldistone, 2009)

In response (2), RachDan makes very similar observations about the dream-like nature of the text to those by DekeDastardly already noted in response (1). However, RachDan also reports several strong emotional responses to the novel, in spite of clearly perceiving the text-world of the fiction as 'disjointed'. This reader describes finding the novel 'powerful', 'fascinating' and 'gripping', but most notably makes a specific reference to a marked shift in perception at a moment of significant world-repair in the novel. The plot twist RachDan is so careful to avoid giving away to other readers (but which, unfortunately, is crucial to my academic account of the text here!) is the point in the final chapter of the novel at which the narrator finally reaches his home village after days of wandering and greets Divney in a local shop. He receives the following response from Divney:

He half-crawled and rolled himself up with grotesque movements of his limbs until he was a crumpled heap on the far side of the fireplace, spilling the bottle of whiskey on his way and sending it clattering noisily across the floor. He moaned and made cries of agony which chilled me to the bone . . . He told me to keep away. He said I was not there. He said that I was dead. He said that what he had put under the boards in the big house was not the black box but a mine, a bomb. It had gone up when I touched it. He had watched the bursting of it from where I had left him. The house was blown to bits. I was dead. He screamed to me to keep away. I was dead for sixteen years.

(O'Brien, 1993: 203)

It becomes evident at this point in the text, then, that the narrator has been dead for the majority of the novel and that the hellish landscape in which he has found himself trapped since Chapter 2 is, indeed, some sort of after-life. This revelation obviously requires the reader to make a considerable re-evaluation of the entire fiction and to repair the text-worlds constructed up to this point in the light of this dramatic twist: the narrator upon whom the reader has depended for all world-building information is suddenly revealed in actual fact to be a prototypical example of Alber et al.'s 'unnatural narrator' (Alber et al., 2012: 353). As RachDan reports, for her this process of world-repair is one which 'completely transforms how you perceive the rest of the novel' and 'made me want to reread the whole thing'. In response (3), Osbaldistone reports feeling disoriented and confused by the novel and having particular unresolved questions around the narrator's obsession with de Selby. Once again, however, he reports that the novel ultimately succeeded in securing his 'support' for the narrator, in spite of him being 'a murderer and robber'. These readers can be seen in various ways, therefore, to be highly aware of the experimental form of *The Third Policeman*, but at the same time to be co-locating some of their most profound and long-lasting emotional responses to the text and its narrator with these experimental textual features. While none of the three responses examined here would appear to contain a report of self-modification, at least not to the same extent as those seen in response to Camus in Chapter 2 of this book, it is nevertheless clear that each of the readers of O'Brien's text has experienced a high level of immersion within a text-world which is stylistically greatly experimental.

Time, space and fictionality

We have now seen evidence at various points throughout this book that readers of absurd fiction frequently undergo intense and often long-lasting emotional experiences as a result of their encounters with texts at the experimental end of the stylistic cline. We have also seen, most probably as a direct consequence of this, that readers value such texts very highly, commonly including experimental absurd works within online lists of life-changing or treasured books under such headings as 'Top ten books to read before you die', 'Novels you can't imagine never having read' and so on, as well as reporting their positive evaluations in more extended discussions and reviews. The elevated esteem in which readers of absurdism hold stylistic experimentalism would seem to go against any popular belief that stylistically innovative literature is in some way exclusive or difficult to comprehend; as Bray et al. point out in their recent companion to experimental literature, the very label 'experimental', in a literary context, is often adopted as 'a term of dismissal and condescension' (Bray et al., 2012: 3). However, it is evident even from the limited survey of readers' everyday interactions with the literary absurd presented within this book that, for a great number of readers, experimental style does not represent a barrier to immersion in a literary text-world or to any consequent emotional effects of that immersion. Indeed, it is apparent that many of the absurd texts considered avant-garde at the time of their publication in the mid to late twentieth century have already taken their place within the literary canon and, as such, are now prized by readers in both academic and non-academic contexts alike. One such example is Kurt Vonnegut's novel *Slaughterhouse-Five*, originally published in 1969 and now widely considered to be a modern American classic. This is not to say, however, that Vonnegut's text is uncontroversial, since even as recently as 2011 its content was considered subversive enough for it to be banned from the Republic State High School in Missouri, USA (see Flood, 2011).

Slaughterhouse-Five is the story of Billy Pilgrim, who serves as a chaplain in the United States army during World War II and is present during the Allied bombing of Dresden as a prisoner of war. Billy is also 'unstuck in time' (Vonnegut, 1991: 17) and leaps from decade to decade throughout the narrative; from his childhood in New York, to Dresden in 1945, to the planet Tralfamadore, where he is put in a zoo by the planet's inhabitants to mate with a beautiful movie starlet, Montana Wildhack. As we have seen in Chapter 2 of this book, *Slaughterhouse-Five* is another prominent text in online readers' lists of absurd fiction, as well as being widely perceived within literary criticism in the same terms (see, for example, Harris, 1972; Hilfer, 1992; Ketterer, 1978; Klinkowitz, 1971; May, 1972; Philmus, 2005; Ward, 2012). Perhaps the most renowned episode in Vonnegut's novel is that in which the destruction of Dresden is narrated backwards, as Billy, located in 1960s New York at the time, watches an old war film while 'slightly unstuck in time':

> It was a movie about American bombers in the Second World War and the gallant men who flew them. Seen backwards by Billy, the story went like this:
>
> American planes, full of holes and wounded men and corpses took off backwards from an airfield in England. Over France, a few German

fighter planes flew at them backwards, sucked bullets and shell fragments from some of the planes and crewmen. They did the same for
wrecked American bombers on the ground, and those planes flew up
backwards to join the formation.

The formation flew backwards over a German city that was in
flames. The bombers opened their bomb bay doors, exerted a miraculous magnetism which shrunk the fires, gathered them into cylindrical
steel containers, and lifted the containers into the bellies of the planes.
The containers were stored neatly in racks. The Germans below had
miraculous devices of their own, which were long steel tubes. They used
them to suck more fragments from the crewmen and planes. But there
were still a few wounded Americans, though, and some of the bombers
were in bad repair. Over France, though, German fighters came up
again, made everything and everybody as good as new.

(Vonnegut, 1991: 53–4)

Billy, of course, has already experienced this filmic sequence in reality and
in normal chronological order, having been sheltered in a meat locker (the
titular Slaughterhouse-Five) as a prisoner of war during the Dresden attack.
He has not, however, *seen* the bombing before and this is the only time that
Vonnegut describes the attack itself in the novel. Since Billy is the reflector of this third-person heterodiegetic narrative, only the aftermath of the
bombing, as discovered by Billy and his fellow prisoners when they emerge
from the meat locker, is described elsewhere in the book. Billy, then, is
witnessing the Dresden attack from a new perspective in this episode, one
which is all the more defamiliarised by its temporal reversal. Vonnegut, of
course, not only reverses the sequencing of the attack here, but also shifts
the agency and causality within the text-world accordingly. As a result, the
Allied bombers not only fly backwards, but appear from Billy's perspective
as life-saving machines, sucking bullets and shrapnel from wounded men,
while the German guns are 'miraculous devices' which make 'everything and
everybody as good as new'.

The text-world of the temporally unstuck war movie is thus completely
coherent in and of itself, in spite of the curious manipulation of time within this
episode. This particular section of the book is also narrated in a neutral style
and includes no modal-worlds and no spatial or temporal world-switches. Its
only challenges to readers, then, are the disruptions it presents to our schematic knowledge of normal human beings' experiences of temporal order and
of war and its consequences. Even those readers with no prior knowledge of
the Allied bombing of Dresden at the start of the novel have had these events
summarised for them earlier in the text. The more detailed presentation of the
bombing at this point in the novel as a movie experienced in reverse by a time-
travelling ex-serviceman, and of war in general as the miraculous restoration
of human life on a massive scale, thus stands in contradiction of readers'

schematic understanding. Once again, then, the absurd opposition of incongruous scripts comes into play here in much the same way as was identified in Donald Barthelme's short story 'Some of Us Had Been Threatening Our Friend Colby', in Chapter 2. Vonnegut's Dresden sequence also fits Attardo's (1997: 409) notion of the low resolvability of script opposition in absurd humour, most markedly by the fact that the above episode in *Slaughterhouse-Five* is immediately followed by the even more implausible event of Billy climbing aboard a spaceship to the planet Tralfamadore.

Vonnegut further complicates readers' attempts to reconcile the opposition of fantastical and traumatic content through his use of a highly intrusive heterodiegetic narrator throughout the text, the presence of whom is made felt through a number of narrative techniques which play with the novel's ontological structure. *Slaughterhouse-Five* begins with an apparently autobiographical account of the text's origins, headed as the first chapter of the novel but sitting outside the central narrative. In this chapter Vonnegut describes his meeting with an old friend, Bernard O'Hare, from his own time serving in the US army during World War II and recounts the promise he made to O'Hare's wife that he would write an unglamourised account of the two friends' experiences in 1940s Germany. The text-world structure which arises from this opening is shown in Figure 4.1. To the far left of the diagram is the discourse-world of the novel, its real-world writing and reception. As noted in Chapter 2 of this book, most literary discourse-worlds are split in this way and Kurt Vonnegut and his reader occupy separate spatial and temporal locations. Although literary discourse lacks face-to-face interaction between participants, readers of a literary fiction will normally nevertheless have a mental representation of the author based on other real-world experiences, such as encounters with other texts by the same writer, television or magazine interviews and so on. This textually based conceptual entity, normally referred to as the implied author in the majority of literary theory, may have a more or less greatly felt presence in the text-world readers construct of the fiction itself. In the case of *Slaughterhouse-Five*, Vonnegut conflates the implied author with the narrator of the fiction by claiming that the novel is based on his own real-world experiences in the opening lines of the first chapter of the text, as follows:

> All this happened, more or less. The war parts, anyway, are pretty much true. One guy I knew really *was* shot in Dresden for taking a teapot that wasn't his. Another guy I knew really *did* threaten to have his personal enemies killed by hired gunmen after the war. And so on. I've changed all the names.
>
> I really *did* go back to Dresden with Guggenheim money (God love it) in 1967. It looked a lot like Drayton, Ohio, more open spaces than Drayton has. There must be tons of human bone meal in the ground.
>
> (Vonnegut, 1991: 1)

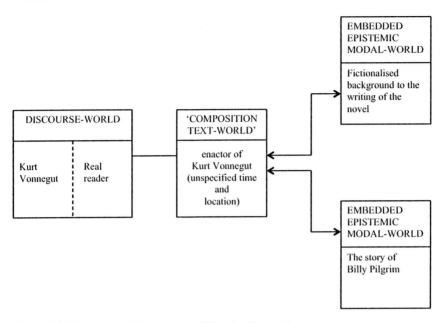

Figure 4.1 The text-world structure of *Slaughterhouse-Five*

From these lines, readers are able to construct a mental representation of a text-world containing a textual enactor of Kurt Vonnegut at the time of his writing the novel. His precise geographical location is not specified, nor is the precise date of writing, but we can infer that this is some time between the visit to Dresden in 1967 and the publication of *Slaughterhouse-Five* in 1969. From this somewhat fuzzy temporal point, shown emerging immediately to the right of the discourse-world in Figure 4.1, Vonnegut goes on to narrate a number of other text-worlds as the text switches between locations in time and space: he describes his initial reunion with O'Hare in one text-world, their visit to Dresden in another, his time as a student of anthropology at the University of Chicago in another and so on.

It is important to remember, however, that despite the presence of enactors with real-world counterparts, the various text-worlds contained within the opening chapter of *Slaughterhouse-Five* are nevertheless still fictionalised, a fact which Vonnegut playfully reminds us of throughout the first pages of the book. For example, the opening lines of the novel above make a direct claim to the text's authenticity while simultaneously undermining it: 'All this happened, more or less. The war parts, anyway, are pretty much true' (Vonnegut, 1991: 1). Note here that the first assertion about the novel's autobiographical status is immediately subverted by the qualifying statement 'more or less', while the second sentence not only reduces the authenticity of the text to just the 'war parts' but also contains a further subversive qualifier in '*pretty much* true'. Indeed, the fact that the whole of the first chapter of *Slaughterhouse-Five* relates to the background motivations and writing of the novel serves only to emphasise the fictionality of the rest of the text. The text-worlds created within the opening chapter of the novel are in fact epistemic modal-worlds, created by the implied author/narrator and embedded within the text-world containing this fictionalised textual entity. They are shown emerging to the top right of this world in Figure 4.1.

Even when Billy Pilgrim's story finally begins in the second chapter, Vonnegut continues to remind the reader of the fictional status of the unfolding account, undermining Billy's reliability as a source of world-building information in particular. Consider the following lines, which open the second chapter of the novel:

> LISTEN:
> BILLY PILGRIM has come unstuck in time.
> Billy has gone to sleep a senile widower and awakened on his wedding day. He has walked through a door in 1955 and come out another one in 1941. He has gone back through that door to find himself in 1963. He has seen his birth and death many times, he says, and pays random visits to all the events in between.
> He says.
> Billy is spastic in time, has no control over where he is going next, and the trips aren't necessarily fun. He is in a constant state of stage fright, he says, because he never knows what part of his life he is going to have to act in next.
>
> (Vonnegut, 1991: 17)

At this point, the text returns from the various world-switches through which Vonnegut has been describing his travels with O'Hare in the first chapter to the world in which he is writing *Slaughterhouse-Five* at a later temporal point and in an unspecified location. The directive 'Listen' exists as a direct address from the enactor of Vonnegut in this text-world to the reader. From this point onwards, another new text-world then becomes embedded within that containing our mental representation of the implied author/narrator. This new world has different temporal and spatial parameters and contains a different set of textual enactors. In Figure 4.1, the embedded narrative of Billy's story can be seen emerging to the bottom right of the text-world containing the enactor of Kurt Vonnegut at the point of his writing of the text. Having then begun an apparently neutral presentation of Billy's predicament, the narrator qualifies the report by subordinating the information just imparted to the reporting clause 'he says'. The same clause is repeated in the next sentence, where it is further emphasised by its graphological isolation. The positioning of this reporting clause, following the reported information rather than preceding it, is also important, since on each occasion it causes a world-repair through which the reader must re-conceptualise the text-world already constructed as the mere reportage of a character in an embedded text-world, rather than information provided by the narrator. This acts to downgrade the authoritativeness of the text-world, a shift which is all the more pronounced because of the direct link established in the first chapter of the novel between the narrator and the author of the text: world-building information provided by the purely textually located Billy Pilgrim seems doubly unreliable through its comparison with that provided by a textual version of the real-world Kurt Vonnegut.

The narrator of *Slaughterhouse-Five* is not only a clearly drawn conflation with the implied author of the text, but one who offers regular evaluative interjections in the story which serve to distance the reader from the main character, Billy Pilgrim, time and again. The most repeated and obvious of these interjections is the phrase 'So it goes', which is used exactly 100 times during the course of the novel and which almost always follows descriptions of traumatic or emotive events experienced by Billy. The following extract provides a typical example:

> He was down in the meat locker on the night Dresden was destroyed. There were sounds like giant foot-steps above. Those were sticks of high-explosive bombs. The giants walked and walked. The meat locker was a very safe shelter. All that happened down there was an occasional shower of calcimine. The Americans and four of their guards and a few dressed carcasses were down there, and nobody else. The rest of the guards had, before the raid began, gone to the comforts of their own homes in Dresden. They were all being killed with their families.
> So it goes.
> The girls that Billy has seen naked were all being killed, too, in a much shallower shelter in another part of the stockyards.
> So it goes.
> A guard would go to the head of the stairs every so often to see what it was like outside, then he would come down and whisper to the other guards. There was a fire-storm out there. Dresden was one big flame. The one flame ate everything organic, everything that would burn.
> It wasn't safe to come out of the shelter until noon the next day. When the Americans and their guards did come out, the sky was black with smoke. The sun was an angry little pinhead. Dresden was like the moon now, nothing but minerals. The stones were hot. Everybody else in the neighborhood was dead.
> So it goes.
>
> (Vonnegut, 1991: 129)

Once again, this episode is narrated in neutral style for the most part, with no use of modality and no insights provided into the thoughts and feelings of Billy, his fellow prisoners or his captors. In these sections, the text fits Simpson's (1993) category of neutrally shaded Category B narration in Narratorial mode, a 'reportage' style which Simpson (1993: 75) notes carries few evaluations of any kind but is dominated instead by unmodalised categorical assertions. There are numerous departures into other text-worlds in the passages above, however, several of which come in the form of metaphors. Blended mental representations are in turn created of explosive giants walking above the prisoners' heads, a personified flame eating the whole of Dresden, an angry pinhead sun, and a moon-like city. Slightly more unnerving, though, are the world-switches which occur with each repetition of 'So it goes'. At these points, there is a shift from the simple past tense of the main narration into a present continuous tense which is aligned with the text-world in which the narrator/implied author is situated. Each time the narrator makes this external evaluative commentary, a switch occurs from the text-world of Billy Pilgrim to that of the enactor of Kurt Vonnegut, telling Billy's story. In many ways what might be usefully described as the 'composition text-world' of *Slaughterhouse-Five* can be seen, in spite of its lack of spatial and temporal detail, to be the most consistent text-world constructed over the course of the novel. The various text-worlds relating to the origins of the novel depart from this conceptual point at the beginning of the fiction, as do all of the multitude of text-worlds relating to Billy Pilgrim's story which make up the main bulk of the novel; the narrative switches back to the matrix text-world over and over again. This relationship is shown in Figure 4.1 by the two-way arrows between the composition text-world and the two sets of embedded modal-worlds containing the story of Billy Pilgrim and the story of the writing of the text. In this way, Vonnegut makes his presence as real author, implied author and narrator felt throughout the text, drawing attention to the fictionality of his creation at regular intervals.

A similar use of metafictional techniques can also be seen at work in Paul Auster's *The New York Trilogy*, first published as a collection in 1987. Auster sets the experimental tone of the entire trilogy immediately in the opening novella, *City of Glass*, which contains the episode below within the first few pages of the text. Here, the main character, Daniel Quinn, a writer of mystery novels, is alone in his New York apartment when the telephone rings:

> He climbed out of bed, walked naked to the telephone, and picked up the receiver on the second ring.
> 'Yes?'
> There was a long pause at the other end, and for a moment Quinn thought the caller had hung up. Then, as if from a great distance, there came the sound of a voice unlike any he had ever heard. It was at once mechanical and filled with feeling, hardly more than a whisper and yet perfectly audible, and so even in tone that he was unable to tell if it belonged to a man or a woman.

'Hello?' said the voice.

'Who is this?' asked Quinn.

'Hello?' said the voice again.

'I'm listening,' said Quinn. 'Who is this?'

'Is this Paul Auster?' asked the voice. 'I would like to speak to Mr Paul Auster.'

'There's no one here by that name.'

'Paul Auster. Of the Auster Detective Agency.'

'I'm sorry',' said Quinn. 'You must have the wrong number.'

'This is a matter of the utmost urgency,' said the voice.

'There's nothing I can do for you,' said Quinn. 'There is no Paul Auster here.'

(Auster, 1988: 7)

Auster's text does not contain the same claims to authenticity as Vonnegut puts forward in his opening chapter, nor is the heterodiegetic narrator of this text explicitly linked to the implied author in the same way as in *Slaughterhouse-Five*. However, both novels play with the boundary between the discourse-world and the text-world in deliberate and interesting ways, which in both cases leads to the foregrounding of the fictional status of the text. In the extract from *City of Glass* above, the mention of the real author's name by a fictional character in the text-world draws attention to the ontological borderline which separates reality from fiction, the real author and real reader from the fictional world of the text. McHale (1987: 34) claims that such ontological foregrounding outlines what he terms the 'semi-permeable membrane' which exists between worlds, whereby Paul Auster appears to have access to the text-world he has created, and his characters appear to have access to the discourse-world from which they spring. In her analysis of hypertext narratives, Bell (2007) goes on to argue,

> While this is not logically possible, the effect is enough to draw attention to the ontological game in which readers normally passively partake ... It is precisely because this [ontological] boundary is so prominent that it is unsettling when fictional entities appear to cross or permeate it.
>
> (Bell, 2007: 50)

McHale identifies this kind of narrative feature as typical of postmodern fiction in particular and, indeed, Auster's work is most often discussed in literary criticism from this perspective (see, for example, Alford, 1995a, 1995b; Briggs, 2003; Dimovitz, 2006; Russell, 1990; Shiloh, 2002; Varvogli, 2001; Zilcosky, 1998). It is important to note, however, that Auster's manipulation of ontological boundaries in *City of Glass* has specific significance to the text's absurdist themes as well. Like Wurlitzer's experimentalism in *Nog*, and indeed like all the stylistic innovation examined throughout this book, Auster's narrative techniques are not merely self-conscious ornamentation but facilitate the exploration of key absurdist questions. Berge (2005) points out that the games Auster plays in his trilogy centre specifically around characterisation and around questions of identity, noting that 'Literature applying such devices emphasizes the reader's awareness of the novel being a construct, and the characterization's objective to explore a theme rather than describe a realistic person' (Berge, 2005: 106; see also Shiloh, 2002).

Auster creates multiple layers of overlapping identities within *City of Glass*. Daniel Quinn writes under a pseudonym, William Wilson, but also invests much of his own personality in his creation of the main character of his detective novels, Max Work. Following the mystery phone call in the middle of the night, he readily takes on, as Berge describes it, 'the absurd-ity of the "Paul Auster" identity' (Berge, 2005: 106) in order to pursue the missing persons case it turns out was the subject of the call. Quinn the writer of detective fiction is thus hired as a real-life detective by Virginia Stillman to find her husband Peter Stillman's abusive father, Peter Stillman Snr (note the shared names here too). It also emerges that Quinn's own dead son was named Peter and the trauma of revisiting memories of his son through his investigations into Peter Stillman soon take their toll on his mental health. Quinn buys a red notebook and makes the following initial notes on the case:

> And then, most important of all: to remember who I am. To remember who I am supposed to be. I do not think this is a game. On the other hand, nothing is clear. For example: who are you? And if you think you know, why do you keep lying about it? I have no answer. All I can say is this: listen to me. My name is Paul Auster. That is not my real name.
>
> (Auster, 1988: 40)

The sudden proliferation of epistemic modality in this first-person section of the text exists in stark contrast to the predominantly positively shaded heterodiegetic narration which forms the bulk of the fiction (Simpson, 1993: 69–71). Although the Reflector mode narrative offers insights into Quinn's perspective and opinions throughout *City of Glass*, the extent of his confu-sion is made fully apparent only in the sections of the text where his notebook entries are directly related. In these parts of the narrative, Quinn's increasing bewilderment and gradual loss of his sense of identity are expressed using the same unstable modal texture as we have now seen in so many other absurdist narratives.

Also noteworthy in the extract above is the second-person address Quinn uses, since it remains ambiguous to whom he is addressing his question 'who are you?' The addressee of this question, and that which immediately follows it, could equally conceivably be himself or the future reader of his notebook within the text-world. However, the illusion of a semi-permeable membrane between the discourse-world and the text-world, which has already been set up by the appearance of Paul Auster's name within the text-world, also suggests that the 'you' here could be the real reader of *City of Glass* in the discourse-world, or even the real-world Paul Auster. None of these different possibilities is confirmed, of course, as, instead, Quinn's futile search for Peter Stillman Snr and for a stable sense of his own identity eventually leads him to meet the 'real' Paul Auster within the text-world. Quinn looks up the Auster Detective Agency he has been impersonating in the phone book and finds only one entry under 'Auster', a writer. When Quinn goes to meet Auster at his apartment, the permeability of the ontological divide between worlds becomes ever more apparent as Auster transforms into a fully realised character in the text-world, rather than just a name. He claims to have read Quinn's novels and says he is an admirer of his work. The two men share a meal and talk about *Don Quixote* for a while, before Quinn meets Auster's wife, Siri, who bears the same name as Paul Auster's wife in the real world (Siri Hustvedt), and his son, Daniel, who has the same first name as Quinn. *City of Glass* can be seen, in this way, as something of a master class in the violation of 'fiction's epidermis', as McHale (1987: 34) puts it. Crucially, however, Auster ensures that resolving the ontological transgressions he institutes remains a Sisyphean quest for his readers. At the end of the fiction, the disembodied and nameless heterodiegetic narrator switches from his third-person account of Quinn's life to a closing first-person account of the delivery into his hands of Quinn's red notebook by one Paul Auster, just before Quinn finally disappeared altogether.

Mixing genres

Vonnegut's *Slaughterhouse-Five* and Auster's *The New York Trilogy* bear resemblance not only in the attention they draw to the semi-permeable membrane between the discourse-world and the text-world and their consequent foregrounded fictionality, but also in the mixing of literary genres with which they both experiment. Vonnegut's World War II novel is intermingled with science fiction, whereas Auster makes use of the genre of detective fiction in order to facilitate his exploration of human identity. It is useful at this point to remind ourselves of Steen's (2011) definition of literary genre as a conceptual category exhibiting the same prototype effects as any other, first examined in Chapter 2 of this book:

> A particular genre event can be a central or marginal case for the category it exemplifies in that it can display better or worse characteristics of the genre it belongs to. Any historical novel, for instance, is (a) a novel but (b) less typical since it is not completely fictive. This perspective therefore allows for the inclusion of a particular genre event

within the class of a genre as more or less typical, or even as a hybrid between two genres, without undermining the complete system. This is in fact how many language users operate with genres that are in a stage of transition or that have ended up on the border between two well-defined but mutually exclusive categories.

(Steen, 2011: 30)

By this reasoning, then, both *Slaughterhouse-Five* and *The New York Trilogy* are clearly hybrids, each of them utilising the textual and thematic features of two different genres. Also by this reasoning, however, both texts can be seen to be less than prototypical of either of the genres they employ, since the combination of two genres within one text dilutes their centrality in one or other of these conceptual categories. This becomes of particular interest when examining readers' responses to the novels in non-academic contexts, where both fictions seem to polarise opinion.

On the online literary discussion site Shelfari, for example, *Slaughterhouse-Five* achieves an average reader rating of four stars out of a possible five, based on 1,103 reviews posted on the site at the time of writing (Shelfari, 2012c). While a considerable majority of these reviews, 749 to be precise, give the book a rating of either four or five stars, a significant number of other readers also report not liking the text at all: 76 readers rate the book at either one or two stars. Shelfari also allows readers to award a text no stars at all but, on closer inspection of their accompanying commentaries, it becomes clear that many such ratings are actually made by readers who are not willing to give a rating or who are undecided. In total, a further sixteen readers rating the novel zero stars actually express a dislike of the text. Most interestingly, from all of those readers commenting negatively on *Slaughterhouse-Five*, the most common response seems to be one based on a lack of comprehension, often along the lines of 'I didn't get it', 'maybe I'm missing something' or 'really confusing'. These kinds of readers also frequently refer to the science-fictional aspects of the novel in the most negative terms. Consider the following typical examples:

[1]
Don't let the name fool you, this book is neither exciting nor about anything in particular. There is no real plot; this book is more of a memoir. In my book, this is not remotely science fiction, either. While there is time travel and other species, they are merely tangents to Billy Pilgrim's life, which is altogether fairly unmemorable.

(Kasey C, 2012)

[2]
I get that it was supposed to be sardonic, yes. Literally, the only part of this book that I enjoyed were some humorous commentaries. Other

than that, I did not enjoy it. It was waaaaaaay too . . . out there . . . so much so that I couldn't even begin to try and grasp what Vonnegut was being sarcastic about. Too weird.

(Brittany S, 2012)

[3]
Billy Pilgrim is a dry, boring, and pathetic character. The fire bombing of Dresden is mentioned throughout the book and only explained in two pages that failed to make a statement. The majority of the book is dedicated to Billy Pilgrim's alien abduction by the Tralfamadorians which make the book too far out to take seriously.

(mary-erin, 2009)

[4]
I don't know what I was thinking when I started this book. I had heard it was strange, and it is definitely that, but I guess I expected more from all that I had heard. It was almost as if it was strange just for the sake of being strange. Billy Pilgrim was insipid and stupid. I saw no point in his being 'unstuck' in time and the addition of the Tralfamadorians.

(Erika M, 2012)

Each of these readers, and many more like them, locate their dissatisfaction with *Slaughterhouse-Five* in one way or another around its use of science fiction. Reviews (2) and (3) both comment that this aspect of the novel undermines its seriousness or makes the text unfathomably eccentric, whereas review (4) makes a similar argument but also regards the addition of aliens in the text as ultimately pointless. Each of these responses suggests that the novel did not fit with the reader's prior expectations of the text and that the juxtapositioning of science fiction with war in *Slaughterhouse-Five* is at the root of the failure of the reading experience for them. Review (1) is even more interesting in that this reader's anticipations about the text seem to have had a reverse orientation and *Slaughterhouse-Five* is perceived as a disappointment here because its science fiction components were not prominent or central enough to the text.

As I argued in Chapter 2, readers' interactions with all literary texts are highly context-dependent and their evaluations of their individual reading experiences are based very much on pre-existing schematic understanding of a given genre. In order to explore this notion a little further, it is possible to make use of Shelfari's bookshelf system to contextualise readers' responses to Vonnegut's text. Users of the site are able to build a virtual bookshelf for themselves, which is public to other users of the site, by adding texts to their profile and rating and reviewing them, as seen above. Interestingly, responses (2), (3) and (4) were all made by readers with a liking for highly prototypical examples of genre fiction of one sort or another: among the most highly rated texts on the bookshelf of mary-erin (reader 3) are the hugely popular Harry Potter series of novels by J.K. Rowling and the Twilight series by Stephanie Meyer; the favourites of Erika M (reader 4) include the fantasy novels of Jim Butcher, the mystery novels of Harlan Coben and Rick Riordan's reworkings of Greek and Roman myths; Brittany S (reader 2) enjoys the Luxe series of fiction for young adults by Anne Godberson, as well as Michael Scott's fantasy texts. Unsurprisingly, Kasey C (reader 1) is also a regular reader of genre fiction and rates prototypical science fiction and fantasy writers, such as Ursula K. Le Guin, Frank Herbert and J.R.R. Tolkien, most highly on her bookshelf. Kasey C's frustration with *Slaughterhouse-Five* is clearly situated within her preference for texts which take a central position within the science fiction genre. The other three readers cited above have similarly situated responses and, even though they appear to read less prototypical science fiction ordinarily than Kasey C, they still express disappointment or irritation with Vonnegut's creation of a mixed-genre text, the hybridity of which positions it on the periphery of both the 'science fiction' and 'war novel' categories.

A very similar pattern of responses can also be seen to Paul Auster's *The New York Trilogy* on Shelfari. Again, overall the text scores four stars out of five based on 113 reviews: sixty-one readers rate the book four or five stars; fifteen give the book a mediocre rating of three stars; seventeen readers rate the text two stars or below (again discounting those readers rating the book zero stars but accompanied with a positive commentary). Once again, those readers rating the trilogy most negatively frequently comment upon its use of genre as a contributing factor to their lack of enjoyment. The following are typical examples of such responses:

[1]
I guess this just isn't my cuppa tea. I don't mind a little mystery but giving no clue on some of the protagonists motivations is just too awkward for me. Too many possibilities. I don't mind a million different ideas on a subject but I'd rather choose the subject myself and be in complete control of everything. With these books you're being set some parameters, they seem set in 'the real world' but then as you think you just figured out how and what and the probable why, you find out you were wrong and that nothing is what it seems . . . I think. But I could be wrong :P Anyway I can understand if people would like a book for the exact same reasons as why I don't like it ;) It's clever just not the clever I like.

(Dicul, 2006)

[2]
Maybe I missed something, in fact, I'm pretty sure I did. Heralded as a work of genius I waited in anticipation for all the pieces to slot into

place . . . they never did. The New York Trilogy is three individual stories based around the idea of someone tracing/watching someone else. Sure, there are some similarities between them – some character names are the same, the idea of tracking and watching is shared throughout and I've no doubt someone much more intelligent than me managed to get even more out of it than that. I didn't.

(Sherri L, 2010)

[3]
I am glad that I gave my copy of these novellas away some time ago (I just hope that I didn't give it to a friend!). Rarely do I say this about a book, but Auster's *The New York Trilogy* really was unadulterated crap. I should have known better, as I really do despise postmodernism in fiction. Anyway, I sure wouldn't recommend this to anyone; and I am likely to delete the book from my list at some point because of what it says about me the reader.

(Christopher H, 2010)

In these examples, a common theme emerges of the 'cleverness' of Auster's text, which is used as a term of negative appraisal. These readers specifically seem to be rejecting the role of implied reader they perceive the novel to be constructing through this cleverness, for example 'clever just not the clever I like' in review (1), 'I've no doubt someone much more intelligent than me managed to get even more out of it than that' in review (2) and 'I am likely to delete the book from my list at some point because of what it says about me the reader' in review (3). Once again, each of the readers above rates prototypical examples of genre fiction most highly on their bookshelf: Dicul enjoys science fiction and fantasy and particularly the work of Neil Gaiman; Sherri L rates J.K. Rowling, Philip Pullman and Frank Herbert all equally highly; and Christopher H is an avid reader of Patrick O'Brien's novels.

At the opposite end of the spectrum of reader evaluations for both *Slaughterhouse-Five* and *The New York Trilogy*, the readers who rate these texts most highly on Shelfari have, on the whole, a more diverse range of books on their virtual bookshelf and tend to give equally high ratings both to prototypical genre fiction from a range of different categories (e.g. science fiction, fantasy, detective fiction, horror) and to hybrid or less prototypical texts within such categories. In the case of *The New York Trilogy*, these readers comment most positively on the collection's metafictional features, its intertextuality and its existential themes in a manner almost diametrically opposed to the readers reporting negative experiences with the text. Kurt Vonnegut's most positive readers on Shelfari similarly report enjoyment of the absurdity of *Slaughterhouse-Five*, its experimentation with disrupted chronology in particular, and they commonly read the inclusion of the Tralfamadorians and of time travel as humorous. Most notably, almost all of the 749 readers who rated Vonnegut's text at four stars or above and almost all the sixty-one readers who rated Auster's trilogy at four stars or above have at least one other prototypically absurdist text rated highly on their bookshelf. By contrast, the readers reporting negative experiences with these authors are more likely to have no other absurdist texts on their shelf or to have rated other absurdism similarly negatively. It would seem, therefore, that many readers' positive evaluations of absurd experimentalism are directly dependent on or develop from previous experiences with similar texts.

Mixing modes

Auster's *City of Glass* and Vonnegut's *Slaughterhouse-Five* bear a final similarity through the use of illustration within the main body of these texts. Auster's novella includes a series of maps that the narrator claims are reproductions of those made by Quinn in his red notebook while tailing Peter Stillman around New York (Auster, 1988: 66–9). These maps appear to be crudely drawn at first using a single pen line. However, by the third drawing, it is clear that the maps form the outlines of the letters O, W and E. The narrator goes on to describe how Quinn drew further maps of his movements, the emerging letters of which Quinn interprets as beginning to spell out TOWER OF BABEL. Vonnegut's novel, on the other hand, contains three illustrations, which appear to have been done by the implied author of *Slaughterhouse-Five*: one of Billy Pilgrim's imagined tombstone, on which the epitaph 'Everything was beautiful, and nothing hurt' is carved (Vonnegut, 1991: 88); one of a sign in an army latrine reading 'Please leave the latrine as tidy as you found it!!' (Vonnegut, 1991: 91); and one of the locket which hangs between Montana Wildhack's breasts and bears another inscription, 'God grant me the serenity to accept the things I cannot change, courage to change the things I can, and wisdom always to tell the difference' (Vonnegut, 1991: 153). Each of the illustrations in Vonnegut's text is in simple monochrome and appears to have been drawn using a felt-tipped pen. The infrequency of the drawings in both *Slaughterhouse-Five* and *City of Glass* adds to their impact when they occur, the first one coming eighty-eight pages into Vonnegut's text and sixty-six pages into Auster's. However, where the maps in *City of Glass* have an obvious and explicitly stated relation to Quinn's notebook, the sudden appearance of illustrations in *Slaughterhouse-Five* is not explained by that text's narrator. As such, the drawings present much more of a challenge to the reader's schematic knowledge of the textual conventions of modern novels, which has been reinforced throughout the rest of Vonnegut's text through the non-appearance of any other illustrations up to this point. In many ways, this challenge to existing and recently reinforced knowledge can be seen essentially as another technique of absurdist script opposition (see Attardo, 1997; Attardo and Raskin, 1991). No warning is given of the sudden switch to a mixed mode of representation and no explanation or resolution of the incongruity follows it.

A later novel by Kurt Vonnegut, *Breakfast of Champions*, originally published in 1973, makes much more frequent and consistent use of illustrations (similar to those in *Slaughterhouse-Five*) from the very start of the text. Indeed, the preliminary pages of this book carry a drawing of a T-shirt bearing the name of the novel, followed by a drawing of a cow with a speech bubble containing the novel's alternative title, 'Goodbye Blue Monday'. The similar style of the drawings is not the only means through which Vonnegut forges intertextual connections between *Breakfast of Champions* and *Slaughterhouse-Five*. *Breakfast of Champions* traces the events which lead up to a meeting between two characters: Kilgore Trout, an ageing writer of obscure science fiction, and Dwayne Hoover, a wealthy but troubled businessman. The novel begins with a Preface, the style and content of which are readily comparable to the opening chapter of *Slaughterhouse-Five*. The Preface is a first-person account of the writing of *Breakfast of Champions* and sets up a conflation between the narrator of the fiction and the real-world author, Kurt Vonnegut, in much the same way as we saw in his earlier novel. Once again, the explanation the Preface provides of Vonnegut's motivations for writing the text acts to foreground the fictionality of the work, as does the direct reference made within this opening chapter to the author's use of illustrations: 'This book is my fiftieth birthday present to myself . . . I am programmed at fifty to perform childishly – to insult "The Star-Spangled Banner", to scrawl pictures of a Nazi flag and an asshole and a lot of other things with a felt-tipped pen' (Vonnegut, 2000: 4–5).

Although Vonnegut claims in the Preface that he is 'throwing out characters from my other books' (Vonnegut, 2000: 5), he nevertheless goes on to include numerous characters in his text who have appeared in previous novels, including Kilgore Trout himself, who was a minor character in *Slaughterhouse-Five*. Furthermore, he begins the story of Kilgore Trout and Dwayne Hoover in a style which is also highly reminiscent of the opening pages of that novel:

This is a tale of a meeting of two lonesome, skinny, fairly old white men on a planet which was dying fast.

One of them was a science-fiction writer named Kilgore Trout. He was a nobody at the time, and he supposed his life was over. He was mistaken. As a consequence of the meeting, he became one of the most beloved and respected human beings in history.

The man he met was an automobile dealer, a *Pontiac* dealer named Dwayne Hoover. Dwayne Hoover was on the brink of going insane.

◆ Listen:

Trout and Hoover were citizens of the United States of America, a country which was called *America* for short.

(Vonnegut, 2000: 7)

Having established another composition text-world, just like that which underpins *Slaughterhouse-Five*, containing an enactor of himself at an unspecified time and location, Vonnegut then begins the embedded narrative of Trout and Hoover in a separate chapter. Further parallels can also be drawn between the two texts through the repetition of the directive 'Listen:', which opened Billy Pilgrim's story and which appears again in the first few lines of the story of Trout and Hoover and at numerous other stages later in the novel. Once again, the embedded story is told in the third person, but here Vonnegut adopts a style which is somewhat less neutral than that which characterises *Slaughterhouse-Five*. Where in his earlier novel Vonnegut's narrating style is typified by a lack of modality and evaluative commentary, in *Breakfast of Champions* his narrator/implied author is much more opinionated. In the extract above, for example, he describes the main characters as 'lonesome, skinny, fairly old', and Trout in particular as 'a nobody'. The passage also contains a fleeting glimpse into Trout's mind, as it reports his inner thoughts through the use of epistemic modality ('*he supposed* his life was over'). The narrator then goes on to insult 'The Star-Spangled Banner' in precisely the manner he has promised he would in the Preface, calling it 'pure balderdash' (Vonnegut, 2000: 8), and the rest of the novel proceeds in a similar vein.

The text-world enactor of Vonnegut in *Breakfast of Champions* can thus be seen to be a more outspoken textual version of the real author than that constructed through the neutral narrative shading in *Slaughterhouse-Five*, with a more keenly felt presence throughout the text. Indeed, when Trout and Hoover finally meet at the end of the novel, the narrator/implied author takes a final forceful step through the text's semi-permeable ontological boundaries. Dwayne Hoover reads one of Kilgore Trout's novels, the narrator of which claims to be the Creator of the Universe, delivering a message that everyone on Earth is a robot except for the reader of that novel, who is the only person in the world with free will. In his fragile mental state, Hoover takes Trout's fiction as reality and goes on a violent rampage around his home city, which Trout happens to be visiting at the time. Afterwards, the narrator/implied author of *Breakfast of Champions* approaches Trout within his text-world to tell him that he is a fictional character, controlled by him through his writing:

'Mr Trout,' I said, 'I am a novelist, and I created you for use in my books.'
'Pardon me?', he said.
'I'm your Creator,' I said. 'You're in the middle of a book right now – close to the end of it, actually.'
'Um,' he said.

(Vonnegut, 2000: 291)

The narrator/implied author then sets Trout 'free', granting him free will along with all Vonnegut's other previous fictional characters, although the narrator/implied author is careful to warn Trout that he is the only one of those characters whom he is telling of his new found liberty.

Vonnegut, then, can be seen to be foregrounding fictionality and playing with intertextuality throughout *Breakfast of Champions*. As already noted, the style of the frequent drawings in the novel is also highly reminiscent of those in *Slaughterhouse-Five*. However, not only are the drawings in Vonnegut's later novel much more numerous, appearing at regular intervals throughout the book, but they play a more integrated role in the narrative itself. In *Slaughterhouse-Five*, the first of the three illustrations (which appear towards the end of the novel), that of Billy's tombstone, is not referred to explicitly in the text. The drawing simply appears mid-way through an episode where Billy and his wife, Valencia, are talking about his experiences in the war. The only reference made to the tombstone at all is as follows:

'I'm *proud* you were a soldier. Do you know that?'
'Good.'
'Was it awful.'
'Sometimes.' A crazy thought now occurred to Billy. The truth of it startled him. It would make a good epitaph for Billy Pilgrim – and for me, too.

(Vonnegut, 1991: 87–9)

It is left to the reader to infer that the 'crazy thought' which has occurred to Billy is the inscription shown in the drawing, which is then referred to anaphorically in the extract above on two further occasions using the pronoun 'it'. Both the drawing of the sign in the latrine and that of Montana Wildhack's locket, which occur later in the novel, are pointed to more explicitly in the text, the former being preceded with 'Here is what the message said:' (Vonnegut, 1991: 90) and the latter with 'Engraved on the outside of the locket were these words:' (Vonnegut, 1991: 152). By contrast, almost all of the 120 drawings in *Breakfast of Champions* are pointed to through explicit linguistic reference in the novel, most frequently using proximal deictic markers, such as '*This* was it' (Vonnegut, 2000: 149), '*Here* is what it said' (Vonnegut, 2000: 249) or 'It looked like *this*' (Vonnegut, 2000: 51).

Vonnegut's later fiction, then, can be seen to be more fully developed in its multimodality than his earlier work, at least in the sense defined by Kress and van Leeuwen, who state that a multimodal text is 'any text whose meanings are realized through more than one semiotic mode' (Kress and van Leeuwen, 2006: 177). The consistent interrelationship between text and image in *Breakfast of Champions* (as opposed to the occasional inclusion of images that are not necessarily deictically connected to the text in *Slaughterhouse-Five*) is an integral component of this text's meaning-making. In her cognitive-poetic account of multimodal fiction, Gibbons (2011) explains that multimodal novels

> complicate the relationship of the concrete to the imaginary, since in contrast to traditional Western literary forms, they are not transparent. They are 'opaque', bearing self-conscious graphic designs that draw attention to their materiality. In doing so, the concrete realisation of word and image upon the printed page participates in the narrative. The innovative appearance of multimodal literature induces the two semiotic modes to collaborate in the literary act, and thus both the verbal and the visual influence the reader's creation of, and potential immersion in, an imagined text-world. Moreover, since multimodal novels exploit the visual surface of the page to communicate their story, the readerly performance of transportation from the discourse-world and submersion in the text-world is not as fixed as with traditional literary forms. Rather, a slippage occurs between discourse-world and text-world, in which the surface of the book's pages also becomes a significant conceptual plane. In other words, multimodal texts demand a dynamic reading strategy in which the reader must 'toggle' between the mediating textual surface and cognitive worlds.
>
> (Gibbons, 2011: 114)

In essence, Gibbons argues that multimodal surfaces obstruct sustained engagement with the imagined content of literary narratives, leading readers to adopt a strategy whereby they are simultaneously aware of the innovative graphic nature of the text and of the text-worlds created through the linguistic component of a narrative. From this perspective, Vonnegut's use of multimodality in *Breakfast of Champions* can be seen as another device through which the materiality, and consequently the fictionality, of the novel is foregrounded.

Figure 4.2 shows a typical example of the way Vonnegut integrates text and image in *Breakfast of Champions* to particular communicative ends. This section of the text describes Bunny Hoover, Dwayne Hoover's son, who plays piano in the lounge of the Holiday Inn. Bunny practises transcendental meditation before each of his performances, a process which is described in this section of the text. The effect of this meditation is related by the heterodiegetic narrator in Reflector mode initially (Simpson, 1993: 69–76), so that an insight is granted into the effects of the meditative practice on both Bunny's body and his mind while the voice of the narrator remains present in the text. Interestingly, the image which follows the textual description of the meditation is also located firmly within Bunny's point of view. This is made explicit in the text ('Here is what it looked like to Bunny Hoover:'), where the close alignment between the reader and Bunny is also emphasised in the proximal deictic 'Here' with which the image is introduced. The image of the word

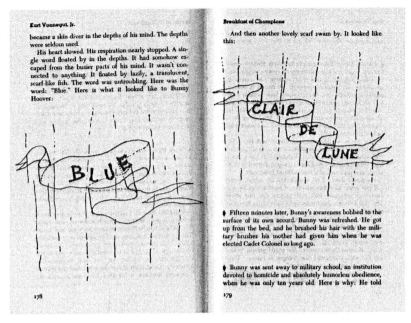

Figure 4.2 Multimodality in Kurt Vonnegut's *Breakfast of Champions* (published by Jonathan Cape, reprinted by permission of The Random House Group Limited)

which follows this text is then a direct depiction of what Bunny sees in his mind so that, for an instant, it seems that the narrator is no longer present as mediator. This, of course, is an illusion, since the narrator claims responsibility for all the images in the text as well as for the text itself, but it is an illusion which nevertheless results in a particularly intimate connection between Bunny and the reader at this moment in the fiction. However, as we have seen Gibbons argue above, this connection is complicated by the multimodal nature of the novel. This leads the reader to be simultaneously immersed in the text-world of Bunny, encouraged by the intimate and involving narrative style, yet highly aware of the materiality of the novel. Gibbons further argues that this requires the reader to 'toggle' between two worlds (Gibbons, 2011: 119–21; see also Gavins, 2007: 152–6; Werth, 1977). In relation to multimodal fiction specifically, she terms this effect 'bi-stable oscillation' (Gibbons, 2011: 114–24) in a development of Lanham's (1993) original term.

The same effect can also be seen to occur through Auster's use of multimodality in *City of Glass* and even in Vonnegut's more limited use of illustration in *Slaughterhouse-Five*. Although the use of drawings in both of these texts is less frequent and, in the case of *Slaughterhouse-Five*, not always fully integrated with the meaning-making of the fiction, the deployment of more than one mode of signification in these novels nevertheless foregrounds the materiality of the text at the same time as a potentially immersive and imaginative text-world is being negotiated. In all these cases, then, the reader is presented with a bi-stable position at which both aspects of the fictions can be experienced simultaneously, but which complicates the transportative effects of the narratives. In this way, the use of multimodality in absurdist texts can be seen as another means through which the discourse-world activity of reading itself is foregrounded and, consequently, the fictionality of the text-worlds created by these books is also emphasised and manipulated.

The literary absurd, so far

In this chapter we have seen a number of the stylistic techniques identified in previous chapters re-emerge through the analysis of a further selection of absurdist texts. It is now clear that the modal texture of a literary fiction plays an important role in the communication of unstable or unreliable narrative perspectives in absurd prose fiction. In particular, we have seen across several chapters how negatively shaded modality, in Simpson's terms (1993), is especially instrumental in the creation of fictional minds that are alienated, bewildered and erratic. This type of modality is often also closely associated with the creation of multiple hypothetical modal-worlds, embedded within the main narrative, through which a character's paranoia and confusion are frequently played out. We have also now seen on several occasions how unreliable first-person narrators of absurd fictions can be responsible for the construction of significant plot twists which require substantial world-repair on the part of the reader in order to rationalise or comprehend new information. Such world-repairs are sometimes delivered by narrators, as in Flann O'Brien's *The Third Policeman*, who are themselves surprised and disoriented by a particular plot development. Alternatively, they can be created by the narrator's own denarration and renarration (see Richardson, 2006) of key components of the text-world, either deliberately (in cases such as in Tom McCarthy's *Remainder*) or as the result of a less obviously intentional psychological instability (such as in Rudolph Wurlitzer's *Nog*).

This chapter has also examined several novels which manipulate spatio-temporal deixis to create text-worlds either with a particularly surrealistic feel or which are difficult for readers to construct coherent mental representations of at all. The hellish landscapes of *The Third Policeman*, the interchangeable identities and shifting time and space in *Nog*, and the reversal of time and causality in *Slaughterhouse-Five* have all been investigated as concrete stylistic examples of Weinberg's notion of an 'absurd surface' (Weinberg, 1970: 11). This absurd surface has also been shown in several other examples to be further exaggerated through the use of multimodality. The analysis of Paul Auster's *City of Glass* and Kurt Vonnegut's novels *Slaughterhouse-Five* and *Breakfast of Champions* in this chapter revealed how the use of more than one mode of signification can create a bi-stable position for the reader, in Gibbons's (2011) terms. Readers are made simultaneously aware of the imaginative content of the text-worlds of a fiction and of its materiality in such cases, complicating immersion in the narrative world and foregrounding the fictional status of the text.

Indeed, foregrounded fictionality has emerged over the course of this chapter as another key feature of the literary absurd. In Chapter 3 we saw how the inclusion of footnotes in Mordecai Richler's *Barney's Version*, attributed to a textual enactor, drew attention to the fictionalised nature of what purports to be an autobiographical account. Similarly, the footnotes in *The Third Policeman* were shown in this chapter to foreground the fictionality of O'Brien's text in much the same way, despite being presented as the work of the narrator, rather than that of another, destabilising character in the text. Further techniques for drawing attention to fictionality were also identified in this chapter in the form of crossings through ontological boundaries in various texts. Both Paul Auster and Kurt Vonnegut were shown to utilise the semi-permeable membrane between the discourse-world and various text-worlds in their fiction to create the illusion that entities ordinarily confined either to reality or to fiction have access across these divides.

None of the stylistic features examined in this or other chapters in this book is the exclusive preserve of absurd prose fiction, of course, and techniques such as the ontological manipulations described above have been argued by other critics to be characteristic of other categories of literature, such as postmodernism (for further discussion see McHale, 1987). However, what makes each of the texts analysed over the course of the present volume absurdist, rather than postmodern or even simply experimental for experimentalism's sake, is the fact that in each case the innovative style of the fiction is in some way and at the same time enabling of the exploration of the philosophical absurd. Each of the experimental novels examined over the course of this book can be seen to fit Weinberg's description of a literary style 'created to embody the inexplicable' (1970: 11).

It is important to note once again, however, that the employment of such exaggerated, surreal and innovative stylistic techniques does not appear to impair immersion in and enjoyment of absurdist literature for a great many readers. We have seen in this chapter how emotional responses comparable with those reported in relation to more realistic fiction in Chapter 2 are also frequently reported by readers of texts at the experimental end of the absurdist cline. The readers who value absurd texts most highly do not seem to view challenging narrative games and practices as a barrier to their transportation to a fictional text-world. We have also seen, however, that responses to absurdist forms from readers reading in non-academic contexts can be polarised and that absurd texts which mix different generic conventions, in particular, can cause frustration and disappointment in some readers. Such genre-mixing works by opposing different frames of knowledge in much the same way as humorous texts create incongruity by juxtaposing different sets of reader expectations. Readers who ordinarily enjoy prototypical examples of particular literary genres, such as horror, detective fiction, science fiction and fantasy, were revealed to react most negatively to the genre hybrids more often created in absurd narratives. Regular readers of experimental absurdism, on the other hand, were seen frequently to locate their enjoyment of these texts specifically with the playful borrowing of tropes and techniques to be found in such literature.

With a more well defined compendium of some of the characteristic stylistic devices to be found in a broad range of absurd prose fiction now in place, as well as an emerging understanding of the typical behaviours and responses of readers of the absurd, the next and final chapter of this book moves on to consider whether these concepts might also be identifiable within poetic discourse. I end the book with a look to the future of research into absurd literary style and the possibility of a wider application of the work begun in this volume to yet more diverse texts, authors and literary forms.

5 Absurd Verses

In this final chapter, I present a summary of the central observations and arguments made about the stylistics of absurd prose fiction in each of the preceding chapters. I provide a survey of the linguistic characteristics discovered to be of significance in the narrative texts examined so far, in order then to take a prospective view of the further avenues of enquiry that stylistic analyses of the literary absurd might explore in the future. In particular, I put forward an argument for a more coherent and rigorous account of the stylistic manifestation of the absurd in poetic texts, based on the template of the stylistics of the literary absurd which has been formulated over the course of this study. I provide example linguistic analyses of poems by Charles Simic, James Tate and Ted Hughes, and also examine responses made to these texts by readers in both academic and non-academic contexts. The discussion here addresses the key question of why literary critics have to date been more reluctant to identify the absurd as a poetic phenomenon than they have been to recognise it as a feature of dramatic and prose fiction texts. Consequently, I revisit the notion of the literary absurd as a situated conceptual category exhibiting prototype effects, first put forward in Chapter 2. I argue that the more precise account of the linguistic characteristics of absurd prose fiction presented over the course of this book may in turn help to clarify our understanding of the phenomenon of the poetic absurd.

The stylistics of absurd prose fiction

My examination of the stylistic features which characterise the literary absurd developed in this book from a starting point at which the term 'absurd' was, as Esslin put it, 'a catchphrase much used and abused' (Esslin, 1965: 7). Over the intervening pages, I have attempted to add systematicity and analytical rigour to existing accounts of the absurd in literature through the examination of some of the most common linguistic features to be found in a range of absurd prose fiction. As I stated in Chapter 1, this book is not intended as a comprehensive survey of the stylistics of the absurd, but rather as a first step towards a better understanding of the textual manifestation of this phenomenon across a significant sample of typical texts. With the aim of presenting the most easily comprehensible and most generally applicable account possible, key absurdist authors and works have not been subject to analysis here and, no doubt, further interesting stylistic characteristics of the absurd will have been overlooked. Nevertheless, the preceding discussion stands as a replicable initial exploration into absurd style from which further investigations may develop. In order to assess the wider applicability of my account of the language of the absurd, and specifically its relevance to poetic forms, it is useful at this stage to summarise the key stylistic and conceptual features of absurd prose fiction which have been uncovered up to this point in my study. In this section of the chapter, and in the section which follows it, I provide a survey of my central findings so far, before going on to extend the application of these ideas to the analysis of poetic texts in the latter half of the chapter.

I began the exploration of the stylistics of the absurd in Chapter 1 with a consideration of the different ways in which readers identify the absurd in literature, depending on the specific context surrounding their reading and their categorisation. The discussion focused initially on the boundary between existentialism and the absurd and on the interesting position occupied there by Albert Camus, author of the seminal *The Myth of Sisyphus* and widely acknowledged as the father of the absurd. The literary absurd was shown to be a conceptual category, like any other genre, with a radial structure which includes both central and more peripheral examples. Also as in any other genre, the conceptual boundaries around the literary absurd are neither fixed nor impermeable: countless texts and authors, Camus included, occupy several genre categories at once for a wide range of readers. Hybrids of two or more literary categories (such as vampire romance, absurdist science fiction, and tragicomedy) also exist as a common means by which readers conceptualise and label their encounters with fictional texts. I argued, as a result, that Camus's position as a key figure in more than one genre was likely to be in great part due to the relatively realistic style of his prose fiction, which has led Esslin, for example, to describe his work as bearing 'the elegantly rationalistic and discursive style of an eighteenth century moralist' (Esslin, 1980: 24). A detailed analysis of the style of Camus's novel *The Outsider* then revealed how the dominant themes of oppression and powerlessness, particularly in the face of overwhelming natural forces, are linguistically constructed in this influential text. The use of negative modal shading (see Simpson, 1993: 46–85) in *The Outsider* was seen to play a crucial role in the communication of Meursault's sense of confusion and fear, with the abundance of epistemic modality in the novel creating a multitude of enactor-accessible modal-worlds embedded within the narrative (see also Gavins, 2007: 109–25). It is through these remote text-worlds that Meursault's shifting perceptions of his reality are played out.

Chapter 1 also put forward an argument that all absurd literature can be positioned along a cline of relative stylistic experimentation, with Camus's rationalistic style closely aligned with that of the existentialists at one end of the spectrum. More avant-garde works are located at the opposite extreme of this cline, where texts and authors whose works employ more innovative styles frequently cross over into the category of postmodern fiction. As a comparison with *The Outsider*, therefore, two of Donald Barthelme's short stories, 'Some of Us Had Been Threatening Our Friend Colby' and 'The Balloon', were subjected to the same detailed stylistic analysis as Camus's novel. 'Some of Us Had Been Threatening Our Friend Colby' was first seen to deploy script opposition to humorous effect (see Attardo, 1997; Attardo and Raskin, 1991), with its lack of incongruity resolution rendering it a perfect example of Attardo's notion of 'absurd humour' (Attardo, 1997: 409; see also Attardo, 2001: 25). Interestingly, however, all three texts were then shown to exhibit a number of other linguistic similarities. Most notably, both of Barthelme's texts are characterised by the same multiple embedding of epistemic modal-worlds as seen in Camus's novel. In much the same way as *The Outsider*, these stories make use of this technique to create a sense of remote foreboding, in the case of 'Some of Us Had Been Threatening Our Friend Colby', or to communicate indeterminacy, as in 'The Balloon'. The latter of these two stories is further characterised by the oddly under-defined spatio-temporal deixis upon which its text-worlds are constructed. 'The Balloon' was also seen to employ a sudden shift from negative modal-shading to neutral modal-shading at a crucial moment in the plot in a manner identical to Camus's *The Outsider*. I argued in Chapter 2 that a full account of these kinds of stylistic family resemblances must form the basis of any advance in our understanding of the conceptual constitution of the literary absurd for a wide range of readers.

The use of shifting epistemic modality in absurd narrative and the often conflicting embedded modal-worlds which result from it were also found to be a key feature of Saul Bellow's novel *The Victim*, in Chapter 3. That chapter focused on the fictional minds constructed in absurd literature and began by examining the role played by intermental and intramental mind-modelling in absurd characterisation (see Palmer, 2002, 2004, 2005, 2007a, 2007b, 2010, 2011; and also Stockwell, 2009: 137–44; Stockwell, 2011). The increasing paranoia of Bellow's central character, Leventhal, was shown to emerge through the multitude of contradictory hypotheses he constructs in order to assess how other fictional consciousnesses, both individual and collective, evaluate him and his behaviour. I made an accompanying argument in this section of the chapter that close associations can be found between post-war Jewish identity and absurd and existential sensitivities more broadly. The chapter then moved on to examine the notion of narratorial unreliability in more detail, a device by now emerging as a key trait in absurdist narratives. My analysis of Mordecai Richler's novel *Barney's Version* once again linked the modal texture of the fiction to the overall unreliability of Barney's viewpoint. The use of fictional footnotes and the denarration and renarration of key events (see Richardson, 2006: 87–9) also acted to destabilise the main narrative in this text. On the whole, however, and in spite of numerous significant world-repairs demanded by this novel (see also Gavins, 2007: 141–5), the unreliability of Richler's narrator was shown to have a generally bonding effect (see Phelan, 2007a). By comparison, the narrator of Tom McCarthy's *Remainder* presents readers with a similarly unreliable narration, but one which has a contrastingly estranging effect. Although using many of the same narrative techniques, and denarration and renarration in particular, McCarthy's choice of a self-obsessed, callous and eventually murderous narrator ultimately discourages any ethical alignment between the reader and this character.

In Chapter 4, fluctuating modality and world-repair were once again discovered to be stylistic techniques that are centrally enabling of the explorations of the absurd effected in Rudolph Wurlitzer's *Nog*, Flann O'Brien's *The Third Policeman*, Kurt Vonnegut's *Slaughterhouse-Five* and Paul Auster's *City of Glass*. I additionally noted that the first three of these texts, along with Kazuo Ishiguro's *The Unconsoled*, exhibit similar curious distortions of the spatio-temporal parameters of their text-worlds and can in this regard be seen to bear further resemblance to Donald Barthelme's odd use of world-building, first outlined in Chapter 2. Footnoting, in O'Brien's novel, and unresolved script opposition, in Vonnegut's text, were also once more underlined as principal absurdist devices in this chapter. I then examined the combination of narrative conventions from more than one genre in *City of Glass* and in *Slaughterhouse-Five* before closing Chapter 4 with a consideration of the conceptual effects of multimodality in both these novels, as well as in Vonnegut's *Breakfast of Champions*. I argued, following Gibbons (2011), that the inclusion of drawings as an integrated component of the narrative in *Breakfast of Champions*, in particular, positions the reader in a bi-stable relationship with the text. Being made acutely aware of the material surface of the fiction in the discourse-world, while at the same time being encouraged to become immersed in its fictional text-worlds, the reader is able to oscillate attention between these two separate conceptual levels. The unifying focus of Chapter 4, then, was on the foregrounded fictionality achieved in several absurdist texts, not only through multimodal bi-stable oscillation, but also through all the other narrative techniques highlighted in this chapter.

Through the precise stylistic analyses completed over the first four chapters of this book, I have attempted to provide a clear delineation of some of the linguistic and narrative features which connect a range of prose fiction texts identified as absurd in various reading contexts. However, the present volume has sought not only to clarify the stylistic composition of such texts and their family resemblances, but also the experience of *reading* them. My approach throughout has been not solely stylistic, but *cognitive*-stylistic, and

I have attempted to illuminate readerly encounters with the literary absurd alongside my analyses of the textual configurations of this phenomenon.

Reading the absurd in prose fiction

From the outset, this book has approached reading as a culturally, historically and personally situated activity, defined and directly affected by the specific context in which it takes place. I have viewed the varying behaviours of readers as inextricably connected to the communities of practice with which those readers engage, and within which they engage in their discussions of reading. One of the most important reading communities for the present study has been that which can be broadly identified as academic literary criticism. Reading which takes places within this context has the potential to influence readings made in countless other reading communities, since its responses and interpretations have been privileged in Western societies for many decades. In Chapter 2, I outlined the expansive and rather imprecise boundaries that readers reading within an academic context have previously drawn around the literary absurd. I observed that the authors most frequently identified as absurdist within this reading situation are generally white and male, but that they nevertheless represent a sizeable spread of work across the late nineteenth, twentieth and early twenty-first centuries, with an emphasis on the post-World War II period of the twentieth century in particular. I also noted that the peripheries of this category extended much further, as far back as Greek tragedy according to some (see Cornwell, 2006: 34–5), and that numerous crossovers between the absurd and other literary genres are tangible to readers reading within this context.

At points throughout this book, I have also looked at the responses of readers discussing literature in online fora as situated within a usefully contrasting context with which to compare readings produced within an academic setting. As I pointed out in Chapter 1, although the opportunities for anonymity offered by such online discourse communities mean that it is not always possible to ascertain precisely who these readers are, it is nevertheless clear that the dynamic, immediate and informal nature of web-based discussions differs greatly from that of formal, peer-reviewed academic publishing. Crucially, the goals, motivations and discursive practices of readers within any informal reading context differ from those of readers writing academic criticism, and this holds true whether the online readers themselves are academics by occupation or not. A brief survey of a selection of online readers in Chapter 2 revealed that their notions of which authors constitute prototypical literary absurdists were, in fact, greatly similar to those of literary critics in their published accounts of the phenomenon and that the boundaries around these readers' conceptual categories of the absurd possessed the same hazy and permeable characteristics. It has also become increasingly clear as my investigations have developed that readers who regularly read and comment upon absurdist texts online value their interactions with these fictions very highly and often report accompanying profound and long-lasting emotional responses to them. In some cases, I have argued, these responses are intense enough to fit Kuiken et al.'s (2004) notions of self-modification, that is, permanently altering readers' perceptions of and beliefs about their everyday existence.

Most importantly, the force of the emotional reactions reported by readers in non-academic contexts in relation to absurd prose fiction does not appear to be diminished by the degree of stylistic experimentation exhibited by the text concerned. None of the readers commenting on their positive engagement with absurdism examined in this book report a decrease in their enjoyment of these texts as a result of innovative narrative techniques and they do not appear to have any difficulty immersing themselves in a fictional world through a text which employs stylistic experimentation. Indeed, for many, the experimental features of an absurdist text are precisely where they locate their most positive reading experiences. Of course, this is not true for *all* readers and in Chapter 4 we saw how absurd experimentation with genre-mixing can cause deep frustration for readers who approach these novels with a particular set of expectations built on previous experiences with more prototypical genre fictions. It is also worth noting that all the readers' responses examined in online literary discussion communities within this book were produced within the last ten years. Not only are readers' behaviours and opinions affected directly by their previous reading experiences, but they are similarly situated historically and culturally. Unfortunately, the necessary limits of the present study mean that a cross-cultural comparison of readers' responses to the absurd in literature remains outside my analytical focus. What is more, the earliest readers' responses accessible for analysis at this point in time are, of course, unavoidably limited to those published by literary critics and reviewers. While the reactions, for example, of much of the 1969 audience which first encountered Kurt Vonnegut's *Slaughterhouse-Five* may be lost to us, the advent of the internet has at least now allowed a wider set of twenty-first-century readings of the absurd to be considered in this book and documented for possible further examination in the future.

Reading the absurd in poetry

Across the academic contexts examined over the course of the present volume a further key pattern of reading the absurd can be identified: a markedly smaller group of readers within this community has categorised and discussed poetry in terms of its absurdist content. Where literary criticism on absurd prose fiction is abundantly available, particularly from the 1960s onwards, academic analyses which approach poetic texts as manifestations of an absurd sensitivity are comparatively scarce. Poets whose works form the subject of the rare exceptions to this rule include Stephen Crane (see Huang, 2004), T.S. Eliot (see Bagchee, 1980; Sinha, 1993), Robert Frost (see Tomlinson, 1984), Thomas Hardy (see May, 1970; Patil, 1999), Ted Hughes (see Meier, 2001), James Joyce (see Lennartz, 2010) and Wallace Stevens (see Silver, 1972). Unsurprisingly, none of these studies offers an account of the linguistic features through which the absurd might be expressed in the poems under scrutiny. It would seem, then, that poetic absurdism exists on the peripheries of the conceptual categories of the literary absurd formulated in a scholarly setting and that, much like absurd prose fiction, little clarification has been offered of its linguistic characteristics within this context. Nevertheless, absurd poetry does exist for at least some literary critics and, however eccentric or under-defined such a categorisation of poetic work may prove to be, as a form of absurdism made manifest through a reading experience, it forms an important part of the core concerns of this book. I have also attempted throughout this study to consider not only the most central examples of the literary absurd, but also those authors and texts which are positioned, for whatever reason, on the boundaries of our understanding of the phenomenon. Comprehending the outer limits of the absurd as a literary concept is an essential part of understanding the parameters within which readers' perceptions of the absurd operate.

To begin the stylistic investigation of absurd poetry with the most central member of this apparently peripheral category of literature, one of the few poets whose work is relatively frequently described by literary critics in terms of its absurdist content is Charles Simic (see, for example, Delville, 1998; Lysaker, 2001, 2002; Maio, 2005; Oakes, 2004). Simic is a Serbian-American poet and former US Poet Laureate whose work is summarised by one critic as follows:

> Behind Simic's disjunctive poetics, one finds not just a sense of the absurdity of human endeavours to make sense of the irrationality of twentieth-century history but, at least as important, a counter-determination to resist that absurdity.
>
> (Delville, 1998: 174)

Interestingly, readers in non-academic reading contexts seem far less reluctant than literary critics to approach Simic's poetry from an absurd perspective. His work is often discussed in terms very similar to those used by Delville above by a much wider range of readers on literary discussion websites. Various readers on Goodreads, for example, describe Simic's poems as 'absurdist Mix & Match', 'Narratives that blend absurdist situations and clear language ... snippets of Samuel Beckett with a sheen of Franz Kafka', and Simic himself as 'the master of the absurd and of hyper-meaning' (Goodreads, 2012c). Thus, as far as the present study is concerned, the most obvious question which arises in response to these typical evaluations of Simic's work is whether any of the linguistic features identified as characteristic of absurd prose fiction can also be found to exist in Simic's poetry. What stylistic family resemblances does Simic's work share with prose fiction that readers describe in the same way? By way of a case study, consider the following poem (from Simic, 2004a):

Dream Avenue
Monumental, millennial decrepitude,
As tragedy requires. A broad
Avenue with trash unswept,
A few solitary speck-sized figures
Going about their business
In a world already smudged by a schoolboy's eraser.

You've no idea what city this is,
What country? It could be a dream,
But is it yours? You've nothing
But a vague sense of loss,
A piercing, heart-wrenching dread
On an avenue with no name.

With a few figures conveniently small
And blurred who in any case
Have their backs to you
As they look elsewhere, beyond
The long row of gray buildings and their many windows,
Some of which appear to be broken.

The first analytical point to make about this poem is the lack of world-building detail it provides for the reader in its first two lines. The monumental decrepitude posited in the opening sentence of the text is temporally positioned (being 'millennial'), albeit rather imprecisely, but not spatially located to begin with. Constructing a mental representation of the poem is not aided much further in the rest of the first stanza, where additional world-building elements are introduced only through indefinite reference ('A broad/ Avenue', 'A few solitary speck-sized figures', 'a world', 'a schoolboy's eraser') and the lack of a main verb in the first few lines means the poem is not temporally anchored through tense. The perspective here is also a distant one, from which human beings appear small and an entire avenue can be seen, and by the end of the stanza the definition of the scene is further effaced by an imagined schoolboy's eraser. Here, Simic constructs an embedded metaphor world in which WORLD forms an input space into a blended mental representation with PICTURE. Specifically, the picture with which the avenue scene is blended is a childish one in the process of being wiped out by its creator.

Nevertheless, in terms of the ways in which attention is directed in this stanza (following Stockwell, 2009: 22–30), it is far easier for the reader to conceptualise the moving hand of a schoolboy over a page in the metaphor world than it is to form a clear mental representation of the remote unspecified figures going about unspecified business in the initial text-world.

Having established a distant viewpoint on a hazy scene of decay and loneliness in the first stanza, Simic switches to a far more intimate second-person address in the second stanza. The immediacy of this address is further enhanced by the present tense which continues in this section of the poem (in 'You've no idea' and 'You've nothing/But a vague sense of loss'). The 'You' Simic uses here is somewhat different from the generalised 'you' we saw at work in Bellow's *The Victim* in Chapter 3. It falls into the category of second-person address which Herman (1994) terms 'doubly deictic', since it acts to conflate the ordinarily separate conceptual levels of the discourse-world and the text-world. Although the line, 'You've no idea what city this is' is clearly connected to the text-world of the poem, indicated in the proximal spatial deictic 'this', the second-person pronoun also reaches into the discourse-world containing the reader of the text. Furthermore, the line can be read two ways: a fictionalised 'you' in the text-world does not know which fictional city he or she is situated in; or, the real reader of the poem does not know which real city is being described within the text. This type of second-person pronoun, Herman argues, 'functions as a cue for superimposing two or more deictic roles, one internal to the discourse situation represented in and/or through the diegesis and the other(s) external to that discourse situation' (1994: 381). In relation to narrative fiction, Herman goes on to explain:

> The novel in the second person makes of the reader a fellow player, who is suspended between a fictive world and his own real world, and who stands simultaneously inside and outside the fiction . . . In doubly deictic contexts, in other words, the audience will find itself more or less subject to conflation with the fictional self addressed by you. The deictic force of you is double; or to put it another way, the scope of the discourse context embedding the description is indeterminate, as is the domain of participants in principle specified or picked out by you.
>
> (Herman, 1994: 406)

This suggested conflation between a fictionalised self and the actual self of the reader continues throughout the latter two stanzas of Simic's text, where 'you' and 'yours' are used a further three times. In line 2 of the second stanza a conflation also occurs between the implied author and the fictionalised 'you'/ real reader. Once the double deixis of the second-person address has been established in the preceding line, 'What country?' in the eighth line of the poem also takes on multiple possible meanings. Although this coordinated clause is conjoined to 'You've no idea what city this is' through a comma in the first line of the stanza, it can also be read as a completely separate question. At this point in the text, the already semi-permeable boundary between the discourse-world and text-world is further infiltrated by the implied authorial voice of the poem: 'What country?' can be read equally plausibly as the conflated entity of the fictionalised 'you'/real reader questioning him/herself within the text-world, or as the implied author questioning the fictionalised 'you'/real reader directly across the boundary between text-world and discourse-world. Such a doubly deictic reading is further encouraged in the third line of the second stanza, where 'But is it yours?' makes a less ambiguous direct address through the ontological 'epidermis' of the text, to use McHale's term (1987: 34).

The reader's ability conclusively to situate the various address forms used in the poem in either one world or another is further impeded throughout the text by the ongoing indefiniteness of the text-world's spatial and temporal deixis. The poem continues in its creation of hazy or indistinct images to its close: the avenue has no name (and note that it remains '*an* avenue', indefinite despite having already been introduced in the first stanza of the poem), there is 'a vague sense of loss', and blurred figures who turn their backs as we struggle to conceptualise them. Indeed, even these figures' gazes are fixed on an unspecified point, somewhere far off but ultimately undefined, beyond the 'long row of gray buildings'. On the whole, there is little that is well formed enough for us to settle our attention on for very long in this text. Only 'The long row of gray buildings' is introduced into the text-world with a definite article, but even this image remains relatively dull and indistinct from the background of the text-world, according to Stockwell's (2009: 25) typology of textual attractors.

Throughout 'Dream Avenue', the repetition of the doubly deictic second-person pronoun conflates the discourse-world and the text-world, the fictionalised 'you' with the real 'you', and this double perspective is also closely aligned with that of the implied author in several places. As well as the moment at the beginning of the second stanza, identified above, where all three separate identities seem to be superimposed on one another, at the end of the poem a single use of epistemic modality once again draws the reader's point of view in the poem into complete unification with both the text-world addressee of the second-person pronoun and the implied author. Having described the 'conveniently small/And blurred' figures from his own external perspective in the first lines of the final stanza, the implied author then uses doubly deictic 'you' again to implicate the fictionalised you/real reader in the text-world at the same deictic point, witnessing these figures turn their backs 'to you'. Furthermore, the final line of the poem, 'Some of which appear to be broken', makes use of epistemic perception modality, with 'appear' referring to a seen phenomenon in order to express a particular level of epistemic commitment. It is not clear, however, which entity is seeing the possibly broken windows in the text-world: the implied author, the fictionalised 'you', or the real reader. In fact, at this point in the text all three perspectives are lined up so that the windows of the 'gray buildings' appear broken across the ontological boundaries which normally separate fictional characters from real-world discourse participants. However, the relatively weak epistemic commitment articulated by this particular modal verb also means that the scene is equally uncertain to all those who have been implicated in this shared perspective.

Following this analysis, it is possible to pick out a number of stylistic features that Simic's poem shares with the absurdist fictions examined in preceding chapters of this book and summarised in the opening of this chapter. First of all, the under-defined nature of much of the world-building in Simic's text bears resemblances to other instances of peculiar deictic configuration identified elsewhere in, for example, Rudolph Wurlitzer's *Nog*, Flann O'Brien's *The Third Policeman* and Donald Barthelme's 'The Balloon'. Of all of these, 'Dream Avenue' is perhaps most strongly reminiscent of Barthelme's short story, in which indefinite reference and deleted agency, in particular, were seen in Chapter 2 to play an important role in the overall lack of definition which is provided about the balloon, its surroundings and the people responsible for it. In the same way, the text-world created in 'Dream Avenue' remains obscure throughout the poem not only because of the indefinite references used to nominate world-building components but also as a result of the general dimness of the location as it is depicted. No individual element is sharply foregrounded against this murky background and the figure which draws the most attention in the text is the moving hand of a schoolboy, again under-specified, located in a separate metaphor world, and engaged in the act of erasing the very scene being described.

In addition to the curious deictic construction of its text-world, 'Dream Avenue' can also be seen to enact the same sorts of ontological transgressions analysed in Chapter 4 in Paul Auster's *City of Glass*, and in Kurt Vonnegut's novels *Slaughterhouse-Five* and *Breakfast of Champions*. As already discussed above, the use of doubly deictic 'you' in Simic's poem appears to conflate the text-world and the discourse-world and in so doing draws attention to the fictionality of the text. In much the same way, Auster's and Vonnegut's novels were seen to be based on an ontological trick whereby discourse-world entities appear to have access to fictional worlds, again foregrounding the fictionality of these novels as a result. However, in a manner which seems to counteract this foregrounded fictionality to some degree, Simic's poem also aligns the real reader with a fictionalised 'you', and occasionally with the implied author as well, by the same stylistic means. Not only is the reader included in the second-person address of the poem, but the simultaneous projection of a fictionalised entity this pronoun creates in the text-world means that a powerful empathetic connection is encouraged between the real reader in the discourse-world and the imagined content of the poem. Through this technique, Simic not only describes a scene of desolation, alienation and uncertainty for his readers, but leads them through a deictic and ontological illusion whereby the boundaries between worlds seem to disintegrate and they appear to experience this absurd landscape first-hand for themselves.

The stylistic family resemblances identified here between Simic's text and a range of absurdist novels are not confined to 'Dream Avenue' alone. Further linguistic analyses of other poems by the same author reveal additional similarities between the stylistic characteristics of absurd poetry and absurd prose fiction. Consider the following poem (also from Simic, 2004a), as another typical example:

Empire of Dreams
On the first page of my dreambook
It's always evening
In an occupied country.
Hour before the curfew.
A small provincial city.
The houses all dark.
The storefronts gutted.

I am on a street corner
Where I shouldn't be.
Alone and coatless
I have gone out to look
For a black dog who answers to my whistle.
I have a kind of Halloween mask
Which I am afraid to put on.

The most obvious connection between this poem and 'Dream Avenue' is the shared theme of dreaming. In conceptual terms, the fact that both poems are explicitly marked as relating to dreams, both in their titles and elsewhere, is important, since it underlines the unreality of the text-worlds they contain. In 'Empire of Dreams', this is done once in the title and then in the first line, where the reference to a 'dreambook' is made. Readers are aware from the start of the text, then, that the world being described is in some way unreal and ephemeral. The text-world here is also a compression of a multitude of other dreams, to use Fauconnier and Turner's (2003: 113–38) term, signalled in the temporal adverb 'always' in the second line of the poem. Its timeless quality is further emphasised by the deletion of main verbs from each of the last four lines of the first stanza ('Hour before the curfew./A small provincial city./The houses all dark./The storefronts gutted.'). This removes the temporal anchoring that verb tenses normally provide in discourse, giving an eternal feel to these images. The overall indefiniteness of other aspects of spatial and temporal deixis in this stanza also aids its sense of universality. The location is given first in very broad and under-specific terms as 'In an occupied country', but it remains a country unnamed and we are never told who is occupying it either. Similarly, the temporal locative 'Hour before the curfew' adds little deictic detail to the general 'evening' setting, since the precise time of the curfew itself is not specified. The spatial perspective zooms in a little in the fifth line with 'A small provincial city', but again the city remains nameless and its component parts, the houses and storefronts, are not defined beyond being dark and gutted.

The first line of the second stanza positions the implied author in the text-world with the use of the first-person pronoun 'I'. Once again, however, the corner on which he is positioned is indefinite and no further information is given about why the speaker should not be there, looking for a similarly indefinite black dog. What makes the black dog even more odd is that it answers to the implied author's whistle but he chooses not to specify it as belonging to him: it remains simply '*a* black dog', rather than *my* black dog, the obedience of which consequently does not seem to be something valued by the speaker. Simic in this way re-frames an everyday, mundane task (walking the dog in the evening) as purposeless and alienating, further emphasising the isolation of the poetic persona through the description of him as 'Alone and coatless'. The indefiniteness of the dog also encourages a reading of this reference as a metaphor for depression, particularly given the prevalence of this image in Western metaphors of mental health. In either reading, Simic displaces a commonplace and normally domestically centred activity into a city under occupation by an unnamed force with the threat of violence only an hour away. Perhaps the most chilling aspect of the poem, however, is the appearance of 'a kind of Halloween mask' in the penultimate line. Note, once again, the fuzziness of this image: it is a 'kind of' mask, not a mask. Simic also here reverses the expected function of Halloween masks so that the wearer becomes the victim, rather than the perpetrator, of the fear it instils. Crucially, the poem ends without ever specifying why the poetic persona has the mask or why he is afraid to put it on.

Although 'Empire of Dreams' does not challenge ontological boundaries in the same way as 'Dream Avenue', it does exhibit a similar use of indefinite world-building in its construction of an unsettling and estranging text-world. Once again, the oddly under-defined spatial and temporal deixis in the poem bears a particular resemblance to that examined in Donald Barthelme's short stories in Chapter 2 of this book. It is worth stressing, however, that such stylistic features are neither confined to nor wholly defining of literary absurdism in any form. Rather, they should be seen as enabling of the presentation or exploration of absurd themes within the text in which they occur. Under-specific world-building, ontological transgressions, doubly deictic 'you' and any of the other stylistic techniques examined over the course of this book may occur in countless literary forms across a multitude of genres. However, in Simic's poems, examined above, as in each of the other texts which have been subjected to stylistic analysis in preceding chapters, these techniques are specifically used to convey the experiences of an isolated and alienated individual within an absurd setting.

Stylistic family resemblances across poetic texts

It would seem, then, from just the initial exploration of the style of some
of Simic's poems above, that thematic and stylistic family resemblances do
exist between these works and a range of absurdist novels and short stories,
and that these resemblances may well be at the heart of some literary critics'
impressionistic classifications of Simic's work as absurd. Online readers, furthermore, appear to detect the absurd quality of Simic's poems much more
frequently than do literary critics. As I have already noted, however, Simic's
position within the conceptual category of absurd poetry can be seen as relatively central. To explore the validity of these provisional claims further, it
is necessary to broaden their application to more peripheral members of the
group. James Tate is another American poet whose work has been discussed
in academic reading contexts in terms of its absurdist content, including by
Charles Simic himself (see Simic, 2004b). Wright (2004) describes the development of Tate's work across his writing career as follows:

> It is as if the young poet had discovered that under the ordered, rational,
> smile-face surface of childhood lurks the Kafkaesque adult world of
> absurdity, despair and alienation. Quite logically, he had written all
> his poetry in a spirit of frustration and revenge . . . Then in mid-life he
> was suddenly broken through to 'a beautiful puissant form and a lucid
> thought': that 'serenity has triumphed in its mindless atrophied way'.
>
> Though this is a comically compromised serenity, it is nevertheless
> a state in which the poet seems to perceive that beneath the existential
> grimace, beneath the social grin, there is another cosmically beatific
> smirk on the face of the deep, that could be signalling that all is still
> meaningless and absurd, but that it is supremely okay.
>
> (Wright, 2004: 168)

This summary of Tate's key poetic concerns is one which is, once again, much
more widely and frequently echoed by readers discussing his work in the non-
academic context of online fora as well. For example, consider the following
typical reader responses to Tate's poems, from the Goodreads site again:

> [1]
> When you're going to read a James Tate book, you need to realize
> that you are entering a world of the fantastic. A surreal world where
> anything the mind can imagine, will, and does happen. A world where
> characters are capable of things not of this earth. It's a dream state that
> touches on the absurd (in a marvelous way), but all the while, hints
> towards a reality that we, as the reader, are part of in our own lives.
> By the end of a poem, we've come to realize something greater about
> ourselves, our society, and our way of life.
>
> (Eryk, 2011)

[2]

It's hard to describe the poems in this book: they are close to prose poems, haunting, folksy, and surreal, like disturbing dreams. The reason I stopped reading it is that the rhythms of his sentences got into my head and I when I put the book down (I read poetry a few poems at a sitting), I found that my thoughts were coming to me in the same rhythms. It was hard to shake off, and I didn't like the feeling at all. So the book went back to the library. A very odd experience.

(John, 2008)

These two readers give similar appraisals of the style of Tate's poems, both commenting on the surrealistic quality of the texts. However, their emotional relationships to this style differ markedly. Reader (1) refers to the innovative nature of Tate's work alongside its absurd themes, but also suggests that his own experiences with these texts have been positive (he rates the book four out of five stars) and self-modifying to some degree. He reports that, for him, Tate's poems often lead to a profound realisation which resonates beyond his initial reading of the text (for other readers' similar responses to this collection, see Goodreads, 2012d). Reader (2), by contrast, reports a strong dislike of the effect that Tate's poems had on him. These effects again appear to be long-lasting and he specifically reports a resonant impact lasting beyond the reading itself and directly altering his perceptions of his everyday world. Interestingly, although this reader states clearly that this was not a pleasant reading experience for him, he nevertheless gives the book (Tate, 2004) the same rating (four out of five stars) as reader (1).

Once again, the key question which arises from both academically and non-academically based readers' responses to Tate's poetry is whether stylistic family resemblances can be identified between it and Simic's work, and consequently between a wider collection of poetic texts and absurd prose fiction in general. In order to compare the style of Tate's poetry specifically with that of Simic to begin with, consider the following poem, taken from the same collection (*Return to the City of White Donkeys*; Tate, 2004) to which Eryk refers in his commentary above:

Red Dirt
An archeological team from a nearby university
asked my permission to dig in my backyard, and I said
no. They promised to restore my lawn to its current
state when finished, and I said no. They said the
university hadn't the money to offer me recompense, but
they personally were willing to offer me five thousand
dollars for my trouble, and I said no. I didn't hear from
them after that. They never told me why my backyard held
such interest for them. And I didn't think to ask. I could

think about nothing else for months to come. Was there an
old Mayan city down there, or Incan, Etruscan, Viking?
It could be anything. I was sitting right on it. Some
nights it was almost too much to bear. I could hear the
screams of the sacrifices. I could see the jaguar god
stoically watching on his throne of gold. How was I supposed
to sleep? I couldn't tell anybody, and I couldn't call the
police. I didn't even want people coming to the house for
fear of the harm that might come to them. My friends thought
I had taken ill, and sent me baskets of fruit. And, I suppose,
I was sick in a way. I had lost my appetite, and had grown
weak. The endless beheadings and mutilations had made me
numb. I had become a servant to the jaguar god, one of
thousands, of course, but I did get to come close enough
to him to see the serene beauty of his eyes. How could I
have ever doubted his cause. At night, I slept with the
other servants in an immense dormitory. We were as peaceful
as seraphim. When the winds blow, fine, red dirt sneaks in
and covers the floor. I dream we are being buried in it,
each day a little more. We go about our many duties, but
the dirt is inching up on us. In its way, it is beautiful,
the waves it makes, like the whistling of time. No one
mentions it. It's best this way. A peasant girl smiled
at me; then, she was gone.

The most noticeable difference between this poem and the Simic texts analysed earlier is that, like all of the poems in this particular collection by Tate,
it takes the form of a prose-poem. As such, it provides considerably more
world-building detail for the reader in its opening lines than either of Simic's
poems offer. The poetic persona describes a request made of him by a local
university to dig up his lawn, not only nominating various characters and
objects as present in the text-world in the process, but also inviting inferences
to be made about his own physical and social situation. In my own mental
representation of the poem, the poetic persona is the implied author, a textual
version of James Tate living in a large house in a middle-class neighbour-
hood of Massachusetts. The text-world I construct from the opening lines of
the poem is built not only from the world-building information provided by
the text, but on my own existing knowledge of James Tate as a poet and a
university professor at the University of Massachusetts. The depth of detail
in my text-world is thus aided to a great extent by the deictic configuration
of the first few lines of the poem (the presence of a university, an archaeological team, a backyard, a lawn, five thousand dollars and so on), while the
inferencing I perform is at the same time enabled by the indefinite references
which nevertheless predominate in the text. Because the university remains

simply 'a nearby university', for example, I am able to impose my own knowledge frames onto this referent and adapt my mental representation of it to fit
my own discourse-world assumptions. As a result, the text-world I construct
from the opening of Tate's poem is more fully defined than that I construct
of 'Dream Avenue' or 'Empire of Dreams', despite their sharing the stylistic
feature of predominantly indefinite reference.

Following the initial description of the poetic persona's interactions
with the university archaeologists, which are related chronologically in
three repeated compound sentence structures, several temporal compressions occur one after another in lines 7–10 of the poem (see Fauconnier
and Turner, 2003: 113–38). Sentences such as 'They never told me why my
backyard held/such interest for them' compress an extended and therefore
difficult to conceptualise period of time into what Fauconnier and Turner
term 'human scale' (2003: 30). Interestingly, these compressed worlds all
contain some form of syntactic negation (e.g. 'I didn't hear from/them after
that', 'They never told me'). As already noted in relation to Camus's *The
Outsider* in Chapter 2, this type of negation leads to a foregrounding of these
worlds, since their contents must first be conceptualised in order to then be
un-conceptualised (see Gavins, 2007: 102; Hidalgo Downing, 2000; Lakoff,
2004). The lack of a reason for the university team's request, then, the lack
of explanation, is particularly emphasised in the poem. Following the series
of temporal compressions, the poetic persona then posits a hypothetical
world, which takes the textual form of a rhetorical question in lines 10 and
11: 'Was there an/old Mayan city down there, or Incan, Etruscan, Viking?'
In fact, this question comprises four separate hypothetical situations, each
relating to a different imagined buried city from a different historical period.
Each hypothetical world, however, is an ontologically unrealised epistemic
modal-world, in Text World Theory terms (see Gavins, 2007: 109–25), since
the archaeological dig, we have been told, has not actually taken place and all
of the imagined scenarios remain thus unconfirmed.

In spite of this, an odd slippage from unrealised possibility to perceived
reality occurs in line 12. At this point in the poem, a further and notably
very vague epistemic modal-world is constructed with 'It could be anything'.
This is then immediately followed by an unmodalised assertion, 'I was sitting
right on it', which suddenly transforms the imagined set of remote possibilities which have been initially constructed as a series embedded modal-worlds
in the text into a concrete reality in the text-world. The precise referent to
which the pronoun 'it' refers, however, remains vague, since none of the
four imagined historical settings is singled out for particular confirmation.
Nevertheless, the transformation from imagined possibility to textual reality
then evolves further into detailed elaborations of this text-world filtered
through the physical senses of the poetic persona: 'I could *hear* the/screams
of the sacrifices. I could *see* the jaguar god/stoically watching on his throne
of gold'. On my own first reading of the poem, I understood the verb 'see'

as being used metaphorically here as an epistemic modal verb equating to 'imagine' (i.e. 'I could see in my mind's eye'). However, later developments in the poem led me, on re-reading the text, to reconceptualise this as a direct witnessing of the jaguar god taking place within the imagined buried city, which is, after all, detailed right down to the nature of his gaze. My first assumption, then, was that a literal use of 'see' was too outlandish to be the most salient interpretation. Once the rest of the poem enacts this literalisation, however, this becomes a far more plausible retrospective reading of the text.

After the initial introduction of the image of the jaguar god, the poem switches back to the matrix text-world, in which the speaker of the poem now worries about how to deal with his situation ('How was I supposed/to sleep? I couldn't tell anybody . . .'). He makes a brief reference in the process to the concerns of the intramental unit of his friends ('My friends thought/I had taken ill'). He also notes the effect of his worries on his health in the same text-world, before finally merging the text-world level completely with the remote epistemic modal-world of the imagined city. This merger is realised by the linking of cause and effect across world boundaries: 'I had lost my appetite, and had grown/weak. The endless beheadings and mutilations had made me/numb'. From this point on in the poem, the poetic persona becomes permanently located in the embedded modal-world of the imagined city: he is now literally a servant to a fully realised jaguar god and sleeps in a dormitory with thousands of other servants, rather than simply imagining the distant sounds of this fantasy underground world from his house above ground and at a separate conceptual level. Once the physical transition of the poetic persona from the text-world into the modal-world is complete, he appears more calm, commenting that he and his fellow servants sleep 'as peaceful/as seraphim'. Following this, there is an odd shift in tense, from the simple-past tense used in most of the rest of the poem to the simple-present tense which predominates in the final lines (e.g. 'red dirt sneaks in', 'I dream', 'We go about our many duties'). The effect of this is a kind of conceptual zooming in, by which the embedded modal-world in which the speaker of the poem is now located, once remote and unrealised, now becomes yet more foregrounded and immediate (see also Damsteegt, 2005).

A final merging of worlds occurs when the poetic persona creates a further embedded epistemic modal-world through his report of a dream. Having described the red dirt which covers the floor of the dormitory when the wind blows, he states, 'I dream we are being buried in it,/each day a little more. We go about our many duties, but/the dirt is inching up on us'. In this sequence, it is difficult to delineate the different worlds being created. Although it is easy to discern the initial dream-world that is explicitly constructed with 'I dream', it is not clear at what point this world switches back to its matrix world: there is some ambiguity whether the servants are going about their many duties in the dream-world or in the world in which this dream originated. Once again, the boundaries between different conceptual levels seem to disintegrate in the poem so that the speaker's dreamt fear of being buried in the red dirt appears to be being realised in the scene in the dormitory.

The final linguistically explicit deictic shift between worlds in the poem comes in the closing two lines, when the tense of the text switches once again, this time from the present tense back to the simple past. However, the temporal switch here does not appear to be one which takes the reader back to the text-world which began the poem and which also had a simple-past temporal signature. The final two lines of the text refer to 'a peasant girl', but it is not easy to locate this girl in the same text-world containing the university archaeologists and (in the case of my own reading) the lawns of middle-class suburban Massachusetts. No mention of a girl was made in the opening lines of the poem and the description of her as 'a peasant' does not seem to fit with any of the other world-building elements of that text-world, nor with the wider inferences drawn from them. The poem's final tense switch, then, is highly disorienting, as a referent which seems more in keeping with the embedded modal-worlds of the ancient buried city appears to have been dislocated into a yet another, different but unclear, spatio-temporal location. There is even a further world-switch suggested, but not made fully explicit, in the final line of the poem. The temporal adverbial in 'then, she was gone' is again ambiguous: it could be being used here in its narrative function, chronologically ordering the girl's smile and her departure in the text-world; alternatively, 'then' could be read as signalling a deictic shift into a past world. The latter of these two possible interpretations is further encouraged by the separation of the two clauses of the sentence with a semi-colon, which isolates the girl's disappearance from the report of her smiling graphologically as well as syntactically.

Despite its contrasting prose-poem form, James Tate's 'Red Dirt' shares a number of stylistic family resemblances both with Charles Simic's poems and with many of the absurd prose fiction texts examined over the course of this book. Most notable among these is the poem's manipulation of temporal and spatial deixis to break down the ontological boundaries between the worlds it contains and to blur the distinctions between reality, fantasy and dreams. The poetic persona composes multiple embedded epistemic modal-worlds, through which his fears and suppositions are enacted, before himself slipping between their borders, literalising the metaphorical and subtly transforming imagined possibilities into concrete actuality. Several ambiguities remain unresolved and unexplained throughout the poem, as do the foregrounded motivations of the archaeological team who initiate the whole disorienting sequence of events. Even as the poem shifts away from the imagined-turned-realised worlds of the buried ancient city in the final lines, the promise of a meaningful connection offered in the peasant girl's smile, like all the other nebulous worlds created in the poem, is never verified. The reader is left only with her ghostly and dislocated lacuna (to use the terms of Stockwell, 2009: 31–5) at the poem's close.

Towards a stylistics of absurd poetry

Through the stylistic case studies presented so far in this chapter, it has become apparent that several points of linguistic commonality can be identified in poetic works that have been classified and discussed as absurd by a relatively limited number of literary critics, but by a greater community of online readers. At this point in the chapter and in the present volume as a whole, I would therefore like to venture a possible explanation for the comparative paucity of literary criticism that has dealt with the absurd as a poetic phenomenon. Readers responding to poetry in non-academic, informal, online environments appear to have little trouble identifying an absurdist quality to certain poetic texts and each of the poems examined above has been branded by a significant number of these readers as fundamentally absurd. However, the nature of the discursive community in which these readers communicate about their literary experiences is such that they are not compelled to offer analytical support for their intuitive responses to literature. In this regard, then, these readers can also be seen to be risking relatively little when volunteering their interpretations of poetry, or of any other literary text, and to be more pioneering in these interpretations as a result. Literary critics, by contrast, share their textual interpretations under a far more exacting set of discoursal expectations and must be prepared to corroborate their responses to literature with textual, historical or cultural evidence for their claims. In the case of prose fiction, literary critics have apparently drawn particular confidence for their interpretations of texts as absurd from Esslin's (1965, 1980) enormously influential accounts of absurd drama which, as I noted in Chapter 2, were grounded in at least a partial account of style. A subsequent critical mass of applications of Esslin's ideas to a broader range of text types also seems to have provided the additional weight needed to support and perpetuate interpretations of some prose as essentially absurdist. However, as I have pointed out at various points throughout this book, these same literary critics have lacked the necessary linguistic terminology and analytical skills to add a systematic and rigorous account of style to their readings of the absurd. This technical deficiency in turn seems to have held the majority of critics back from extending the boundaries of absurd criticism beyond prose and drama and into poetry.

By contrast, having now established a clear set of stylistic family resemblances shared between a significant sample of absurd prose fiction and poetic texts, I am confident in broadening the boundaries of the absurd to encompass a wider range of poetry than has previously been examined in these terms in an academic context. To demonstrate the potential of such an augmentation of the academic concept of the literary absurd, I would like to turn to the work of Ted Hughes, a poet who has recently been described as 'represent[ing] "the author" in an unusually heightened state of negotiation' (Hibbett, 2005: 416). Hibbett goes on to explain that Hughes's relatively recent death and his complex personal life have inevitably led to his identity as a poet, and perhaps as a poetic icon, being subject to much current debate. Hibbett also argues that Hughes's name is itself 'an extraordinarily loaded sign, the meaning of which will vary depending on the knowledge one brings to it' (2005: 414). Other studies of Hughes do exist in which readings of the existential content of his poetry are put forward (see, for example, Davis, 2004; Gifford, 2009; Grealish, 1972; Robinson, 1989), but previous critics have on the whole stopped short of linking Hughes's philosophical concerns with his poetic style and developing this reading into an identification of absurdity in his work (for an exception, see Meier, 2001). A more thorough investigation of the stylistic characteristics of Hughes's poetry, however, reveals that many of the existential moments in his texts are enabled by or at least closely connected to linguistic features which have been identified as characteristic of absurd literary texture over the course of this book.

Consider, for example, the following poem by Ted Hughes (from Hughes, 2003: 262–3), originally published in the collection *Crow Wakes* in 1971:

Bedtime Anecdote
There was a man
Who got up from a bed that was no bed
Who pulled on his clothes that were no clothes
(A million years whistling in his ear)
And he pulled on shoes that were no shoes
Carefully jerking the laces tight – and tighter
To walk over floors that were no floor
Down stairs that were no stairs
Past pictures that were no pictures
To pause
To remember and forget the night's dreams that were no dreams

And there was the cloud, primeval, the prophet;
There was the rain, its secret writing, the water-kernel
Of the tables of the sun;
And there was the light and its loose rant;
There were the birch trees, insisting and urging.
And the wind reproach upon reproach.
At the table he cupped his hands
As if to say grace

Avoiding his reflection in the mirror
Huddled to read news that was no news
(A million years revolving on his stomach)
He entered the circulation of his life
But stopped reading feeling the weight of his hand
In the hand that was no hand

And he did not know what to do or where to begin
To live the day that was no day

And Brighton was a picture
The British Museum was a picture
The battleship off Flamborough was a picture
And the drum-music the ice in the glass the mouths
Stretched open in laughter
That was no laughter
Were what was left of a picture

In a book
Under a monsoon downpour
In a ruinous mountain hut

From which years ago his body was lifted by a leopard.

Hughes's text opens with two indefinite references, the first to 'a man' and the second to 'a bed'. In world-building terms, since little other detail about the spatial or temporal parameters of the text-world is provided at this stage, these terms can be conceptualised only with reference to existing knowledge frames and, as a result, they lack specificity and definition. In any case, Hughes immediately complicates conceptualisation of the poem further by beginning a pattern of repeated denarration which continues throughout the rest of the text. Having nominated 'a bed' as present in the text-world in line 2, for example, he instantly qualifies this nomination with 'that was no bed', revoking the mental representation the reader has just constructed for this world-building element. The world-repair that this and all the other denarrations in the text demand is also characterised by the fact that no subsequent information is provided as to what the denarrated items are if they are not what they were initially nominated to be. With the bed in the second line, for example, we are not told what it is if 'it was no bed', but are instead left to infer a new or restructured mental representation without further guidance from the text. In my own reading of the poem, for example, I inferred that some of the defining characteristics of the bed must be missing, rather than that the bed did not exist at all. In my text-world of the poem, then, the man gets up from a bed which has given him no rest, but the bed itself remains present, if somewhat indistinct, in my mental representation. Similarly, the man's clothes offer him no comfort or warmth, although he does still put them on, and his shoes offer no stability or protection.

In this way, the text-world of 'Bedtime Anecdote' contains all of the world-building elements Hughes originally nominates but the core functions of which seem not to be behaving as one would ordinarily expect. Even the title of the poem enacts a slight shift of expectations from 'Bedtime Story' to 'Bedtime Anecdote'. The floor that the man walks on thus becomes unstable once the text-world is fleshed out by discourse-world inferencing; the stairs are similarly precarious and the pictures on the walls are drab and unappealing. Interestingly, half of the world-building components introduced into the text-world in the first stanza lack a pre-modifying article: though 'a man', 'a bed', 'the laces' and 'the night's dreams' are deictically anchored in this way, 'shoes', 'floors', 'stairs' and 'pictures' are given no definite, indefinite or possessive quality. This pattern shifts in the second stanza, where the definite article is used consistently to introduce world-building elements for the first time (e.g. 'the cloud, 'the prophet', 'the rain' and so on). However, it remains ambiguous where these items are located and what spatial, temporal and ontological relationships they have with the man in the poem. The last line of the first stanza, 'To remember and forget the night's dreams that were no dreams', is conjoined to the first line of the second stanza with 'And', which suggests that the cloud, the prophet, the rain and so on are all elements of the dreams being remembered and forgotten. Some of these elements also have distinctly dream-like qualities. For example, there is an odd compounding in 'the water-kernel' of individually easy to conceptualise items which when combined become far more difficult to visualise. The run-on into the next line here reveals that 'the water-kernel' is actually furthermore 'Of the tables of the sun', a highly abstract metaphor again composed of familiar physical items which lose their definition through their blending. The personification of other natural elements, such as the ranting light and the insisting and urging birch trees, add to the dreaminess of this section of the poem.

The boundary between the dreamed components of the text and the world in which they are being recollected and forgotten by the man is not at all clear. In my own first reading of the poem, I inferred that the spatial deixis of the prepositional phrase 'At the table' in the penultimate line of the second stanza signalled a shift out of the dream-world. However, the fact that a table is not nominated in the main text-world of the poem in the first stanza, but one *is* present in the dream-world in 'the tables of the sun', makes this inference questionable and the shift between worlds not fully defined to begin with. As the third stanza progresses and a similar pattern of repeated denarration to that established in the first stanza emerges, it becomes clearer, although through a kind of slow diffusion, that this stanza relates to the main text-world and not a separate world of recollected dreams. Once again, world-building elements are introduced one by one in this section of the poem only to be immediately denarrated and reconceptualised as somehow dysfunctional (e.g. 'news that was no news', 'the hand that was no hand', 'the day that was no day'). In this stanza, however, the man appears to experience a moment of heightened existential realisation, as he stops reading and acutely feels the weight of his own hand. This moment is given an added sense of universality by the description of the man's life as a 'circulation', a term which plays both on the image of rotation in '(A million years revolving on his stomach)' and on the semantic field of newspapers and reading which is prevalent throughout this stanza. The man's complete lack of motivation, his inertia in the face of his own existential potential, is particularly foregrounded through the use of negation, as an epistemic modal-world is created in negative form in 'he did not know what to do or where to begin'.

The repeated references to pictures in the fourth stanza return attention to the 'pictures that were no pictures' which first figured in the poem's opening lines, bringing greater definition to these initially vacant frames. The gaps are now filled, but with clichéd picture-postcard scenes of Brighton, the British Museum and the battle of Flamborough Head, arguably images themselves so hackneyed as to be empty of meaning, presented in a monotonous syntactic structure ('And Brighton was a picture/The British Museum was a picture/The battleship off Flamborough was a picture'). An odd conjunction occurs here too between the timeworn illustrations and 'the drum-music the ice in the glass the mouths', where the lack of punctuation makes this series of figures difficult to delineate. Again, Hughes uses denarration in these lines to complicate comprehension further, as it becomes apparent that the mouths stretched open in laughter (denarrated again in 'that was no laughter'), the drum-music and the ice in the glass all belong to a separate picture which appears to be in tatters ('what was left of a picture'). Once again, Hughes uses a prepositional phrase, 'In a book', in the first line of the fifth stanza to suggest some sort of shift in worlds. However, this is immediately followed in the next line by another prepositional phrase, 'Under a monsoon downpour', which makes the location, extent and end-point of the first apparent deictic shift ambiguous. It is unclear in these closing lines whether the drum-music, the ice in the glass and the stretched mouths are part of a picture which also depicts a monsoon downpour and a ruinous mountain hut, or whether the book in which all these elements appear is located under a monsoon downpour in a ruinous hut. In either case, the shift from the humdrum English images (Brighton, the British Museum, Flamborough Head) to an apparently South East Asian context is marked. The final line of the poem, which is fragmented from the rest of the text, does little to resolve the ambiguity, as it is unclear here, too, to whom the possessive pronoun in 'his body' refers. Furthermore, the tropical scene which ends the poem, complete with leopard, seems to echo the images of nature and the 'primeval' cloud and rain which defined the earlier dream section of the text. By its close, then, the poem has blurred each transition in turn from reality to remembered dream, from remembered dream back to reality, from reality to perceived image, and from image to dream again.

Hughes's poem, then, is not one which expresses straightforwardly existential concerns through a rationalistic style, but one which makes use of surrealistic imagery and blurred spatio-temporal and ontological boundaries to create a sense of altered perception and of helpless inertia. In much the same way as Tate and Simic, Hughes creates permeable and often indistinguishable borders between worlds, between dreams and reality, imagination and perception, and manipulates the deictic configuration of the text-worlds of 'Bedtime Anecdote' to disorienting effect. Hughes's use of denarration is particularly noteworthy here, not just for its obvious parallels with some of the absurd narratives analysed in Chapter 4 of this book, but for the fact that it does not enable world-repair in the same way as these prose fictional texts were seen to do. No reimagining of the text-world is encouraged or assisted through the text of Hughes's poem, no resolution of its ambiguities. Rather, key world-building elements remain denarrated but still present, persistent and perceivable in their core dysfunction, poetic figures that are no figures.

The literary absurd, so far

I have, of course, chosen an absurd interpretation of Ted Hughes as a deliberately provocative note on which to end this book. As Scigaj puts it, 'So much is stitched into the torn richness of Hughes's verse' (1992: 33), and we have already seen Hibbett, too, argue that readings of his work 'vary depending on the knowledge one brings to it' (2005: 414). My own interpretation of 'Bedtime Anecdote' is indeed very much defined by its personal, cognitive and disciplinary situatedness. I am an avid reader of absurd literature and a committed and cognitively focused stylistician, all of which influences how I read and analyse texts of all kinds. However, what I have attempted to demonstrate throughout this book is that I am no different from any other reader in any other reading context in this respect. I see absurdism everywhere – in poetry and in prose, in drama, television and film – and this is greatly the result of the predisposition to absurd reading which I have developed and refined over years of interaction with these particular kinds of texts. I seek absurdism out, because I enjoy the reading experience it offers me, and the more I seek it, the more I find it, and the more I am led to seek it again. Crucially, though, this is how *all* readers read, regardless of the individual situation of their reading; all readings are directly affected by the motivations, the pre-conceived ideas and the literary appetites of those who produce them. We have seen time and again throughout this volume how readers, in various contexts, bring their previous experiences and expectations to bear on the texts with which they interact. We have also seen, however, that patterns of reading, common reactions, interpretations and perceptions, are plainly identifiable within particular communities of practice. It is these patterns of shared experience that shape our notions of literary genre, but they are only one side of the story: what is indispensable in the pursuit of a better understanding of how readers identify, categorise and discuss literary texts is a systematic and transparent explanation of how those texts are structured and how they function.

As I have emphasised at points throughout this book, my aim here has not been to present an encyclopaedic account of the literary absurd. I have instead outlined and put into initial practice a replicable analytical means through which the absurd in literature may be described linguistically and understood in context. The model of the stylistic characteristics of absurd prose fiction and poetry formulated over the preceding chapters provides an emerging, but not yet fully tested, template against which the absurdity of texts not examined in this book may be measured in future investigations. Within these pages, this template has facilitated a clearer understanding of the linguistic family resemblances which unify the diverse texts which, in one context or another, have been categorised as absurd over the last century. It has also enabled a richer appreciation of the stylistic means through which various authors have fulfilled Camus's original appeal for an absurd creativity which embodies 'revolt, freedom and diversity' (Camus, 1975: 106). Far more remains to be done, of course, particularly in order to advance further the account of the stylistics of the poetic absurd offered for the first time in these pages. However, what has already been achieved is a systematic description of the textual characteristics which underpin a significant body of absurd literature and which govern the prototypical positioning of particular texts and authors in readers' conceptualisations of this category of experience. Through this, it is now possible to assess in a disciplined way and through precise explanation the relative centrality or peripherality of particular works within the genre of the literary absurd.

Most importantly, the present volume has approached the literary absurd as an experiential phenomenon inextricably situated in specific reading and writing contexts which play a direct role in shaping our perceptions of the absurd. I have attempted to account not only for the language through which the absurd is enacted in literature but also for the conceptual structures which arise from these linguistic enactments. I have based my arguments not only on my own introspective interactions with absurd texts but also on the reported experiences of other academics and of a far broader community of readers situated in non-academic reading contexts. By observing and analysing the habitual reading practices of readers in such unmanipulated environments it has been possible to reach an understanding of the absurd as a literary phenomenon with which many readers experience long-lasting and profound emotional interactions. Significantly, it has become apparent over the course of this study that the experimental nature of many absurd texts does not constitute a barrier to the majority of readers' immersion in and enjoyment of this form of literature. Rather, readers of the literary absurd in the twenty-first century have shown themselves to be, in the main, accepting of stylistic innovation, frequently locating their most positive reading experiences with experimental elements of absurd texts. In this way, such readers can be seen also to embody Camus's call for 'revolt, freedom and diversity' (Camus, 1975: 106) in their celebratory and adventurous readings of the absurd.

References

Aarons, V. (2011) 'American Jewish fiction'. In: J.N. Duvall (ed.), *The Cambridge Companion to American Fiction After 1945*. Cambridge: Cambridge University Press, 129–41.

Alber, J. (2009) 'Impossible storyworlds and what to do with them'. *StoryWorlds: A Journal of Narrative Studies*, 1: 79–96.

Alber, J., Skov Nielsen, H. and Richardson, B. (2012) 'Unnatural voices, minds, and narration'. *The Routledge Companion to Experimental Literature*. London: Routledge, 351–67.

Alford, S.E. (1995a) 'Mirrors of madness: Paul Auster's *The New York Trilogy*'. *Critique: Studies in Contemporary Fiction*, 37(1): 17–33.

Alford, S.E. (1995b) 'Spaced-out: signification and space in Paul Auster's *The New York Trilogy*'. *Contemporary Literature*, 36(4): 613.

Allington, D. (2011) '"It actually painted a picture of the village and the sea and the bottom of the sea": reading groups, cultural legitimacy, and description in narrative (with particular reference to John Steinbeck's *The Pearl*)'. *Language and Literature*, 20(4): 317–32.

Allington, D. (2012) 'Private experience, textual analysis, and institutional authority: the discursive practice of critical interpretation and its enactment in literary training'. *Language and Literature*, 21(2): 211–25.

Allington, D. and Swann, J. (2009) 'Researching literary reading as social practice'. *Language and Literature*, 18(3): 219–30.

Amazon (2012) *The Outsider* by Albert Camus. Available via http://www.amazon.co.uk

Andringa, E. (1996) 'Effects of "narrative distance" on readers' emotional involvement and response'. *Poetics*, 23(6): 431–52.

Antor, H. (2005) 'Postcolonial laughter in Canada: Mordecai Richler's *The Incomparable Atuk*'. In: S. Reichl and M. Stein (eds), *Cheeky Fictions: Laughter and the Postcolonial*. Amsterdam: Rodopi, 89–106.

Apperly, I. (2011) *Mindreaders: The Cognitive Basis of 'Theory of Mind'*. Hove: Psychology Press.

Aronson, R. (2004) *Camus and Sartre: The Story of a Friendship and the Quarrel That Ended It*. Chicago: University of Chicago Press.

Attardo, S. (1997) 'The semantic foundations of cognitive theories of humor'. *Humor*, 10(4): 395–420.

Attardo, S. (2001) *Humorous Texts: A Semantic and Pragmatic Analysis*. Berlin: Walter de Gruyter.

Attardo, S. and Raskin, V. (1991) 'Script theory revis(it)ed: joke similarity and joke representation model'. *Humor*, 4(3–4): 293–347.

Auster, P. (1988) *The New York Trilogy*. London: Faber and Faber.

Bagchee, S. (1980) '"Prufrock": an absurdist view of the poem'. *English Studies in Canada*, 6: 430–43.

Baker, B. (2006) *Masculinity in Fiction and Film: Representing Men in Popular Genres, 1945–2000*. London: Continuum International Publishing Group.

Baker, R.E. (1993) *The Dynamics of the Absurd in the Existentialist Novel*. New York: Peter Lang.

Balogun, F.O. (1984) 'Characteristics of absurdist African literature: Taban lo Liyong's *Fixions* – a study in the absurd'. *African Studies Review*, 27(1): 41–55.

Barge, L. (1977) '"Coloured Images" in the "black dark": Samuel Beckett's later fiction'. *PMLA*, 92(2): 273–84.

Barnes, H.E. (1962) *Humanistic Existentialism: The Literature of Possibility*. Lincoln, NE: University of Nebraska Press.

Baron-Cohen, S. (1995) *Mindblindness: An Essay on Autism and Theory of Mind*. Cambridge, MA: MIT Press.

Barsalou, L.W. (1985) 'Ideals, central tendency, and frequency of instantiation as determinants of graded structure in categories'. *Journal of Experimental Psychology: Learning, Memory, and Cognition*, 11: 629–54.

Barsalou, L.W. (2003) 'Situated simulation in the human conceptual system'. *Language and Cognitive Processes*, 18(5–6): 513–62.

Barsalou, L.W. (2009) 'Simulation, situated conceptualization, and prediction'. *Philosophical Transactions of the Royal Society of London, Series B: Biological Sciences*, 364(1521): 1281–9.

Barsalou, L.W., Huttenlocher, J. and Lamberts, K. (1998) 'Basing categorization on individuals and events'. *Cognitive Psychology*, 36(3): 203–72.

Barsalou, L.W., Solomon, K.O. and Wu, L-L. (1999) 'Perceptual simulation in conceptual tasks'. In: M.K. Hiraga, C. Sinha and S. Wilcox (eds), *Cultural, Psychological and Typological Issues in Cognitive Linguistics*. Amsterdam: John Benjamins, 209–28.

Barta, S. (1999) 'The comedy of the tragic: anticipations of the Theatre of the Absurd in William Butler Yeats's *The Death of Cuchulain*'. *AnaChronist*, 5: 137–49.

Barth, J. (1958) *The End of the Road*. New York: Doubleday.

Barthelme, D. (1982) *Sixty Stories*. New York: G.P. Putnam and Sons.

Barthelme, D. (1989) *Forty Stories*. Harmondsworth: Penguin.

Bartley, P. (2009) 'Book tagging on LibraryThing: how, why, and what are in the tags?' *Proceedings of the American Society for Information Science and Technology*, 46(1): 1–22.

Bates, J. and Rowley, J. (2011) 'Social reproduction and exclusion in subject indexing: a comparison of public library OPACs and LibraryThing folksonomy'. *Journal of Documentation*, 67(3): 431–48.

Bell, A. (2007) '"Do you want to hear about it?" Exploring possible worlds in Michael Joyce's hyperfiction, *afternoon, a story*'. In: P. Stockwell and M. Lambrou (eds), *Contemporary Stylistics*. London: Continuum, 43–55.

Bellow, S. (2008) *The Victim*. Harmondsworth: Penguin.

Belmonte, M.K. (2008) 'Does the experimental scientist have a "Theory of Mind"'. *Review of General Psychology*, 12(2): 192–204.

Bennett, M.Y. (2011) *Reassessing the Theatre of the Absurd*. Basingstoke: Palgrave Macmillan.

Berge, A.M.K. (2005) 'The narrated self and characterization: Paul Auster's literary personae'. *Nordic Journal of English Studies*, 4(1): 101–20.

Berkenkotter, C. and Huckin, T.N. (1993) 'Rethinking genre from a sociocognitive perspective'. *Written Communication*, 10(4): 475–509.

Berry, M. (1977) *An Introduction to Systemic Linguistics*. London: Batsford.

Bersani, L. (1970) '*The Stranger*'s secrets'. *NOVEL: A Forum on Fiction*, 3(3): 212–24.

Booker, M.K. (1991) 'Science, philosophy, and *The Third Policeman*: Flann O'Brien and the epistemology of futility'. *South Atlantic Review*, 56(4): 37–56.

Bortolussi, M. and Dixon, P. (2003) *Psychonarratology: Foundations for the Empirical Study of Literary Response*. Cambridge: Cambridge University Press.

Bowen, J. (1971) 'Alienation and withdrawal are not the absurd: renunciation and preference in "Bartleby the Scrivener"'. *Studies in Fiction*, 8: 633–5.

Braun, L. (1974) *Witness of Decline: Albert Camus, Moralist of the Absurd*. Madison: Fairleigh Dickinson University Press.

Bray, J. (2007) 'The "dual voice" of free indirect discourse: a reading experiment'. *Language and Literature*, 16(1): 37–52.

Bray, J., Gibbons, A. and McHale, B. (2012) 'Introduction'. In: J. Bray, A. Gibbons and B. McHale (eds), *The Routledge Companion to Experimental Literature*. London: Routledge, 1–18.

Briggs, R. (2003) 'Wrong numbers: the endless fiction of Auster and Deleuze and Guattari and . . .' *Critique: Studies in Contemporary Fiction*, 44(2): 213–24.

Brittany S. (2012) *Slaughterhouse-Five* by Kurt Vonnegut. Available at http://www.shelfari.com/books/11877/Slaughterhouse-Five/reviews?sort=3&Page=93.

Britton, C. (2010) 'How does Meursault get arrested?' *French Studies Bulletin*, 31(114): 1–3.

Brod, H. and Kaufman, M. (1994) *Theorizing Masculinities*. London: Sage.

Brodwin, S. (1972) 'The humor of the absurd: Mark Twain's Adamic diaries'. *Criticism: A Quarterly for Literature and the Arts*, 14: 49–64.

Brombert, V. (1948) 'Camus and the novel of the "absurd"'. *Yale French Studies*, 1: 119–23.

Brône, G. and Vandaele, J. (eds) (2009) *Cognitive Poetics: Goals, Gains and Gaps*. Berlin: Walter de Gruyter.

Brothers, B.H. (1977) 'Henry Green: time and the absurd'. *boundary 2*, 5(3): 863–76.

Burton, D. (1980) *Dialogue and Discourse: A Sociolinguistic Approach to Modern Drama Dialogue and Naturally Occurring Conversation*. London: Routledge and Kegan Paul.

Camus, A. (1942) *L'Etranger*. Paris: Gallimard.

Camus, A. (1956) *The Rebel*. New York: Alfred Knopf.

Camus, A. (1975) *The Myth of Sisyphus*. London: Penguin.

Camus, A. (1982) *The Outsider*. Harmondsworth: Penguin.

Carroll, D. (2007) 'Rethinking the absurd: *Le Mythe de Sisyphe*'. In: E.J. Hughes (ed.), *The Cambridge Companion to Camus*. Cambridge: Cambridge University Press, 53–66.

Carruthers, P. (2000) 'The evolution of consciousness'. In: P. Carruthers and
  A. Chamberlain (eds), *Evolution and the Human Mind: Modularity, Language and
  Meta-Cognition*. Cambridge: Cambridge University Press, 254–75.
Carruthers, P. and Smith, P.K. (1996) *Theories of Theories of Mind*. Cambridge:
  Cambridge University Press.
Christensen, N. (1962) '*L'Etranger*: the unheroic hero'. *College English*, 24(3):
  235–6.
Christopher H (2010) *The New York Trilogy* by Paul Auster. Available at http://www.
  shelfari.com/books/11902/The-New-York-Trilogy/reviews?sort=3&Page=11.
Clissmann, A. and Clune, A. (1975) *Flann O'Brien: A Critical Introduction to His
  Writings*. London: Gill and Macmillan.
Cohen, S.B. (1981) 'The comedy of urban low life: from Saul Bellow to Mordecai
  Richler'. *Thalia: Studies in Literary Humour*, 4(2): 21–4.
Cooper, D.E. (1990) *Existentialism: A Reconstruction*. Oxford: Basil Blackwell.
Corfariu M and Rovenţa-Frumuşani D (1984) 'Absurd dialogue and speech acts –
  Beckett's *En Attendant Godot*'. *Poetics*, 13(1–2): 119–33.
Cornwell, N. (ed.) (1991a) *Daniil Kharms and the Poetics of the Absurd*. London:
  Macmillan.
Cornwell, N. (1991b) 'Daniil Kharms, black miniaturist'. In: N. Cornwell (ed.), *Daniil
  Kharms and the Poetics of the Absurd*. London: Macmillan, 3–21.
Cornwell, N. (2006) *The Absurd in Literature*. Manchester: Manchester University
  Press.
Craniford, A. (2006) *Mordecai Richler: A Life in Ten Novels*. Lincoln, NE: iUni-
  verse.
Cronshaw, R. (2001) 'Blacking out holocaust memory in Saul Bellow's *The Victim*'.
  Saul Bellow Journal, 16(2): 215–52.
cura (2012) *The Stranger* by Albert Camus. Available at http://www.shelfari.com/
  books/18660/The-Stranger/discussions.
Cuthbertson, G. (1974) 'Freedom, absurdity, and destruction: the political theory of
  Conrad's *A Set of Six*'. *Conradiana: A Journal of Joseph Conrad*, 6: 46–52.
Damsteegt, T. (2005) 'The present tense and internal focalization of awareness'.
  Poetics Today, 26(1): 39–78.
Darling, M.E. (ed.) (1986) *Perspectives on Mordecai Richler*. Toronto: ECW Press.
Davis, A. (2004) 'Romanticism, existentialism, patriarchy: Hughes and the vision-
  ary imagination'. In: K. Sagar (ed.), *The Challenge of Ted Hughes*. Basingstoke:
  Macmillan, 70–90.
Davis, C. (2003) 'The cost of being ethical: fiction, violence, and altericide'. *Common
  Knowledge*, 9(2): 241–53.
Davis, C. (2007) 'Violence and ethics in Camus'. In: E.J. Hughes (ed.), *The Cambridge
  Companion to Camus*. Cambridge: Cambridge University Press, 106–17.
DekeDastardly (2011) Review: *The Third Policeman* by Flann O'Brien. Available at
  http://www.librarything.com/work/7104.
Delville, M. (1998) *The American Prose Poem: Poetic Form and the Boundaries of
  Genre*. Gainesville: University Press of Florida.
Derksen, C. (2002) 'A feminist absurd: Margaret Hollingsworth's *The House that
  Jack Built*'. *Modern Drama*, 45(2): 209–30.
Dicul (2006) *The New York Trilogy* by Paul Auster. Available at http://www.shelfari.
  com/books/11902/The-New-York-Trilogy/reviews?sort=3&Page=10.

Dimovitz, S.A. (2006) 'Public personae and the private I: de-compositional ontology in Paul Auster's *The New York Trilogy*'. *MFS Modern Fiction Studies*, 52(3): 613–33.

Doherty, F. (1989) 'Flann O'Brien's existentialist hell'. *Canadian Journal of Irish Studies*, 15(2): 51–67.

Ebert, T. (1991) 'Postmodern politics, patriarchy, and Donald Barthelme'. *The Review of Contemporary Fiction*, 11(1): 75–82.

Ebewo, P. (2008) '*Holding Talks*: Ola Rotimi and the Theatre of the Absurd'. *Marang: Journal of Language and Literature*, 18(1): 153–60.

Eckert, P. (2000) *Linguistic Variation as Social Practice: The Linguistic Construction of Identity in Belten High*. Oxford: Blackwell.

Eckert, P. and McConnell-Ginet, S. (1992) 'Think practically and look locally: language and gender as community-based practice'. *Annual Review of Anthropology*, 21: 461–90.

Ehrmann, J. (1960) 'Camus and the existentialist adventure'. *Yale French Studies*, 25: 93–7.

Emmott, C. (1997) *Narrative Comprehension*. Oxford: Oxford University Press.

Emmott, C., Sanford, A.J. and Morrow, L.I. (2006) 'Capturing the attention of readers? Stylistic and psychological perspectives on the use and effect of text fragmentation in narratives'. *Journal of Literary Semantics*, 35(1): 1–30.

Emmott, C., Sanford, A. and Dawydiak, E. (2007) 'Stylistics meets cognitive science: studying style in fiction and readers' attention from an interdisciplinary perspective'. *Style* (special issue on style in fiction), 41(2): 204–26.

Emmott, C., Sanford, A. and Alexander, M. (2010) 'Scenarios, characters' roles and plot status: readers' assumptions and writers' manipulations of assumptions in narrative texts'. In: J. Eder, F. Jannidis and R. Schneider (eds), *Characters in Fictional Worlds: Understanding Imaginary Beings in Literature, Film and Other Media*. Berlin: De Gruyter, 377–99.

Erika M (2012) *Slaughterhouse-Five* by Kurt Vonnegut. Available at http://www.shelfari.com/books/11877/Slaughterhouse-Five/reviews?sort=3&Page=97.

Eryk (2011) A review of *Return to the City of White Donkeys*. Available at http://www.goodreads.com/review/show/121044574.

Esslin, M. (1965) *Absurd Drama*. Harmondsworth: Penguin Books.

Esslin, M. (1980) *The Theatre of the Absurd*. London: Penguin.

Fauconnier, G. and Turner, M. (2003) *The Way We Think: Conceptual Blending and the Mind's Hidden Complexities*. New York: Basic Books.

Ferrebe, A. (2006) *Masculinity in Male-Authored Fiction, 1950–2000: Keeping It Up*. Basingstoke: Palgrave Macmillan.

Feuerlicht, I. (1963) 'Camus's *L'Etranger* reconsidered'. *PMLA*, 78(5): 606–21.

Fink, H.L. (1998) 'The Kharmsian absurd and the Bergsonian comic: against Kant and causality'. *Russian Review*, 57(4): 526–38.

Flegar, Ž. (2010) 'A bakery in the mind: sound and emotion in David Ives's *Philip Glass Buys a Loaf of Bread*'. *Cambridge Quarterly*, 39(2): 122–41.

Flood, A. (2011) '*Slaughterhouse-Five* banned by US school'. At http://www.guardian.co.uk/books/2011/jul/29/slaughterhouse-five-banned-us-school.

Forsdick, C. (2007) 'Camus and Sartre: the great quarrel'. In: E.J. Hughes (ed.), *The Cambridge Companion to Camus*. Cambridge: Cambridge University Press, 118–30.

Fowler, R. (1986) *Linguistic Criticism*. Oxford: Oxford University Press.

Freeman, J. (1996) 'Holding up the mirror to mind's nature: reading Rosencrantz "beyond absurdity"'. *Modern Language Review*, 91(1): 20–39.

Friedman, B.J. (1962) *Stern*. New York: Grove Press.

Friedman, M. (1964) *The Worlds of Existentialism: A Critical Reader*. London: Random house.

Frohock, W.M. (1949) 'Camus: image, influence and sensibility'. *Yale French Studies*, 4: 91–9.

Fuchs, D. (1974) 'Saul Bellow and the modern tradition'. *Contemporary Literature*, 15(1): 67–89.

Gadhi, A. (1989) 'A Heideggerian evaluation of humanism in Mordecai Richler's "The Street"'. *Recherches Anglaises et Nord-Americaines*, 22: 99–104.

Galloway, D. (1964) 'The absurd man as picaro: the novels of Saul Bellow'. *Texas Studies in Literature and Language*, 6: 226–54.

Galloway, D. (1966) *The Absurd Hero in American Fiction: Updike, Styron, Bellow, Salinger*. Austin: Texas University Press.

Gavins, J. (2000) 'Absurd tricks with bicycle frames in the text world of *The Third Policeman*'. *Nottingham Linguistic Circular*, 15: 17–33.

Gavins, J. (2007) *Text World Theory: An Introduction*. Edinburgh: Edinburgh University Press.

Gavins, J. (2010) '"Appeased by the certitude": the quiet disintegration of the paranoid mind in *The Mustache*'. In: B. Büsse and D. McIntyre (eds), *Language and Style*. Basingstoke: Palgrave Macmillan, 402–18.

Gavins, J. (2012) 'The literary absurd'. In: J. Bray, A. Gibbons and B. McHale (eds), *The Routledge Companion to Experimental Literature*. London: Routledge, 62–74.

Gavins, J. and Steen, G. (eds) (2003) *Cognitive Poetics in Practice*. London: Routledge.

Geherin, D. (1964) 'Nothingness and beyond: Joan Didion's *Play It As It Lays*'. *Critique: Studies in Modern Fiction*, 16(1): 64–78.

Genette, G. (1980) *Narrative Discourse*. Ithaca: Cornell University Press.

Gerrig, R.J. (1993) *Experiencing Narrative Worlds: On the Psychological Activities of Reading*. New Haven: Westview Press.

Gerzymisch-Arbogast, H.E. (1988) 'The absurd in the dramas of Harold Pinter: attempt at a clarification from a linguistic viewpoint'. *Die Neueren Sprachen*, 87(4): 405–21.

Gibbons, A. (2011) *Multimodality, Cognition, and Experimental Literature*. London: Routledge.

Gifford, T. (2009) *Ted Hughes*. London: Routledge.

Gillen, F. (1972) 'Donald Barthelme's city: a guide'. *Twentieth Century Literature*, 18(1): 37–44.

Gilmore, T.B. (1982) 'Allbee's drinking'. *Twentieth Century Literature*, 28(4): 381–96.

Golden, D. (1981) 'Mystical musings and comic confrontations: the fiction of Saul Bellow and Mordecai Richler'. *Essays on Canadian Writing*, 22: 62–85.

Goldman, A.I. (1992) 'In defense of the simulation theory'. *Mind and Language*, 17(1–2): 104–19.

Goodreads (2012a) *The Stranger* by Albert Camus. Available at http://www.goodreads.com/book/show/49552.The_Stranger.

Goodreads (2012b) 'Some of Us Had Been Threatening Our Friend Colby'. Available at http://www.goodreads.com/book/show/10562181-some-of-us-had-been-threatening-our-friend-colby.

Goodreads (2012c) 'Review of *The World Doesn't End* by Charles Simic'. Available at http://www.goodreads.com/book/show/539143.The_World_Doesn_t_End.

Goodreads(2012d) *Return to the City of White Donkeys* by James Tate. Available at http://www.goodreads.com/book/show/162412.Return_to_the_City_of_White_Donkeys.

Gordon, A. (1979) '"Pushy Jew": Leventhal in *The Victim*'. *Modern Fiction Studies*, 25: 129–38.

Grealish, G.E. (1972) *The Existential Strain in the Poetry of Ted Hughes*. Scranton: University of Scranton.

Green, M.C. (2004) 'Transportation into narrative worlds: the role of prior knowledge and perceived realism'. *Discourse Processes*, 38(2): 247–66.

Green, M.C. and Brock, T.C. (2000) 'The role of transportation in the persuasiveness of public narratives'. *Journal of Personality and Social Psychology*, 79: 701–21.

Green, M.C., Strange, J.J. and Brock, T.C. (2002) *Narrative Impact: Social and Cognitive Foundations*. Mahwah, NJ: Lawrence Erlbaum Associates.

Green, M.C., Brock, T.C. and Kaufman, G.F. (2004) 'Understanding media enjoyment: the role of transportation into narrative worlds'. *Communication Theory*, 14(4): 311–27.

Grol-Prokopczyk, R. (1979) 'Slawomir Mrozek's Theatre of the Absurd'. *Polish Review*, 24(3): 45–56.

Gunn, L.A.H. (2008) 'Arrested development and the Theatre of the Absurd'. *Velox: Critical Approaches to Contemporary Film*, 21(1): 14–20.

Halliday, M.A.K. and Mathieson, C. (2004) *An Introduction to Systemic Functional Linguistics*. London: Continuum.

Hanauer, D. (1998) 'Reading poetry: an empirical investigation of formalist, stylistic, and conventionalist claims'. *Poetics Today*, 19(4): 565–80.

Haney, W.S. (2001) 'Beckett out of his mind: the Theatre of the Absurd'. *Studies in the Literary Imagination*, 34(2): 39–54.

Hanţiu, E. (2010) 'Humor and satire in Edgar Allan Poe's absurd stories'. *Edgar Allen Poe Review*, 11(2): 28–35.

Harris, C.B. (1972) *Contemporary American Novelists of the Absurd*. Lanham: Rowman and Littlefield.

Hauck, R. (1971) *A Cheerful Nihilism: Confidence and 'The Absurd' in American Humorous Fiction*. Bloomington: Indiana University Press.

Hausdorff, D. (1966) 'Thomas Pynchon's multiple absurdities'. *Wisconsin Studies in Contemporary Literature*, 7(3): 258–69.

Heller, J. (1962) *Catch-22*. London: Jonathan Cape.

Herman, D. (1994) 'Textual "you" and double deixis in Edna O'Brien's *A Pagan Place*'. *Style*, 28(3): 378–410.

Herman, D. (2011) 'Post-Cartesian approaches to narrative and mind'. *Style*, 45(2): 265–71.

Herman, V. (1998) *Dramatic Discourse: Dialogue as Interaction in Plays*. London: Routledge.

Herrero-Olaizola, A. (1998) 'Revamping the popular in *Snow White* and *Pubis Angelical*: the residual fictions of Donald Barthelme and Manuel Puig'. *The Journal of Popular Culture*, 32(3): 1–16.

Hibbett, R. (2005) 'Imagining Ted Hughes: authorship, authenticity, and the symbolic work of "Collected Poems"'. *Twentieth Century Literature*, 51(4): 414–36.

Hidalgo Downing, L. (2000) *Negation, Text Worlds, and Discourse: The Pragmatics of Fiction*. Stamford: Ablex.

Hilfer, A.C. (1992) *American Fiction Since 1940*. London: Longman.

Hinchliffe, A.P. (1972) *The Absurd*. London: Methuen.

Hinden, M. (1981) 'Jumpers: Stoppard and the Theater of Exhaustion'. *Twentieth Century Literature*, 27(1): 1–15.

Hoffmann, G. (1986) 'The absurd and its forms of reduction in postmodern American fiction'. In: D.W. Fokkema and J.W. Bertens (eds), *Approaching Postmodernism*. Amsterdam: John Benjamins Publishing Company, 185–210.

Hopper, K. (1995) *Flann O'Brien: A Portrait of the Artist as a Young Post-Modernist*. Cork: Cork University Press.

Huang, J. (2004) 'Stephen Crane's poetry of the absurd'. In: W. Zhong and R. Han (eds), *Re-Reading America: Changes and Challenges*. Cheltenham: Reardan, 131–5.

Hudgens, M.T. (2001) *Donald Barthelme, Postmodernist American Writer*. New York: Edwin Mellen Press.

Hughes, T. (2003) *Collected Poems*. London: Faber and Faber.

Hunt, R.L. (1989) 'Hell goes round and round: Flann O'Brien'. *Canadian Journal of Irish Studies*, 14(2): 60–73.

Hyles, V. (1985) 'The metaphorical nature of the ambience: absurdist SF and fantastic fabulation'. *Publications of the Arkansas Philological Association*, 11(2): 39–47.

Ishiguro, K. (1995) *The Unconsoled*. London: Faber and Faber.

Jakovljevic, B. (2010) 'The Theater of the Absurd and the historization of the present'. In: H. Bial and S. Magelsson (eds), *Theater Historiography: Critical Interventions*. Ann Arbor: University of Michigan Press, 61–73.

Janoff, B. (1974) 'Black humor, existentialism, and absurdity: a generic confusion'. *Arizona Quarterly: A Journal of American Literature, Culture, and Theory*, 30: 293–304.

John (2008) Review of *The Ghost Soldiers*. Available at http://www.goodreads.com/review/show/33257079.

John, S. (1955) 'Image and symbol in the work of Albert Camus'. *French Studies* 9(1): 42–53.

Karst, R. (1975) 'The reality of the absurd and the absurdity of the real: Kafka and Gogol'. *Mosaic: A Journal for the Interdisciplinary Study of Literature*, 9(1): 67–81.

Kasey C. (2012) *Slaughterhouse-Five* by Kurt Vonnegut. Available at http://www.shelfari.com/books/11877/Slaughterhouse-Five/reviews?sort=3&Page=93.

Kavanagh, T.M. (1972) 'Kafka's *The Trial*: the semiotics of the absurd'. *NOVEL: A Forum on Fiction*, 5(3): 242–53.

Kearney, R. (2006) *Navigations: Collected Irish Essays, 1976–2006*. Syracuse: Syracuse University Press.

Keen, S. (2006) 'A theory of narrative empathy'. *Narrative*, 14(3): 207–36.

Keen, S. (2007) *Empathy and the Novel*. Oxford: Oxford University Press.

Kesey, K. (1962) *One Flew Over the Cuckoo's Nest*. Harmondsworth: Penguin.

Ketterer, D. (1978) 'Take-off to cosmic irony: science-fiction, humor and the absurd'. In: S.B. Cohen (ed.), *Comic Relief: Humor in Contemporary American Literature*. Urbana: University of Illinois Press, 70–86.

Kiberd, D. (1986) 'Beckett and Kavanagh: comparatively absurd?' *Hermathena: A Trinity College Dublin Review*, 141: 45–55.

Kierkegaard, S. (trans. C.S. Evans and S. Walsh) (2006) *Fear and Trembling*. Cambridge: Cambridge University Press.

Killinger, J. (1961) 'Existentialism and human freedom'. *English Journal*, 50(5): 303–13.

Kleppner, A. (1964) 'Philosophy and the literary medium: the existentialist predicament'. *Journal of Aesthetics and Art Criticism*, 23(2): 207–17.

Klinkowitz, J. (1971) 'Kurt Vonnegut, Jr. and the crime of his times'. *Critique: Studies in Modern Fiction*, 12(3): 38–53.

Klinkowitz, J. (1991) *Donald Barthelme: An Exhibition*. New York: Duke University Press.

Knopp, J. (1974) 'Wiesel and the absurd'. *Contemporary Literature*, 15(2): 212–20.

Komaromi, A. (2002) 'Daniil Kharms and the art of absurd life-creation'. *Russian Literature*, 52(4): 419–37.

Kosinski, M. (1979) 'Mark Twain's absurd universe and "The Great Dark"'. *Studies in Short Fiction*, 16: 335–40.

Kramer, R. (2008) *Mordecai Richler: Leaving St Urbain*. Montreal: McGill-Queen's University Press.

Kress, G.R. and van Leeuwen, T. (2006) *Reading Images: The Grammar of Visual Design*. London: Routledge.

Kuiken, D., Miall, D.S. and Sikora, S. (2004) 'Forms of self-implication in literary reading'. *Poetics Today*, 25(2): 171–203.

Kusnir, J. (2004) 'Subversion of myths: high and low cultures in Donald Barthelme's *Snow White* and Robert Coover's *Briar Rose*'. *European Journal of American Culture*, 23(1): 31–49.

Lakoff, G. (1987) *Women, Fire, and Dangerous Things: What Categories Reveal About the Mind*. Chicago: University of Chicago Press.

Lakoff, G. (2004) *Don't Think Of An Elephant! Know Your Values and Frame the Debate*. White River Junction: Chelsea Green Publishing.

Lakoff, G. and Johnson, M. (1980) *Metaphors We Live By*. Chicago: University of Chicago Press.

Lakoff, G. and Turner, M. (1989) *More Than Cool Reason: A Field Guide to Poetic Metaphor*. Chicago: University of Chicago Press.

Lanham, R.A. (1993) *The Electronic Word: Democracy, Technology, and the Arts*. Chicago: University of Chicago Press.

Lea, D. and Schoene-Harwood, B. (2003) *Posting the Male: Masculinities in Post-War and Contemporary British Literature*. Amsterdam: Rodopi.

Lebowitz, N. (1971) *Humanism and the Absurd in the Modern Novel*. Evanston: Northwestern University Press.

Lee, S-H. (2002) 'Jewish consciousness of the self and Saul Bellow's *The Victim*, *Herzog* and *Mr. Sammler's Planet*'. *Saul Bellow Journal*, 18(1): 55–65.

Lehan, R. (1959) 'Existentialism in recent American fiction: the demonic quest'. *Texas Studies in Literature and Language*, 1: 181–92.

Lemon, R. (2011) 'The comfort of strangeness: correlating the Kafkaesque and the Kafkan in Kazuo Ishiguro's *The Unconsoled*'. In: S. Corngold and R. Gross (eds), *Kafka for the Twenty First Century*. Rochester: Camden House, 207–21.

Lennartz, N. (2010) '"The ache of modernism": James Joyce's *Pomes Penyeach* and their literary context'. *James Joyce Quarterly*, 47(2): 197–211.

Leslie, A.M. (1991) 'The theory of mind impairment in autism: evidence for a modular mechanism of development?' In: A. Whiten (ed.), *Natural Theories of Mind*. Oxford: Blackwell, 63–78.

LibraryThing (2012) Homepage at http://www.librarything.com.

Liu, Y. (2006) 'Middle English romance as prototype genre'. *Chaucer Review*, 40(4): 335–53.

Lysaker, J.T. (2001) 'White dawns, black noons, twilit days: Charles Simic's poems before poetry'. *TriQuarterly*, 110–11: 525–80.

Lysaker, J.T. (2002) *You Must Change Your Life: Poetry, Philosophy, and the Birth of Sense*. University Park: Penn State Press.

MacNamara, E. (1968) 'The absurd style in contemporary American literature'. *Humanities Association Review*, 19(1): 44–9.

Macquarrie, J. (1972) *Existentialism*. Philadelphia: Westminster.

Maio, S. (2005) *Creating Another Self 2/E: Voice in Modern American Personal Poetry*. Kirksville: Truman State University Press.

Malinowska, B. (1992) 'Beyond the absurd: language games in the theatre of Maria Irene Fornés, Samuel Beckett, and Eugène Ionesco'. *Text and Presentation: The Journal of the Comparative Drama Conference*, 12: 55–60.

Malle, B.F. and Hodges, S.D. (2005) *Other Minds: How Humans Bridge the Divide Between Self and Others*. New York: Guilford Press.

mary-erin (2009) *Slaughterhouse-Five* by Kurt Vonnegut. Available at http://www.shelfari.com/books/11877/Slaughterhouse-Five/reviews.

Maxymuk, J. (2007) 'Whose space?' *Bottom Line: Managing Library Finances*, 20(2): 97–100.

May, C. (1970) 'Thomas Hardy and the poetry of the absurd'. *Texas Studies in Literature and Language*, 12: 63–73.

May, J.R. (1972) 'Vonnegut's humor and the limits of hope'. *Twentieth Century Literature*, 18(1): 25–36.

Mazzullo, C. (1995) 'Flann O'Brien's hellish otherworld: from *Buile Suibhne* to *The Third Policeman*'. *Irish University Review*, 25(2): 318–27.

McCaffery, L. (1979) 'Meaning and non-meaning in Barthelme's fictions'. *Journal of Aesthetic Education*, 13(1): 69–79.

McCaffery, L. (1982) *The Metafictional Muse: The Works of Robert Coover, Donald Barthelme, and William H. Cass*. Pittsburgh: University of Pittsburgh Press.

McCarthy, P. (1988) *Albert Camus, The Stranger*. Cambridge: Cambridge University Press.

McCarthy, T. (2007) *Remainder*. London: Alma.

McGregor, R.R. (1993) 'Camus's "Le Renégat": an allegory of the existentialist pilgrimage'. *French Review*, 66(5): 742–51.

McGregor, R.R. (1994) 'Camus's "La Femme Adultère": a metaphor of the fall from the absurd'. *French Review*, 67(3): 478–85.

McGregor, R.R. (1995) 'Camus's "Jonas ou L'Artiste au Travail": a statement of the absurd human condition'. *South Atlantic Review*, 60(4): 53–68.

McHale, B. (1987) *Postmodernist Fiction*. London: Methuen.

McHale, B. (1992) *Constructing Postmodernism*. London: Routledge.

McHale, B. (2012) 'Postmodernism and experiment'. In: J. Bray, A. Gibbons and B. McHale (eds), *The Routledge Companion to Experimental Literature*. London: Routledge, 141–53.

Meier, F. (2001) 'Laughter and the absurd in Ted Hughes's crow-poems'. In: W. Witalisz (ed.), *'And Gladly Wolde He Lerne and Gladly Teche.' Studies on Language and Literature in Honour of Professor Dr Karl Heinz Göller*. Krakow: Wydawnictwo Uniwersytetu Jagiellońskiego, 101–15.

Miall, D.S. (2008) 'Feeling from the perspective of the empirical study of literature'. *Journal of Literary Theory*, 1(2): 377–93.

Miall, D.S. and Kuiken, D. (1994) 'Foregrounding, defamiliarization, and affect: response to literary stories'. *Poetics*, 22(5): 389–407.

Miall, D.S. and Kuiken, D. (2002a) 'The effects of local phonetic contrasts in readers' responses to a short story'. *Empirical Studies of the Arts*, 20(2): 157–75.

Miall, D.S. and Kuiken, D. (2002b) 'A feeling for fiction: becoming what we behold'. *Poetics*, 30(4): 221–41.

Michel, L.A. (1961) 'The absurd predicament in Conrad's political novels'. *College English*, 23(2): 131–6.

Miller, J.E. (1967) *Quests Surd and Absurd: Essays in American literature*. Chicago: University of Chicago Press.

mingus(2006)*SixtyStories*byDonaldBarthelme.Availableathttp://www.amazon.com/product-reviews/0141180935/ref=cm_cr_dp_syn_footer?k=Sixty%20Stories%20%28Penguin%20Twentieth%20Century%20Classics%29&showViewpoints=1.

Mistri, Z. (1988) 'Absurdist contemplations of a sperm in John Barth's "Night-Sea Journey"'. *Studies in Short Fiction*, 25(2): 151–2.

Morreale, G. (1967) 'Meursault's absurd act'. *French Review*, 40(4): 456–62.

Moss, J. (1983) 'Introduction'. In: J. Moss (ed.), *The Canadian Novel: A Critical Anthology*. Toronto: NC Press, 7–15.

Murphy, G.L. (2004) *The Big Book of Concepts*. Cambridge, MA: MIT Press.

Nealon, J. (2005) 'Disastrous aesthetics: irony, ethics, and gender in Barthelme's *Snow White*'. *Twentieth Century Literature: A Scholarly and Critical Journal*, 51(2): 123–41.

New, O. and New, W.H. (2003) *A History of Canadian Literature*. Toronto: McGill-Queen's University Press.

Newton, A. (1996) 'From exegesis to ethics: recognition and its vicissitudes in Saul Bellow and Chester Himes'. *South Atlantic Quarterly*, 95(4): 989–1007.

Nilsen, H.N. (1979) 'Anti-Semitism and persecution complex: a comment on Saul Bellow's *The Victim*'. *English Studies*, 60(2): 183–91.

Nobelprize.org (2012) 'The Nobel Prize in Literature 1976'. Available at http://www.nobelprize.org/nobel_prizes/literature/laureates/1976/.

nyssa (2011) 'September reviews in writer's workshop'. Available at http://www.shelfari.com/groups/87296/discussions/385757/September-Reviews?showall=true#9159769.

Oakes, E.H. (2004) *American Writers*. New York: Infobase Publishing.

Oberman, W. (2002) 'John Barth's *The End of the Road* and Donald Barthelme's "A Shower of Gold": two views of Sartrean existentialism'. *Notes on Contemporary Literature*, 32(2): 7–9.

O'Brien, F. (1993) *The Third Policeman*. London: Harper Collins.

O'Connell, M. (2009) '"How to handle eternity": infinity and the theories of J.W. Dunne in the fiction of Jorge Luis Borges and Flann O'Brien's *The Third Policeman*'. *Irish Studies Review*, 17(2): 223–37.

Olsen, L. (1986) 'Linguistic pratfalls in Barthelme'. *South Atlantic Review*, 51(4): 69–77.

O'Neill, J. (1967) 'The absurd in Samuel Beckett'. *Personalist: An International Review of Philosophy*, 48: 56–76.

O'Neill, P. (1983) 'The comedy of entropy: the contexts of black humour'. *Canadian Review of Comparative Literature/Revue Canadienne de Littérature Comparée*, 10(2): 145–66.

Osbaldistone (2009) Review: *The Third Policeman* by Flann O'Brien. Available at http://www.librarything.com/work/7104.

Ostashevsky, E. and Yankelevich, M. (2002) 'OBERIU: Russian absurdism of the 1930s'. *New American Writing*, 20: 122–53.

Palmer, A. (2002) 'The construction of fictional minds'. *Narrative*, 10(1): 28–46.

Palmer, A. (2004) *Fictional Minds*. Lincoln, NE: University of Nebraska Press.

Palmer, A. (2005) 'Intermental thought in the novel: the Middlemarch mind'. *Style*, 39(4): 427–39.

Palmer, A. (2007a) 'Universal minds'. *Semiotica*, 165(1–4): 205–25.

Palmer, A. (2007b) 'Attribution theory: action and emotion in Dickens and Pynchon'. In: P. Stockwell and M. Lambrou (eds), *Contemporary Stylistics*. London: Continuum, 81–92.

Palmer, A. (2010) *Social Minds in the Novel*. Columbus: Ohio State University Press.

Palmer, A. (2011) 'Social minds in fiction and criticism'. *Style*, 45(2): 196–240.

Palmer, W. (1974) 'Abelard's fate: sexual politics in Stendhal, Faulkner and Camus'. *Mosaic: A Journal for the Interdisciplinary Study of Literature*, 7(4): 29–41.

Patil, M. (1999) *Thomas Hardy's Poetry and Existentialism*. New Delhi: Atlantic Publishers.

Penner, D. (1978) '*Invitation to a Beheading*: Nabokov's absurdist initiation'. *Critique: Studies in Modern Fiction*, 20(3): 27–38.

Peplow, D. (2011) '"Oh, I've known a lot of Irish people": reading groups and the negotiation of literary interpretation'. *Language and Literature*, 20(4): 295–315.

Phelan, J. (1996) *Narrative as Rhetoric: Techniques, Audiences, Ethics, Ideology*. Columbus: Ohio State University Press.

Phelan, J. (2007a) 'Estranging unreliability, bonding unreliability, and the ethics of Lolita'. *Narrative*, 15(2): 222–38.

Phelan, J. (2007b) 'Rhetoric/ethics'. In: D. Herman (ed.), *The Cambridge Companion to Narrative*. Cambridge: Cambridge University Press, 203–16.

Philmus, R.M. (2005) *Visions and Re-visions: (Re)constructing Science Fiction*. Liverpool: Liverpool University Press.

Pifer, E. (1991) *Saul Bellow Against the Grain*. Philadelphia: University of Pennsylvania Press.

Posner, M.I. (2004) *Cognitive Neuroscience of Attention*. New York: Guilford Press.

Pratt, A. (1993) '"People are equally wretched everywhere": Candide, black humor and the existential absurd'. In: A. Pratt (ed.), *Black Humor: Critical Essays*. New York: Garland, 181–93.

Pynchon, T. (1963) *V*. London: Jonathan Cape.

Quennet, F. (2002) 'Humour and Jewish Canadian writing: Mordecai Richler's *Barney's Version* as ethnic humour'. In: M. Kuester and W.R. Keller (eds), *Writing Canadians: The Literary Construction of Ethnic Identities*. Marburg: Universitätsbibliothek Marburg, 107–19.

Rabinowitz, P.J. (1977) 'Truth in fiction: a reexamination of audiences'. *Critical Enquiry*, 4: 121–41.

RachDan (2009) Review: *The Third Policeman* by Flann O'Brien. Available at http://www.librarything.com/work/7104.

Read, G. (1981) 'Absurdist humor in the Spanish American short story'. *Perspectives on Contemporary Literature*, 7: 81–7.

Rebein, R. (2011) 'Contemporary realism'. In: J.N. Duvall (ed.), *The Cambridge Companion to American Fiction After 1945*. Cambridge: Cambridge University Press, 30–43.

Richardson, B. (2006) *Unnatural Voices: Extreme Narration in Modern and Contemporary Fiction*. Columbus: Ohio State University Press.

Richler, M. (1997) *Barney's Version*. London: Chatto and Windus.

Robinson, C. (1989) *Ted Hughes as Shepherd of Being*. Basingstoke: Macmillan.

Rosch, E. (1975) 'Cognitive representations of semantic categories'. *Journal of Experimental Psychology*, 104: 193–233.

Rosch, E. (1977) 'Human categorization'. In: N. Warren (ed.), *Studies in Cross-Cultural Psychology*. London: Academic Press, 1–49.

Rosch, E. (1978) 'Principles of categorization'. In: E. Rosch and B. Lloyd (eds), *Cognition and Categorization*. Hillsdale: Lawrence Erlbaum Associates, 27–48.

Rosch, E. and Mervis, C.B. (1975) 'Family resemblances: studies in the internal structure of categories'. *Cognitive Psychology*, 7(4): 573–605.

Rosenberg, W. (2009) *Legacy of Rage: Jewish Masculinity, Violence, and Culture*. Amherst: University of Massachusetts Press.

Rother, J. (1976) 'Parafiction: the adjacent universe of Barth, Barthelme, Pynchon, and Nabokov'. *boundary 2*, 5(1): 21–44.

Russell, A. (1990) 'Deconstructing *The New York Trilogy*: Paul Auster's anti-detective fiction'. *Critique: Studies in Contemporary Fiction*, 31(2): 71–84.

Safer, E. (1983a) 'The allusive mode, the absurd and black humor in William Gaddis's *The Recognitions*'. *Studies in American Humor*, 1(2): 103–18.

Safer, E. (1983b) 'The absurd quest and black humor in Ken Kesey's *Sometimes a Great Notion*'. *Critique: Studies in Modern Fiction*, 24(4): 228–40.

Safer, E. (1989) 'John Barth, the university, and the absurd: a study of *The End of the Road* and *Giles Goat-Boy*'. In: B. Siegel (ed.), *The American Writer and the University*. Newark, NJ: University of Delaware Press, 88–100.

Safer, E. (1994) 'Pynchon's world and its legendary past: humor and the absurd in a twentieth-century *Vineland*'. In: G. Green, D.J. Greiner and L. McCaffery (eds), *The Vineland Papers: Critical Takes on Pynchon's Novel*. Normal: Dalkey Archive Press, 46–67.

Sagi, A. (2002) *Albert Camus and the Philosophy of the Absurd*. Amsterdam: Rodopi.

Salinger, J.D. (1951) *The Catcher in the Rye*. New York: Little Brown.

Sanford, A.J.S., Sanford, A.J., Molle, J. and Emmott, C. (2006) 'Shallow processing and attention capture in written and spoken discourse'. *Discourse Processes*, 42(2): 109–30.

Sartre, J-P. (1938) *Nausea*. Paris: Gallimard.

Sartre, J-P. (1943) *Being and Nothingness*. Paris: Gallimard.

Schank, R. and Abelson, R. (1977) *Scripts, Plans, Goals and Understanding*. Hillsdale, NJ: Lawrence Erlbaum Associates.

Scigaj, L.M. (1992) 'Introduction'. In: L.M. Scigaj (ed.), *Critical Essays on Ted Hughes*. New York: G.K. Hall, 1–38.

Sedo, D.R. (2003) 'Readers in reading groups: an online survey of face-to-face and virtual book clubs'. *Convergence: The International Journal of Research into New Media Technologies*, 9(1): 66–90.

Sefler, G.F. (1974) 'The existential vs. the absurd: the aesthetics of Nietzsche and Camus'. *Journal of Aesthetics and Art Criticism*, 32(3): 415–21.

Seltzer, L.F. (1967) 'Camus's absurd and the world of Melville's *Confidence-Man*'. *PMLA*, 82(1): 14–27.

Semino, E. and Culpeper, J. (eds) (2002) *Cognitive Stylistics: Language and Cognition in Text Analysis*. Amsterdam: John Benjamins.

Shaffer, B.W. (2008) *Understanding Kazuo Ishiguro*. Columbia: University of South Carolina Press.

Shelfari (2012a) Homepage at http://www.shelfari.com.

Shelfari (2012b) Discussions of *The Stranger*. Available at http://www.shelfari.com/books/18660/The-Stranger/discussions.

Shelfari (2012c) Readers and reviews of *Slaughterhouse-Five* by Kurt Vonnegut. Available at http://www.shelfari.com/books/11877/Slaughterhouse-Five/readers-reviews.

Sherri L. (2010) *The New York Trilogy* by Paul Auster. Available at http://www.shelfari.com/books/11902/The-New-York-Trilogy/reviews?sort=3&Page=10.

Sherzer, D. (1978) 'Dialogic incongruities in the Theater of the Absurd'. *Semiotica*, 22(3–4): 269–86.

Sherzer, D. (1979) 'Literary and social language'. *Language and Style*, 12(4): 228–44.

Shiloh, I. (2002) *Paul Auster and Postmodern Quest: On the Road to Nowhere*. Berlin: Peter Lang.

Shulman, R. (1968) 'The style of Bellow's comedy'. *PMLA*, 83(1): 109–17.

Sikorska, L. (1994) 'The language of entropy: a pragma-dramatic analysis of Samuel Beckett's *Endgame*'. *Studia Anglica Posnaniensia*, 28: 195–208.

Silver, R.H. (1972) *The Absurd in Wallace Stevens' Poetry: A Method of Explicating Modern Poetry*. Walden: Walden University Press.

Simic, C. (2004a) *Selected Poems, 1963–2003*. London: Faber and Faber.

Simic, C. (2004b) 'Review of Memoir of the Hawk'. In: B. Henry (ed.), *On James Tate*. Ann Arbor: University of Michigan Press, 171–3.

Simon, J.K. (1960) 'The glance of idiots: the novel of the absurd'. *Yale French Studies*, 25: 111–19.

Simpson, P. (1993) *Language, Ideology and Point of View*. London: Routledge.

Simpson, P. (1997) 'The interactive world of *The Third Policeman*'. In: A. Clune and T. Hurson (eds), *Conjuring Complexities: Essays on Flann O'Brien*. Belfast: Institute of Irish Studies, 73–81.

Simpson, P. (1998) 'Odd talk: studying discourses of incongruity'. In: M. Short, J. Culpeper and P. Verdonk (eds), *Exploring the Language of Drama: From Text to Context*. London: Routledge, 34–53.

Simpson, P. (2000) 'Satirical humour and cultural context: with a note on the curious case of Father Todd Unctuous'. In: T. Bex, M. Burke and P. Stockwell (eds), *Contextualised Stylistics: In Honour of Peter Verdonk*. Amsterdam: Rodopi, 243–66.

Simpson, P. (2003) *On the Discourse of Satire: Towards a Stylistic Model of Satirical Humor*. Amsterdam: John Benjamins Publishing.

Sinclair, J. and Cardew-Hall, M. (2008) 'The folksonomy tag cloud: when is it useful?' *Journal of Information Science*, 34(1): 15–29.

Sinha, N. (1993) 'Eliot's "Prufrock" and the absurd'. *Aligarh Journal of English Studies*, 15(1–2): 87–92.

Sloboda, N. (1996) 'American post-modern extensions: Donald Barthelme's picture/text mosaic'. *New Novel Review*, 3(2): 85–102.

Sloboda, N. (1997) 'Heteroglossia and collage: Donald Barthelme's *Snow White*'. *Mosaic: A Journal for the Interdisciplinary Study of Literature*, 30(4): 109–23.

Snipe, A.J. (1997) 'Flann O'Brien'. In: A.G. Gonzalez (ed.), *Modern Irish Writers: A Bio-Critical Sourcebook*. London: Greenwood Publishing Group, 289–95.

Solimini, M. (2001) 'The outsider in Camus' *Létranger*'. *Semiotic*, 136: 369–75.

Sollars, M. (2010) 'Franz Kafka's *The Trial* and civil disobedience'. In: H. Bloom (ed.), *Civil Disobedience*. New York: Infobase Publishing, 253–62.

Sotirova, V. (2006) 'Reader responses to narrative point of view'. *Poetics*, 3(2): 108–33.

Spector, R.D. (1961) 'Melville's "Bartleby" and the absurd'. *Nineteenth-Century Fiction*, 16(2): 175–7.

Spergel, J. (2005) 'Constructing a multicultural identity at the Canadian frontier: Mordecai Richler and Jewish-Canadian writing'. *Revue LISA/LISA e-journal*, 3(2): 131–45.

Sprintzen, D. and van den Hoven, A. (2004) *Sartre and Camus: A Historic Confrontation*. London: Prometheus Books.

Srigley, R.D. (2011) *Albert Camus' Critique of Modernity*. Columbia: University of Missouri Press.

Srivastava, A.K. (1974) 'The crooked mirror: notes on the Theatre of the Absurd'. *Literary Criterion*, 11(2): 58–62.

Stafford, B.M. (2007) *Echo Objects: The Cognitive Work of Images*. Chicago: University of Chicago Press.

Steen, G. (2011) 'Genre between the humanities and sciences'. In: M. Callies, W.R. Keller and A. Lohöfer (eds), *Bi-Directionality in the Cognitive Sciences*. Amsterdam: John Benjamins, 21–41.

Stengel, W. (1992) 'Irony and the totalitarian consciousness in Donald Barthelme's *Amatuers*'. In: R. Patterson (ed.), *Critical Essays on Donald Barthelme*. New York: G.K. Hall, 145–52.

Stockwell, P. (1999) 'The inflexibility of invariance'. *Language and Literature*, 8(2): 125–42.

Stockwell, P. (2000) '(Sur)real stylistics: from text to contextualizing'. In: P. Stockwell, M. Burke and T. Bex (eds), *Contextualised Stylistics: In Honour of Peter Verdonk*. Amsterdam: Rodopi, 15–38.

Stockwell, P. (2002a) *Cognitive Poetics: An Introduction*. London: Routledge.

Stockwell, P. (2002b) 'Surreal figures'. In: J. Gavins and G. Steen (eds), *Cognitive Poetics in Practice*. London: Routledge, 13–26.

Stockwell, P. (2009) *Texture: A Cognitive Aesthetics of Reading*. Edinburgh: Edinburgh University Press.

Stockwell, P. (2011) 'Changing minds in narrative'. *Style*, 45(2): 288–91.

Stockwell, P. (2012) 'The surrealist experiments with language'. In: J. Bray, A. Gibbons and B. McHale (eds), *The Routledge Companion to Experimental Literature*. London: Routledge, 48–61.

Styles, E.A. (2005) *Attention, Perception and Memory: An Integrated Introduction*. Hove: Psychology Press.

Styles, E.A. (2006) *The Psychology of Attention*. Hove: Psychology Press.

Swann, J. and Allington, D. (2009) 'Reading groups and the language of literary texts: a case study in social reading'. *Language and Literature*, 18(3): 247–64.

Swanson, E. (1971) 'Samuel Beckett's *Watt*: a coming and a going'. *Modern Fiction Studies*, 17: 264–8.

Swardson, H.R. (1976) 'Sentimentality and the academic tradition'. *College English*, 37(8): 747–66.

Tate, J. (2004) *Return to the City of White Donkeys*. New York: Ecco.

Thomas, M., Caudle, D.M. and Schmitz, C. (2010) 'Trashy tags: problematic tags in *LibraryThing*'. *New Library World*, 111(5–6): 223–35.

Thompson, G. (2004) *Introducing Functional Grammar*. London: Arnold.

Tigges, W. (1988) *An Anatomy of Literary Nonsense*. Amsterdam: Rodopi.

Tomlinson, S. (1984) 'Frost's "The Draft Horse"'. *Explicator*, 42(4): 28–9.

Van Peer, W. (1983) 'Poetic style and reader response: an exercise in empirical semics'. *Journal of Literary Semantics*, 12(2): 3–18.

Van Peer, W. (2008) *The Quality of Literature: Linguistic Studies in Literary Evaluation*. Amsterdam: John Benjamins.

Van Peer, W. and Andringa, E. (1990) 'Stylistic intuitions: an empirical study'. *Language and Style*, 23(2): 235–46.

Varvogli, A. (2001) *World That Is the Book: Paul Auster's Fiction*. Liverpool: Liverpool University Press.

Vassilopolou, K. (2008) '"Why get upset over a few cases of rhinoceritis?" Possible worlds in the Theatre of the Absurd'. In: G. Watson (ed.), *The State of Stylistics*. Amsterdam: Rodopi, 155–75.

Vatulescu, C. (2010) *Police Aesthetics: Literature, Film, and the Secret Police in Soviet Times*. Stanford: Stanford University Press.

Viggiani, C.A. (1956) 'Camus' *L'Etranger*'. *PMLA*, 71(5): 865–87.

Villar Flor, C. (2000) 'Unreliable selves in an unreliable world: the multiple projections of the hero in Kazuo Ishiguro's *The Unconsoled*'. *Journal of English Studies*, 2: 159–69.

Vonnegut, K. (1991) *Slaughterhouse-Five*. London: Vintage.

Vonnegut, K. (2000) *Breakfast of Champions*. London: Vintage.

Wade, S. (1999) *Jewish American Literature Since 1945: An Introduction*. Edinburgh: Edinburgh University Press.

Waldmeir, J.J. (1964) 'Two novelists of the absurd: Heller and Kesey'. *Wisconsin Studies in Contemporary Literature*, 5(3): 192–204.

Ward, J. (2012) 'Following in the footsteps of Sisyphus: Camus, Vonnegut and rationale emotive behavior therapy'. *Interdisciplinary Literary Studies*, 14(1): 79–94.

Weinberg, H. (1970) *The New Novel in America: The Kafkan Mode in Contemporary Fiction*. Ithaca: Cornell University Press.

Wenger, E. (1998) *Communities of Practice*. Cambridge: Cambridge University Press.

Werth, P. (1977) 'The linguistics of double-vision'. *Journal of Literary Semantics*, 6: 3–38.

Werth, P. (1999) *Text Worlds: Representing Conceptual Space in Discourse*. Harlow: Longman.

Whiteley, S. (2010) *Text World Theory and the Emotional Experience of Literary Discourse*. Unpublished PhD thesis, University of Sheffield.

Whiteley, S. (2011a) 'Text world theory, real readers and emotional responses to *The Remains of the Day*'. *Language and Literature*, 20(1): 23–42.

Whiteley, S. (2011b) 'Talking about "An Accommodation": the implications of discussion group data for community engagement and pedagogy'. *Language and Literature*, 20(3): 236–56.

Wilde, A. (1976) 'Barthelme unfair to Kierkegaard: some thoughts on modern and postmodern irony'. *boundary 2*, 5(1): 45–70.

Wilde, A. (1982) '"Strange displacements of the ordinary": Apple, Elkin, Barthelme, and the problem of the excluded middle'. *boundary 2*, 10(2): 177–99.

Winston, M. (1972) 'Humour noir and black humor'. In: H. Levin (ed.), *Veins of Humor*. Cambridge, MA: Harvard University Press, 269–84.

Wittgenstein, L. (1953) *Philosophical Investigations*. New York: Macmillan.

Wright, C. (2004) 'Review of *Worshipful Company of Fletchers*'. In: B. Henry (ed.), *On James Tate*. Ann Arbor: University of Michigan Press, 166–8.

Wurlitzer, R. (2009) *Nog*. Granville, OH: Two Dollar Radio.

Yeh, W. and Barsalou, L.W. (2006) 'The situated nature of concepts'. *American Journal of Psychology*, 119(3): 349–84.

Young, G. (1975) 'Chance and the absurd in Conrad's "The End of the Tether" and "Freya of the Seven Isles"'. *Conradiana: A Journal of Joseph Conrad*, 7: 253–61.

Zilcosky, J. (1998) 'The revenge of the author: Paul Auster's challenge to theory'. *Critique: Studies in Contemporary Fiction*, 39(3): 195–206.

Zunshine, L. (2003) 'Theory of mind and experimental representations of fictional consciousness'. *Narrative*, 11(3): 270–91.

Zunshine, L. (2006) *Why We Read Fiction: Theory of Mind and the Novel*. Columbus: Ohio State University Press.

Zunshine, L. (2008) 'Theory of Mind and fictions of embodied transparency'. *Narrative*, 16(1): 65–92.

Zyngier, S., Bortolussi, M., Chesnokova, A. and Auracher, J. (eds) (2008) *Directions in Empirical Literary Studies: In Honor of Willie Van Peer*. Amsterdam: John Benjamins.

Index